MODES OF PERCEIVING AND PROCESSING INFORMATION

A volume based on conferences
sponsored by the Committee on Cognitive Research
of the Social Science Research Council

Edited by
HERBERT L. PICK, JR.
ELLIOT SALTZMAN
University of Minnesota

 LAWRENCE ERLBAUM ASSOCIATES, PUBLISHERS
1978   Hillsdale, New Jersey

DISTRIBUTED BY THE HALSTED PRESS DIVISION OF

JOHN WILEY & SONS

New York   Toronto   London   Sydney

Lawrence Erlbaum Associates, Inc., Publishers
62 Maria Drive
Hillsdale, New Jersey 07642

Distributed solely by Halsted Press Division
John Wiley & Sons, Inc., New York

Library of Congress Cataloging in Publication Data

Main entry under title:

Modes of perceiving and processing information.

"Product of two workshops (held in the spring of 1974
and 1975) organized by the Committee on Cognition of the
Social Science Research Council."
Includes bibliographical references and indexes.
1. Perception—Congresses.   2. Human information
processing—Congresses.   I. Pick, Herbert L.   II. Saltzman,
Elliot.   III. Social Science Research Council.
Committee on Cognition.
BF311.M57   153.7   77-21025
ISBN 0-470-99342-1

Printed in the United States of America

Contents

Preface

Since World War II the field of perception has developed in two major directions. The first evolved out of the traditional psychophysical approach and is manifest today in the new psychophysics. On the response side, the new psychophysics is characterized by the powerful analytic techniques of signal detectibility theory. On the stimulus side it is characterized by the adaptation of Fourier analysis to stimulus description—most recently in the visual domain.

The second direction is in the increasing bond between the fields of perception and cognition. The traditional empiricist view of perception has always regarded perception as a learning and problem-solving-like behavior. However, the data and experiments to this effect, and more important, the generative impact of this view, were never very convincing. The more recent, and, we believe, more productive ties between perception and cognition have evolved from the impact of cybernetics, information theory, communications, and artificial intelligence. These approaches have combined with a biological—functional orientation to produce significant advances in areas such as speech perception, space perception, and perceptual-motor coordination. From a biological—functional orientation it is not unreasonable to suppose that man has evolved general dispositions or modes of processing stimulation specialized for his vital daily activities—communicating, problem solving, etc.

This volume grew out of the context of this second direction, a particular product of two workshops (held in the Spring of 1974 and 1975), organized by the Committee on Cognitive Research of the Social Science Research Council. The Committee on Cognition was organized in 1971 to encourage communication and interaction on specific problems in the area of cognition among the various social sciences. It has been the hope of the Committee to range broadly across the substantive topics of cognition while including various approaches such as developmental and cross-cultural points of view.

Members of the Committee at the time of the workshops included Roy D'Andrade, Joseph Glick, Frank Palmer, Eleanor Rosch, David Slobin, and Naomi Quinn. David Jenness was the Social Science Research Council staff member of the Committee. He deserves great credit for guiding its organization. The workshops were partially supported by a grant from the Spencer Foundation whose support is gratefully acknowledged. The staff of the Center for Research in Human Learning of the University of Minnesota, especially Ms. Kathy Casey, was of immeasurable help with both the logistics of the workshop and the preparation of the manuscript for this volume.

HERBERT L. PICK, JR.
ELLIOT SALTZMAN
University of Minnesota

1

Modes of Perceiving and Processing Information

Herbert L. Pick, Jr.
Elliot Saltzman

University of Minnesota

SUBJECTIVE OBSERVATIONS ON OBJECTIVE MODES

Consider mankind's day-to-day activity. A large amount of time is spent performing a few very general kinds of behavior. Much of the day is expended in moving from place to place, in manipulating objects, in interacting (especially communicating with others), and so on. It would not be surprising then to find systems of perception or perceptual–motor coordination specialized for dealing with such general activities. Indeed, in the late sixties, this sort of specialization was explicitly suggested by work on speech perception first done at the Haskins Laboratory, and by Trevarthen's (1968) discussion of two visual systems.

In the case of speech perception, a set of sounds would be heard as speech and processed in the "speech mode" by a speaker of a given language, but an acoustically comparable set of sounds not heard as speech would be processed in quite a different way. Furthermore, there seemed to be different neural systems mediating these alternative ways of processing sounds. Both auditory-evoked potentials and a right-ear advantage in dichotic-listening tasks implicated the left cerebral hemisphere in verbal functioning; similarly, right-hemisphere specialization was suggested for nonverbal tasks. This specialization was also supported by the results of dichoptic memory tasks and deficits resulting from differential hemispheric lesions. In the case of two visual systems, different aspects of an integral visual field provided information for two completely different functions: general orientation and focused manipulative behavior. General orientation is associated with behaviors that change the relation of the body to spatial aspects of environment, for example, locomotion and postural adjustments. It involves vision over a wide field, but may not require high resolution. Focused manipulative behavior involves rather localized vision with a premium on high resolution and pattern identification. Again these functions seemed to be mediated by different neural systems. So, in summary, two aspects of this specialization are most impressive: the functional distinctiveness that includes a close tie between perception and action; and the generality of the alternative ways of processing information.

Definition of Mode

More abstractly, different modes of perceiving may be implied: (1) when one type of information rather than another is extracted from a given pattern of stimulation; and (2) when a specific type of information is extracted from very different patterns of stimulation. In the first case, the functional distinctiveness of information is critical. The stimulation itself is ambiguous, that is, it can be read for one meaning or another. In terms of the example of speech perception when one is in the speech mode, auditory stimulation is processed for phonemically relevant categories, that is, categorical perception occurs. Under other conditions, the acoustic stimulation is not processed categorically and finer discriminations can be made along the same acoustic dimensions. In the second case, the generality is critical. If the implication of a spatial orientation mode from Trevarthen's (1968) two-visual systems is realistic, might not there be similar specialization of function in other sense modalities? Evans (1974) has summarized evidence for analogous distinct-auditory systems, one of which seems to mediate auditory spatial orientation. These auditory systems are anatomically distinct at the brain-stem level with the ventral pathway preserving temporal and intensity information necessary for auditory localization. Furthermore, there appears to be convergence of auditory and visual spatial receptive fields at higher (visual) cortical levels which may provide a site for a common orientation function.

In general then, perceptual mode is defined in terms of information extracted by the perceiver. This is information in Gibson's (1966) sense, aspects of the stimulation telling the perceiver something about the environment or something about himself or herself.

Can the Concept of Mode Be Generalized to Other Domains?

Whether, in fact, the one is extracting information about the environment or about oneself is perhaps itself the essence of a primary modal distinction, a subjective—objective distinction. There is considerable evidence that the same stimulation may be processed quite differently depending on whether information is extracted to monitor one's own state or actions, or whether the perceiver's purpose is to extract information about the environment. A classic example (which has by itself evoked several models and instigated numbers of research programs) is the difference in perception of retinal image displacement depending on whether it is caused by displacement of the visual environment (or parts thereof), or by eye movements. A particular aspect of this issue is examined in Arien Mack's chapter in this volume. The more general issue was implied for visual perception by the distinction between the visual field and the visual world (Gibson, 1950). The visual world might be thought of as the information provided by visual stimulation for the significant aspects of the environment—surfaces, objects, people, and so on. And the visual field might be thought of as information about the distribution of energy impinging on the receptor surface.[1]

Another relevant example of a domain of stimulation carrying ambiguous information involves representational displays. To what extent do representational displays require different perceptual processing when the perceiver extracts information about the thing being represented versus the situation in which the perceiver extracts information about the display itself? Pictures, for example, are objects in their own right while they may simultaneously be representing other objects and events. Are there alternative modes of perceiving in these two cases? Written language is also largely a representation of spoken language and yet the perception of text in reading is quite different than perception of print as black and white design. For example, both Posner, Lewis, and Conrad (1972) and LaBerge and Samuels (1974) (as well as others) have distinguished between matching physical shape versus understanding symbolic identity of letters. (Note, however, that physical and symbolic forms may be combined as, for example, in Dylan Thomas' poem "Vision and Prayer," (1952) in which the textual layout has the shape of the symbolic objects, specifically, diamonds and hour glasses. Should these be considered different modes? Is there something common in the processing for represented meaning of all such representational systems including for example, maps, blueprints, circuit diagrams, music notation, and the like? No attempt is made here to answer that general question, but Hagen (in this volume) examines the special case of picture perception in some detail.

The rather different information provided by social and physical objects suggests still another possible modal distinction. A social object, that is, another person, can be perceived simply as a physical object as one might perceive a wax mannequin, simply noting its size, shape, color, and so on. On the other hand, introspectively our perception of other people ordinarily appears to be quite

---

[1] The distinction between visual world and visual field meant here is not equivalent to the classical distinction of sensation and perception. The visual stimulation and (stimulation of other modalities) ordinarily provides information both for objects and events in the world and for distribution of energy and/or events at the receptor surface. This is different information provided by the stimulation and the term perception should be used for both. The sensing of distribution of energy does not add up to perception.

different both in the kind of information registered and in its encoding. One seems to perceive expressions reflecting emotional states, intentions, etc. This is not a novel idea. Heider (1944) suggested there was information for social interaction in dynamic displays of moving geometric shapes. And ethologists have long made the point that certain "social" displays are especially perceptually prepotent. More recently rather systematic experimental evidence has been accumulating. In one study, Hess and Pick (1974) suggested that something like categorical perception may occur in perception of facial expression. The discrimination of degrees of curvature is better for lines in isolation than it is for the lines embedded in a facial context and perceived as smiling mouths. In a series of experiments, Diamond and Carey (in press) have argued that perception of faces is "special." They have noted, for example, Rock's (1973) observations that geometric rotation of pictures of faces disrupts recognition and identification more than does rotation of other visual stimuli. This difference between perception of faces and perception of other stimuli seems to be related to processing the faces as an integral gestalt rather than as a set of separate features. Developmentally, the difference in processing doesn't seem to appear until about the age 10 years and the difference seems to be reduced or eliminated in subjects with right-hemisphere damage. Experimenters have found that split-brain patients also indicate right-hemisphere involvement in face perception (Levy, Trevarthen, & Sperry, 1972; Trevarthen, this volume). That functional differences in perception of facial and nonfacial stimuli exist, and that these differences occur developmentally (possibly alone with neural structure development), form the basis of Diamond and Carey's (1977) suggestion that face perception is unique. Both Diamond and Carey and Trevarthen suggest the difference between face perception and other perception may be due to sensitivity to general gestalt qualities as opposed to sensitivity to isolated features of patterns. On the other hand, there might be differences in sensitivity to elastically transforming (animate) stimuli as opposed to sensitivity to rigid or nonelastically transforming (inanimate) stimuli. (See Ellis, 1975, for an interpretation that perception of faces is not special.)

Trevarthen (Chapter 6, this volume) argues that there is an even more general perceptual mode than face perception—a primitive, but pervasive intersubjective mode that is present in young infants. This mode involves both particular sensitivity to "social" stimulation and particular actions to which others are especially sensitive and responsive. Such a view is reinforced by Halliday's analysis (Chapter 5, this volume) of the functions of early language. One function is simply social binding.

In summary, besides modal distinctions for speech versus nonspeech, auditory perception, and general visual—auditory orientation versus focused manipulative and identification functions, other modal perceptual distinctions might include subjective versus objective perception, perception of objects or events via representational displays versus direct perception of things in themselves, and social versus physical perception. Given such modal distinctions, one can raise the question as to how they are organized. Is the operation of various modes of perceiving mutually exclusive or might the operation of modes be organized in some hierarchical fashion? For example, one might consider a priori that a perceiver would make some sort of decision whether to process for subjective or objective information. If the decision is to extract objective information, it could be information for spatial relations among objects or it could be for pattern identification. Correspondingly, if subjective information is being extracted, it could be information for orientation, like a body's relation to gravity, or external objects or for identification of body-part configuration, as in guidance of manipulation. If objective information is being extracted, a further decision might be to extract social or physical information, and so on. If such a hierarchical organization is to be taken seriously, one would have to have some direct evidence for levels of processing and multiple sequential decisions. This might be obtainable, but to our knowledge, no such evidence has been sought.

What Are the Distinguishing Characteristics of Modes?

In the examples of modal processing that have been mentioned (speech versus nonspeech; orientation versus identification and manipulation; representation versus real object; physical versus social; subjective versus objective), the main defining characteristic has been the processing and extraction of specific information for different *functions*. We would like to suggest that ideally, along with this functional difference in processing, there should be different neural systems or mechanisms mediating different modes. Then it would also be reasonable to find that patterns of individual differences would be different for different modes, and that the ontogenetic development of modal processing might have a different course for different modes.

In the above examples, we have noted some of the suggested neurally based differences, for example, the left-hemispheric association with speech perception; the suggestion of right-hemispheric association with face perception; and the different neural pathways for orientation information and for identification and manipulation. So far no such neural systems have been suggested for other hypothesized modes.

There are some rather interesting individual differences that may be implicated in the modal examples given above. The most dramatic of these were discovered by Day (1970, 1973) in the area of language processing. The criterion task used by Day involves dichotic listening to a pair of words, one to each ear; for example, *banket* in one ear and *lanket* in the other ear. A common perceptual experience reported by some subjects is fusion of the two words. In the example, they would perceive *blanket*. Some subjects fuse most pairs while other subjects fuse pairs rarely or not at all. Even if the task is changed so that it no longer is necessary to report one's perceptual experience but rather to report which phoneme came first, the same bimodal distribution occurs. (In this task the dichotic stimuli are started with slight asynchrony.) In this bimodal distribution, the high-fusing subjects are also poor judges of temporal order and the low-fusing subjects are good judges of temporal order. Day refers, tentatively, to the high fusers as language bound. In addition to the bimodal performance on the fusion and temporal-order tasks, there are highly correlated differences in a digit-memory-span task. The low fusers tend to do better at a digit-memory-span task and do not show a typical serial-position curve. An initial hypothesis by Day was that in many such tasks, language-bound subjects are constrained by linguistic properties even when they are not necessary for the particular task. The low fusers are not so constrained and, for example, in the digit-span task can use both a verbal and a visual encoding system. Marslen-Wilson (1973) discussed another striking example of individual differences in language processing. He used a shadowing task in which subjects were asked to repeat ongoing speech as rapidly as possible. Subjects divide into 2 groups in terms of the latencies with which they can do this. One group has modal latencies around 250 msec while the other group has modal latencies of 350 msec or greater. The relation between these individual differences and those of Day are not yet known.

Somewhat more tenuous and probably more controversial studies are also accumulating on individual differences in spatial orientation. One body of work suggests sex-linked genetic differences in some spatial abilities, such as mental rotation of shapes (Bock & Kolakowski, 1973; Carter-Saltzman, 1976; Garron, 1970; Stafford, 1961). A second body of work that is possibly related suggests spatial orientation deficiencies in girls with Turner's syndrome. This is a genetic anomaly in which one X chromosome of girls is absent or defective (Garron, 1970; Money, 1968; Schaffer, 1962). Girls with Turner's syndrome have been found to be retarded on the performance scales of standard intelligence tests relative to their scores on the verbal scale. This performance deficit seems to be especially great in tasks involving sense of direction, figure retention, and figure copying.

There also may be marked individual differences in the ability of subjects to utilize (and not utilize) pictorial information especially for distance and depth. Some reports have indicated that rural and/or uneducated non-Westerners have difficulty seeing depth in pictures (e.g., Deregowski, 1968; Hudson, 1967). There is some question whether the stimulus materials and the task procedures used permit strong inferences to be made. Not withstanding these problems, susceptibility to certain geometric illusions has been found to be much greater in Westerners than in non-Westerners who have had little exposure to pictures. These geometric illusions, like the Ponzo illusion (converging lines that might be seen as a perspective representation of a road) are often seen as representations of real depth by Westerners (Kilbride & Leibowitz, 1975; Segall, Campbell, & Herskovits, 1966). If so, the results would indicate that Westerners cannot inhibit responding to such line drawings as representations. It would seem that picture perception (at least for depth) is a special mode of perceiving for educated Westerners who have had considerable exposure to pictures. In this case, unlike that of the spatial performance of Turner's-syndrome girls, the development of the individual differences apparently depends on rather specific cultural experience.

Another example of differences attributable to cultural experience is the inability of Japanese to distinguish *r*s and *l*s occurring in both the production and perception of the sounds (Miyawaki, Strange, Verbrugge, Liberman, Jenkins, & Fujimura, 1975). This almost certainly is a function of experience during development since Japanese raised in English-speaking countries seem to make these discriminations and productions quite well.

Diamond and Carey (in press), as noted previously, reported a rather sharp change in the perception of face pictures occurring at about age 10. Before that age, there is little difference between the perception of faces and other stimuli. After the age of 10, perception of picture faces is disrupted by geometric rotation more than is the perception of other objects.

There may also be an interesting developmental trend in the ability to utilize pictorial depth information. Bower (1965) has reported that infants 40–60 days old are sensitive to motion parallax and stereoscopic depth information, but they are not sensitive to pictorial depth information like perspective and relative size. On the other hand, children 3–5 years old have been shown to be sensitive to relative size and interposition cues in pictorial depth (Olson, 1975), and they have been shown to make size judgments consistent with pictorial depth by 3 years (Yonas & Hagen, 1973). There may be some critical amount of experience with pictures that one has to have in order to be facile in seeing pictorial depth. Given that this is true, the cross-cultural studies of illusions mentioned previously would suggest that after a certain amount of exposure to pictures, it becomes very difficult to inhibit responding to pictorial depth, that is, not to perceive two-dimensional drawings in a picture mode.

What Are the Mechanisms by Which Modes Operate?

Ultimately the mechanisms underlying perceptual modes must be neural. However, we would like to consider briefly mechanisms at a more functional level. In particular, we would like to discuss two possible types of mechanisms, the first of which emphasizes the relation of perception to capacity for action; while the second emphasizes the role of mental operations in perceiving. The first mechanism consists of privileged stimulus–response relations. These are strikingly illustrated by the literature on ideo–motor and stimulus–response compatibility. Operationally ideo–motor compatibility (Greenwald, 1970; 1972; Greenwald & Schulman, 1973; James, 1890) consists of stimulus–response relations in which the feedback from the response is similar to the stimulus. For example, if a stimulus is an auditory, acoustic, or spoken word and the response is repeating the word, the auditory feedback is similar to the initial stimulus. Again if the stimulus is a target appearing in a particular spatial location and the response is a hand movement to that spatial location, the visual feedback has some of the same properties as the initial stimulus. Greenwald has demonstrated in various experiments that different ideomotor compatible acts do not interfere with each other when performed simultaneously. They also do not show the typical psychological refractory periods when performed in close succession.

Another kind of privileged stimulus–response relation is characterized in the research on spatial stimulus–response compatibility. For example, in a manual two-choice reaction time task, several investigators have shown that subjects can respond faster to a stimulus if both the stimulus and the responding hand are on the same side of the subject's midline–sagittal body plane. That is, if the subject's right hand is on his right side and his left hand is on his left side, he will be able to respond faster with his right hand if the appropriate stimulus appears on the right, and faster with his left hand if the second stimulus appears on the left. One might think, then, that privileged relations exist between the side of stimulus onset and the anatomically side-labeled hands. However, when the subject crosses his hands, the effect is seemingly reversed both for visual stimuli (Brebner, 1973; Brebner, Shephard, & Cairney, 1972; Wallace, 1971, 1972) and for auditory stimuli (Callan, Klisz, & Parsons, 1974; Klisz & Parsons, 1975; Simon, Hinrichs, & Craft, 1970). In this case (hands crossed), when the stimulus appears on the right, the subject is now able to respond faster with his *left* hand (which is on the right side) and conversely, when the stimulus appears on the left. Thus, this stimulus–response compatibility effect seems to depend on mechanisms that operate primarily within a body-*spatial* frame of reference (a reference system defined with respect to the spatially defined frontal, longitudinal, and sagittal axes of the body) rather than within a body-*anatomical* frame of reference (a reference system defined with respect to the anatomically defined proximodistal, rostrocausal, and dorsoventral axes of the body). It therefore appears that certain privileged relations exist between perception and action which map in a relatively automatic way the perceived locus of a stimulus in body space onto those response mechanisms that are best prepared to act upon that body-spatially defined locus.

This description of the spatial stimulus–response compatibility effect is actually an oversimplified and incomplete one, since it has recently been shown (Hedge & Marsh, 1975) that the effect can be reversed given an appropriate task, that under certain conditions subjects respond faster when stimuli and responses occur on *opposite* sides of the body midline. However, this finding does not seem to change in any crucial way the assertion that we are dealing with a modal phenomenon involving the relatively automatic operation of mechanisms that preferentially relate stimulus and response locations within the body-spatial frame of reference.

The second functional mechanism by which modes may operate involves the use of perceptual activities and strategies to structure the information being processed. With this mechanism, an initial direction is taken (voluntarily or involuntarily) and after that, processing goes on in such a way that one type of information is accepted and information of other types is rejected. An interesting example of such a process occurs in a study by Neisser and Becklen (1975). A subject is presented with two dynamic episodes, one in which two people pass a basketball back and forth, the other in which an adult and child play pattycake. The two episodes are then overlaid on a television monitor. The subject is given the task of following one or another of the episodes; for example, to count the number of ball passes. When the subject is thus engaged in following one episode, he or she is relatively unaware of events occurring in the other episode, even missing such things as change of actor. Neisser and Becklen suggest that a person is able to attend to one or another episode because he or she is actively constructing a schema of expectancies that constrain the possible information that can be processed meaningfully. It is a way of staying oriented to a particular episode. Events in the episode being followed can be processed in the context of these expectancies. Events in the alternative episodes are uninformative, like any random noise. A similar interpretation is implied by Gibson and Levin (1975) in their discussion of the process of reading. In reading, as in the Neisser and Becklen (1975) situation, a person is often faced with perception of sequentially dependent events, as in reading across a line of text. Gibson and Levin also suggest that the context constrains the possible alternative subsequent events. In their view, then, the skilled perceiver can attend to the most economical set of features for specifying the event. Gibson and Levin tend to emphasize the guidance of search as opposed to the construction of a schema that includes expectancies.

Such a mechanism involving perceptual activity might explain a phenomenon that traditional filter theories of attention have not been able to. In the earliest form of these theories (Broadbent, 1958), it was supposed that persons could attend to one or another channel of information and the information to the other channel was lost. The difficulty was that certain key words, like the person's own name, could be detected on the nonattended channel. In later theories of attention (e.g., Triesman, 1969), it was suggested that stimulation in the nonattended channel was not eliminated completely, but only attenuated. However, with Neisser and Becklen's (1975) or Gibson and Levin's (1975) approach, a subject would always be tuned in for certain critical stimulus features (like those that specify his name), but could dynamically adjust the other features for attention according to the context activity.

Is Perceptual Mode a Distinct Concept?

The problem of selective attention raises the general question of the distinctiveness of the concept of perceptual mode. Mode appears to be one of that category of concepts concerned with direction of perception: set, Aufgabe, Einstellung, selective attention, and so on. We would like to suggest that a major novel aspect of mode is generality which arises out of a close relation between perception and physical or mental action. With respect to the stimulus–response compatibility, the association is perception for action. With respect to the selective processing of information, illustrated by Neisser and Becklen (1975), the association is activity for perception. Set, selective attention, and so on, all tend to be used in a narrow and passive sense.

They tend to emphasize selectivity rather than different processing. If the filter analogy for selective attention is taken as a case in point, one thinks of filters for one ear or the other ear; for a particular voice quality; for particular words; but not for speech characteristics of an acoustic stream; or for information for "where," as opposed to "what"; and so on. Similarly, set seems to be used in a very specific sense. Recent studies on set, for example, from the Russians include experiments in which a person is set for German words as opposed to Russian words, or a person is set for a specific weight and then lifts a different one, and so on (Natadze, 1969). This use also seems to be similar to the use of Aufgabe and Einstellung by the Würzberg school (see Humphrey, 1963). Even Neisser's concept of a schema also seems to imply a rather specific construction, instead of accepting more general types of information or general ways of processing stimulation of a specific type. The concept of mode as we intend it, implies the engaging of a general mechanism, and perhaps initiation of complex behavior for the guidance of perception, in a way that simply setting a passive filter does not.

In order for mode to be a useful concept, it is important to specify the functional distinctiveness of the various modes. This should ultimately include demonstrations not only that different modes have different types of information, intake, and processing, but that within one mode, different types of stimulation are processed similarly. In addition, for mode to be more useful than the classical directional concepts in perception, it is important to go further. The mechanisms that underlie modal processing must be specified and the way these mechanisms get triggered must be understood.

At present we conceive of mode as involving an approach to behavior that recognizes the importance of *non*arbitrary relations between different types of information, perceiving, and acting. That is, an organism's behavior is viewed as being significantly determined or affected by different informational subsystems that *predispose* the organism to perceive and act upon a certain type of information in a characteristically distinct way from that used to perceive and act upon a different type of information. These nonarbitrary and predispositional qualities of mode evoke a parallel between the concept of mode as presented in this chapter (and volume) and the concept of biological boundaries of learning as stated and elaborated in a book by Seligman and Hager (1972). According to this latter view, the formation of associations between stimuli and responses in a laboratory situation cannot be explained through a single general theory of learning in which any stimulus can be arbitrarily associated with any response. Rather, there are *non*arbitrary species-specific constraints on learning that must be taken into consideration when one attempts to predict and/or explain the outcome of a typical learning experiment in the laboratory. In a review of Seligman and Hager's book, Schwartz (1974) comments:

> Organisms came biologically equipped to make some (prepared) associations, and biologically very ill-equipped to make others (contraprepared). In the middle are the arbitrary (unprepared) associations, which have been studied traditionally in learning laboratories. The concept of preparedness is thus a label for an ease of learning continuum, and Seligman and Hager suggest that the very laws of learning may vary with the place on the preparedness continuum that particular experiments sample [pp. 184–185].

The usefulness of these principles in describing or explaining the outcomes of learning experiments in a particular species is illustrated in the literature on taste-aversion learning in rats (Garcia & Koelling, 1966). These experimenters showed that rats:

> ... differentially associate tastes as CSs with stomach illness as the US (prepared), and exteroceptive CSs with shock as the US (unprepared), but fail to associate taste with shock and exteroceptive stimuli with stomach illness (contraprepared) [Schwartz, 1974, p. 185].

In summary, then, Seligman and Hager approach the problem of learning from a perspective that recognizes the significant contributions of nonarbitrary species-specific informational constraints to learning. In a similar way, one can view modes as a concept that emphasizes the significant contributions of information-specific constraints to perceiving and acting. However, at the same time we must stay aware not only of the danger of ignoring the presence of nonmodal mechanisms that must surely interact with modal ones in the production of behavior, but also of the danger of reifying the concept of mode. In the sense of the latter, it should be pointed out that just because one can specify a few cases of distinctive information processing does not *necessarily* mean that it will be fruitful to divide the domains of perception and action into a potentially unbounded proliferation of modes. Nevertheless the concept of mode with its entailed perspective on behavior seems to provide an approach that is well worth exploring.

OBJECTIVE OBSERVATIONS ON SUBJECTIVE MODES

As part of our empirical contribution to these issues, we want to focus on a possible distinction between objective and subjective perception. In the first part of the discussion we examine evidence that suggests that differences in *identification* of stimulation are dependent on use of a subjective or objective frame of reference. In the second part of our discussion we examine evidence that suggests perception in *control* of one's own behavior may be different from perception of similar information produced by another.

The Use of Subjective and Objective Reference Systems

Let us first consider the subjective–objective reference systems in the recognition or identification of patterns of stimulation. Attneave and his colleagues (Attneave & Benson, 1969; Attneave & Olson, 1967; Attneave & Reid, 1968) several years ago described some intriguing observations on identification of shapes of objects in various orientations. Specifically, they taught subjects to identify with nonsense names visually presented bars in various orientations: horizontal, vertical, left, and right diagonals. Subjects were asked to respond as rapidly as possible with the name when the bar was presented. The first interesting result was that subjects responded to horizontal and vertical bars with faster reaction times than they did to diagonals. This difference in reaction time was more closely associated with environmental horizontal and vertical orientation than with retinal horizontal and vertical orientation since the same results were obtained when subjects learned the identification with their head tilted 45°. More generally, subjects seemed to learn these identifications in relation to environmental reference systems. After initial learning with head either upright or tilted 45°, subjects were changed to the other head orientation. With their heads in the new orientation, subjects might be asked to identify the lines using the same names relative to gravity or the same names relative to their retinal orientation. Identification was very slow when the same names in relation to a retinal orientation were required. Subjects could, if instructed in the initial learning of the identification, adopt a retinal reference system for orientation so that when they changed to the new head orientation it was easy to respond with names that were the same in relation to the retina. Nevertheless it seemed that there was a marked bias toward using an objective or gravity-based reference system for the identification of differently oriented visual stimuli.

A similar bias toward an objective reference system was found in a different experiment involving tactual stimulation of the fingers of the hand (Attneave & Benson, 1969). The fingers of one hand were placed over a set of vibrators arranged vertically and the fingers of the other hand were placed over a set of vibrators arranged horizontally. Subjects were taught to associate nonsense labels with stimulation by the vibrators of the different fingers. After they had learned these labels, the two hands shifted positions. The fingers covering the horizontal vibrators were shifted to the vertical and vice versa. Subjects were again asked to give the associated nonsense labels upon presentation of stimulation to the different fingers. Most did so in terms of which vibrator stimulated the finger, that is, they were biased towards the objective spatial position, not the specific finger being stimulated. However, if the subjects had their eyes closed during the original learning of the nonsense syllables the bias was reduced and they were just as likely to respond in terms of the finger stimulated as in terms of the spatial position or specific vibrator.

Might there be a case in which the bias toward objective identification would not be so strong or could even be reversed? Perhaps the ambiguity of the tendency in this last vibrator experiment without vision provides a lead. A study in collaboration with Rieser (Rieser & Pick, 1976) was modeled after those of Attneave and his colleagues but involved identification of tactual and haptic stimuli. In one experiment the subjects were again taught to identify stimuli in various orientations with nonsense names. The haptic stimuli were presented in the form of bars which the subjects, with eyes closed, grasped while the tactual stimuli were smaller bars impressed on the forehead. Subjects learned the names for these stimuli either lying on their side or standing upright. They were then changed to the other posture and asked to continue applying the same names. All the tactual subjects responded with the same names in relation to a *subjective,* that is, anatomical or body spatial-reference system (see previous discussion on stimulus–response compatibility and 11 out of 12 haptic subjects responded in terms of an objective (or gravity) reference system. In a subsequent experiment, tactual and haptic subjects were instructed during initial learning of the labels to think in terms of reference systems counter to these subjective and objective biases. The tactual subjects were instructed to think of up–down and right–left in terms of gravity and the haptic subjects were instructed to think of up–down in relation to their own body. As evidenced by their continued labeling when posture was changed, about half the haptic subjects did change their reference system, whereas none of the tactual subjects changed. They continued to respond in terms of a subjective or body-reference system.

Why should subjects initially show this different bias for the two forms of stimulus presentation? The haptic stimuli are, in fact, palpable objects in the real world. They elicit an appropriate mode of processing, one that exhibits a constancy like behavior—identification is independent of body orientation. The tactual stimuli are irritations on the skin and in that sense seem relevant mainly to a subjective mode of processing. Haptic sensitivity seems designed to take into account the position of the body in relation to external stimuli and forces, as for example, in our own finely tuned antigravity postural reflexes. On the other hand, tactual sensitivity provides information about what and where something is scratching and/or biting.

Why should subjects be able to shift voluntarily to a tactual reference system but not to a haptic system? The use of an objective reference system for identification of haptic stimuli implies that both the orientation of the body and the orientation of the object relative to the body are taken into account. Since the response is made after this convergence of information, it is not surprising that both are available. Subjects can, to some extent, voluntarily shift the basis for their identification. On the other hand, no such convergence is required for tactual identification and that may account for the difficulty subjects have in shifting the basis of their tactual identification.

Congruent with the present tactual and haptic results is recent evidence of a convergence in a primary cortical vestibular projection area of vestibular and joint afference (Schwarz & Fredrickson, 1971). Of the units examined 80% were sensitive to both vestibular and kinesthetic stimulation, but none responded to tactile stimulation. The vestibular-projection area included the lower lip of the distal end of the intraparietal sulcus. This general area was also implicated by Pohl (1973) in tasks involving use of external reference systems in spatial-layout problems. Pohl found that monkeys who had bilateral posterior parietal lesions had considerable difficulty with reversals of place learning discriminations but they could reverse response learning discriminations relatively easily. Animals with prefrontal lesions had an opposite pattern.[2] While one is tempted to think of the posterior parietals association areas as a site for integration of spatial information from different sense modalities, some recent analysis by Mountcastle, Lynch, Georgopoulos, Sakata, and Acuna (1975) suggests there may be relatively little convergence of memory information. Mountcastle and coworkers suggest that this area might be better conceived of as a general-directing or command center for certain types of hand and eye movements.

In any event it appears that tactual stimulation under some circumstances is referred to an anatomical or body spatial-reference system and is processed quite differently from formally similar haptic stimulation. Furthermore there is at least suggestive evidence that this difference is mediated by different neural systems.

Self-Perception in the Control of Speech Production

As a second kind of subjective–objective perceptual distinction we would like to consider evidence about perception which occurs during our own actions. There is considerable evidence that perception while we are engaged in activity (perhaps perception in the service of guiding such activity) is different from perception under more passive, or simply receptive conditions. There are lots of examples of this sort in visual perception. A dramatic one is the decreased sensitivity during saccadic eye movements. Why and how this happens is still a

[2] Mendoza and Thomas (1975) disagree with Pohl's interpretation. They have shown that Pohl's landmark reversal problem also contained a factor of separation of landmark cue and reward location which probably caused the difficulty of the problem for the posterior parietals. Their argument is not completely convincing. First Mendoza and Thomas' prefrontal animals as well as posterior parietal animals *both* had difficulty with their problems; and second, the discrimination problem they used was of a very different kind involving a *pattern* of separated objects. It is possible that this pattern itself involves some sort of appreciation of external spatial layout.

matter of much controversy. However, the suggestion has been made that the suppression is partly a by-product of the amount of attention devoted to recomputation of the visual frame of reference so that the visual system can properly interpret the change of retinal stimulation due to self-produced image movement. In a closely related domain is the perception during pursuit eye movements as studied by Arien Mack (Chapter 8, this volume). Similarly, Lee's (1974) research is very relevant. He shows that optical stimulation during locomotion provides information for guiding that movement.

The reafference concept of von Holst (1954), especially as used by Held (Held and Hein, 1958), to explain certain aspects of adaptation to visual distortion, is also relevant here. Perception based on exafferent stimulation (externally produced) is quite different from perception based on the formally similar reafferent (self-produced) stimulation.

Some evidence in a different domain, audio—motor behavior as compared to visual—motor behavior, suggests perception during our own vocal productions is different from that during perception of similar stimulation from another person.

A common observation in children's speech is that misarticulations may not be corrected even when called to the attention of the speakers. For example a child we know often referred to his friends, Mike and Sally as *Sike and Mally*. If an adult responded in kind with some reference to Sike and Mally he would indignantly say, "*Not Sike and Mally, Sike and Mally!*" Such behavior, which is not at all unusual, appears to be a good example of a case where perception of one's own articulation does not match similar perception of another's. Such examples have often been subject to the criticism that the child's own production of the two *Sike* and *Mally* tokens may be subtly different and we adults don't hear the difference. Recently that criticism has been put to an experimental test. Locke and Kutz (1975) recorded kindergarteners' productions of words like *sing* and *wing, run* and *one*, and so on. Half of the children had articulation difficulties that involved their substitutions of /w/ for /r/ such as in Bugs Bunny, the wabbit. These recordings were then played back to the children for identification. (They had to choose the correct of two pictures describing the word.) Both the good and poor articulators identified correctly the experimenter's productions. However, the poor articulators were very poor at identifying their own productions of words like *ring, run, right,* and so on.

In a completely different paradigm, Lackner (1974) has explored the verbal transformation effect during speech production. This verbal transformation effect is the very unusual perceptual phenomenon that occurs when one listens to the same word repeated over and over again very rapidly—like "ring, ring, ring, ring, ring, . . ." The perception begins to change after some time and one might hear "ring, ring, wing, wing, sing, . . ." This effect is very compelling and even the greatest skeptics who know what the effect is can't avoid the experience. Lackner (1974) asked subjects to produce strings of repetitions of the same consonant—vowel syllables. They were able to do this with very few articulation errors but they reported that they experienced no verbal transformation effect. When they listened to recordings of their own productions, on the other hand, they did in fact experience the usual transformation effects. Again, perception during production appears to be different from perception of external stimulation.

In our own research in collaboration with Gerald Siegel and Sharon Garber, we have been interested in the role of auditory feedback in speech production. Initially we focused on the effects of amplification of auditory feedback and of masking auditory feedback on intensity of vocal production (Siegel & Pick, 1974). Our initial question was whether subjects would compensate for changes in signal to noise ratio of their own productions. If we amplified their auditory feedback, would they reduce their intensity and if we added noise to their auditory feedback would they raise their voices? With some qualifications about factors that effect the magnitude of the changes, the answer in both cases is positive. We have also begun work on distorting the frequency of auditory feedback by means of filtering. Subjects will raise their fundamental frequency when the high frequencies in their auditory feedback are attenuated. However, this may be due to the fact that they increase their vocal intensity and may not be a direct compensatory effect for the frequency filtering. Elliott and Niemoller (1970), and Ward and Burns (1975) present additional evidence that suggests that subjects are unable to modulate frequency very well without auditory feedback. Elliott and Niemoller asked subjects to match particular sample frequencies and then presented intense masking noises while subjects unsuccessfully tried to perform their match. Ward and Burns similarly found that subjects performed very poorly when asked to sing scales under masking conditions.

In spite of considerable evidence like this, that subjects use or need auditory feedback to modulate intensity and frequency, there seems to be very little evidence that auditory feedback is involved in modulation of articulation:

1. In spite of a great deal of observation of large numbers of our subjects and ourselves speaking under various degrees of noise, we have never observed any appreciable, that is, obvious, increase in number of articulation errors.

2. We have seen two adventitiously, profoundly deaf individuals whose articulation appeared quite normal even several years after they became deaf. Of course, we didn't have predeaf speech samples from them, however, their articulation would certainly have been judged normal by naive listeners; but it is possible that there may have been very slight abnormalities in intonation patterns.

3. Studies in which auditory feedback and deprivation of tactual and proprioceptive feedback are both involved show relatively little reduction of intelli-

gibility (Ringel, 1970). If auditory feedback were important for modulating articulation, its absence would manifest itself most obviously when other sensory feedback was eliminated or reduced.

Our own introspection in speaking under intense masking noise is that it is not at all obvious when one can hear or cannot hear oneself. Phenomenally we know what we are saying and it is not clear whether we hear what we have said or we hear what we know we are saying. The mind's ear is at work.

There are a number of possible ways to test experimentally whether we monitor our own articulation using auditory feedback. One is to examine the number of articulation errors that occur speaking with and without auditory feedback. Working in collaboration with Jacqueline Rockler, we have been attempting to induce more errors than normal. Subjects are asked to recite tongue twisters with and without masking noise. Preliminary results suggest that subjects do not make any more errors under noise, but they do make fewer self-corrections of errors. Such a result, if it continues to be maintained, would very reasonably suggest that auditory feedback operates on articulation not to correct ongoing vocal gestures since it would be too late. Rather, it operates to correct errors already made or possibly to vary the way the whole task is being performed, as for example when the drunk is careful not to slur his or her words.

Nevertheless it seems paradoxical that the relatively simple but absolute qualities of intensity and frequency are sensitive to manipulation of auditory feedback; the very complex articulation features which presumably we focus on in perceiving another's speech are, and because of timing, must be, robust when we lack auditory feedback. We would like to argue that it is the very complexity of articulation that permits its survival in the absence of feedback. Proper articulation depends on the patterning of movements and they can be programmed in relation to one another and don't need the support of external feedback. The simple and absolute qualities of intensity and frequency are not programmed relationally, and hence depend on auditory feedback.

In summary we have tried to illustrate from two very different domains of perception how the information extracted might characterize a subjective, as opposed to an objective perceptual mode. In both the case of the tactual and haptic identification of line stimuli, and in the case of the auditory perception during one's own and another's speech, the stimulation is formally very similar. But the information for the perceiver is quite different, depending on the mode by which the stimulation is processed in a given task.

ACKNOWLEDGMENTS

The preparation of this paper and research reported herein was supported by a Program Project Grant HD-05027 from the National Institutes of Health to the Institute of Child

Development of the University of Minnesota and by the Center for Research in Human Learning of the University of Minnesota.

REFERENCES

Attneave, F., & Benson, B. Spatial coding of factual stimulation. *Journal of Experimental Psychology,* 1969, *81,* 216–222.
Attneave, F., & Olson, R. K. Discriminability of stimuli varying in physical and retinal orientation. *Journal of Experimental Psychology,* 1967, *74,* 149–157.
Attneave, F., & Reid, K. W. Voluntary control of frame of reference and slope equivalence under head rotation. *Journal of Experimental Psychology,* 1968, *78,* 153–159.
Bock, R. D., & Kolakowski, D. Further evidence of sex-linked major gene influences on human spatial visualizing ability. *American Journal of Human Genetics,* 1973, *25,* 1–14.
Bower, T. G. R. Stimulus variables determining space perception in infants. *Science,* 1965, *149,* 88–89.
Brebner, J. S–R compatibility and changes in RT with practice. *Acta Psychologica,* 1973, *37,* 93–106.
Brebner, J., Shephard, M., & Cairney, P. Spatial relationships and S–R compatibility. *Acta Psychologica,* 1972, *36,* 1–15.
Broadbent, D. E. *Perception and communication.* New York: Pergamon Press, 1958.
Callan, J., Klisz, D., & Parsons, O. A. Strength of auditory stimulus response compatibility as a function of task complexity. *Journal of Experimental Psychology,* 1974, *102,* 1039–1045.
Carter-Saltzman, L. A theoretical consideration of sex differences in spatial visualizing abilities. Unpublished manuscript. University of Minnesota, 1976.
Day, R. S. Temporal order judgements in speech: Are individuals language-bound or stimulus-bound? Haskins Laboratories, *Status Reports,* 1970, *SR-21/22,* 71–87.
Day, R. S. Digit-span memory in language-bound and stimulus-bound subjects. Haskins Laboratories, *Status Reports,* 1973, *SR-34,* 127–139.
Deregowski, J. B. Difficulties in pictorial depth perception in Africa. *British Journal of Psychology,* 1968, *59,* 195–204.
Diamond, R., & Carey, S. Developmental changes in representation of faces. *Journal of Experimental Child Psychology,* 1977, *23,* 1–22.
Elliot, L., & Niemoller, A. The role of hearing in controlling voice fundamental frequency. *International Audiology,* 1970, *9,* 47–52.
Ellis, H. D., Recognizing faces. *British Journal of Psychology,* 1975, *66,* 409–426.
Evans, E. F. Neural processes for the detection of acoustic patterns and for sound localization. In F. O. Schmitt & F. G. Worden (Eds.), *The neurosciences: Third study program.* Cambridge, Mass.: M.I.T. Press, 1974. Pp. 131–145.
Garcia, J., & Koelling, R. Relation of cue to consequence in avoidance learning. *Psychonomic Science,* 1966, *4,* 123–124.
Garron, D. C. Sex-linked recessive inheritance of spatial and numerical abilities and Turner's Syndrome. *Psychological Review,* 1970, *77,* 147–152.
Gibson, E. J., & Levin, H. *The psychology of reading.* Cambridge, Mass.: M.I.T. Press, 1975.
Gibson, J. J. *The perception of the visual world.* Cambridge, Mass.: Riverside Press, 1950.
Gibson, J. J. *The senses considered as perceptual systems.* Boston: Houghton Mifflin, 1966.
Greenwald, A. G. Sensory feedback mechanisms in performance control: With spatial reference to the ideo-motor mechanism. *Psychological Review,* 1970, *77,* 73–99.
Greenwald, A. G. On doing 2 things at once: Time-sharing as a function of ideomotor compatibility. *Journal of Experimental Psychology,* 1972, *94,* 52–57.

Greenwald, A. G., & Schulman, H. G. On doing 2 things at once: II. Elimination of the psychological refractory period effect. *Journal of Experimental Psychology*, 1973, *101*, 70–76.

Hedge, A., & Marsh, N. W. A. The effect of irrelevant spatial correspondences on two-choice response time. *Acta Psychologica*, 1975, *39*, 427–439.

Heider, F. Social perception and phenomenal causality. *Psychological Review*, 1944, *51*, 358–374.

Held, R., & Hein, A. Adaptation of disarranged hand-eye coordination contingent upon reafferent stimulation. *Perceptual and Motor Skills*, 1958, *8*, 87–90.

Hess, V. L., & Pick, A. D. Discrimination of schematic faces by nursery school children. *Child Development*, 1974, *45*, 1151–1154.

Hudson, W. The study of the problem of pictorial perception among unacculturated groups. *International Journal of Psychology*, 1967, *2*, 89–107.

Humphrey, G. *Thinking: An introduction to its experimental psychology.* New York: Wiley, 1963.

James, W. *Principles of psychology* (Vol. 2). New York: Henry Holt, 1890.

Kilbride, P., & Leibowitz, H. W. Factors affecting the magnitude of the ponzo perspective illusion among the Baganda. *Perception & Psychophysics*, 1975, *17*, 543–548.

Klisz, D. K., & Parsons, O. A. Ear asymmetry in reaction time tasks as a function of handedness. *Neuropsychologia*, 1975, *13*, 323–330.

LaBerge, D., & Samuels, S. J. Toward a theory of automatic information processing in reading. *Cognitive Psychology*, 1974, *6*, 293–323.

Lackner, J. Speech production: evidence for collary discharge stabilization of perceptual mechanisms. *Perceptual and Motor Skills*, 1974, *39*, 899–902.

Lee, D. N. Visual information during locomotion. In R. B. MacLeod & H. L. Pick, Jr. (Eds.), *Perception: Essays in honor of James J. Gibson.* Ithaca, N. Y.: Cornell University Press, 1974.

Levy, J., Trevarthen, C., & Sperry, R. W. Perception of bilateral chimeric figures following hemispheric deconnexion. *Brain*, 1972, *95*, 61–78.

Locke, J. L., & Kutz, K. J. Memory for speech and speech for memory. *Journal of Speech and Hearing Research*, 1975, *18*, 176–191.

Marslen-Wilson, W. Linguistic structure and speech shadowing at very short latencies. *Nature*, 1973, *244*, 522–523.

Mendoza, J. E., & Thomas, R. K., Jr. Effects of posterior parietal and frontal neocortical lesions in the squirrel monkey. *Journal of Comparative & Physiological Psychology*, 1975, *89*, 170–182.

Miyawaki, K., Strange, W., Verbrugge, R., Liberman, A. M., Jenkins, J. J., & Fujimura, O. An effect of linguistic experience: The discrimination of [r] and [l] by native speakers of Japanese and English. *Perception & Psychophysics*, 1975, *18*, 331–340.

Money, J. Cognitive deficits in Turner's Syndrome. In S. G. Vandenburg (Ed.), *Progress in human genetics.* Baltimore: Johns Hopkins Press, 1968.

Mountcastle, V. B., Lynch, J. C., Georgopoulos, A., Sakata, H., & Acuna, C. Posterior parietal association cortex of the monkey: Commmand functions for operations within extrapersonal space. *Journal of Neurophysiology*, 1975, *38*, 871–908.

Natadze, R. G. Experimental foundations of Usnadze's theory of set. In M. Cole & I. Maltzman (Eds.), *A handbook of contemporary Soviet psychology.* New York: Basic Books, 1969. Pp. 603–624.

Neisser, U., & Becklen, R. Selective looking: Attending to visually specified events. *Cognitive Psychology*, 1975, *7*, 480–494.

Olson, R. K. Children's sensitivity to pictorial depth information. *Perception and Physics*, 1975, *17*, 59–64.

Pohl, W. Dissociation of spatial discrimination deficits following frontal and parietal lesions in monkeys. *Journal of Comparative & Physiological Psychology*, 1973, *82*, 227–239.

Posner, M. I., Lewis, J., & Conrad, C. Component processes in reading: a performance analysis. In J. Kavenagh & I. Mattingly (Eds.), *Language by ear and eye.* Cambridge, Mass.: M.I. T. Press, 1972.

Rieser, J. J., & Pick, H. L., Jr. Reference systems and the perception of tactual and haptic orientation. *Perception and Psychophysics, 1976, 19,* 117–121

Ringel, R. L. Oral sensation and perception: A selective review. *American Speech and Hearing Association,* 1970, *5,* 188–206.

Rock, I. *Orientation and form.* New York: Academic Press, 1973.

Schaffer, W. J. A specific cognitive deficit observed in gonadal aplasia (Turner's Syndrome). *Journal of Clinical Psychology,* 1962, *18,* 403–406.

Schwartz, E. On going back to nature: A review of Seligman and Hager's *Biological boundaries of learning. Journal of the Experimental Analysis of Behavior,* 1974, *21,* 183–198.

Schwarz, D. W. F., & Fredrickson, J. M. Rhesus monkey vestibular cortex: A bimodal primary projection field. *Science,* 1971, *172,* 280–281.

Segall, M. H., Campbell, D. T., & Herskovits, D. T. *The influence of culture on visual perception.* Indianapolis, Ind.: Bobbs-Merrill, 1966.

Seligman, M. E. P., & Hager, J. L. *Biological boundaries of learning.* New York: Appleton-Century-Crofts, 1972.

Siegel, G. M., & Pick, H. L., Jr. Auditory feedback in the regulation of voice. *Journal of the Acoustical Society of America,* 1974, *56,* 1618–1624.

Simon, J. R., Hinrichs, J. V., & Craft, J. L. Auditory S–R compatibility: Reaction time as a function of ear-hand correspondence and ear-response location correspondence. *Journal of Experimental Psychology,* 1970, *86,* 97–102.

Stafford, R. E. Sex differences in spatial visualization as evidence of sex-linked inheritance. *Perceptual and Motor Skills,* 1961, *13,* 428.

Thomas, D. Vision and prayer. In O. Williams (Ed.), *A little treasury of modern poetry.* New York: Charles Scribner's Sons, 1952.

Triesman, A. M. Strategies and model of selective attention. *Psychological Review,* 1969, *76,* 282–299.

Trevarthen, C. B. Two mechanisms of vision in primates. *Psychologische Forschung,* 1968, *31,* 299–337.

von Holst, E. Relations between the central nervous system and the peripheral organs. *British Journal of Animal Behaviour,* 1954, *2,* 89–94.

Wallace, R. J. S–R compatibility and the idea of a response code. *Journal of Experimental Psychology,* 1971, *88,* 354–360.

Wallace, R. J. Spatial S–R compatibility effects involving kinesthetic cues. *Journal of Experimental Psychology,* 1972, *93,* 163–168.

Ward, W. D., & Burns, E. M. Pitch performance in singing without auditory feedback. *Journal of Acoustical Society of America,* 1975, *58,* (Supplement No. 1), 5–116. (Abstract).

Yonas, A., & Hagen, M. Effects of static and motion parallax depth information on perception of size in children and adults. *Journal of Experimental Child Psychology,* 1973, *15,* 254–265.

Part I

PERCEPTION OF COMMUNICATIVE INFORMATION

The first section of this book consists of four chapters concerning perception of information relevant to communication. In order for people to communicate with each other, it is efficient to have a procedure that abstracts relevant aspects of real situations and events and presents them in ways that are easily manipulated and easily understood. Mankind has developed at least two media with associated forms of behavior that are particularly well suited to communication. One is pictorial representation, and the other is language. Representative pictures might be thought of as analogue representations. In pictorial processing, a perceiver can capitalize on the same perceptual processing he or she uses for dealing with the real world to the extent that the same features of stimulation are present in the picture as are present in the object or event being represented. However, the observer, presumably, also must know that he or she is viewing a picture. Language, on the other hand, is not an analogue representation in the same sense; and the perception or comprehension of meaning in language is not so likely to involve the same form of processing as is involved in dealing with the nonlinguistic world.

The authors of the first four chapters examine whether the perception of pictorial and linguistic information reflect any special characteristics of their own. Hagen focuses on possible differences between perception of pictures and the real events being depicted. Paivio treats as similar the perception of pictures and real objects and focuses on the difference in the processing of verbal material as opposed to real and pictured objects.

MacNeilage and Halliday discuss specifically the possible special characteristics of vocal speech as opposed to the graphic forms of language. If, as suggested here, language perception cannot only depend on the same mechanism as perception of nonlinguistic natural events, is there a special speech processor? This is the question considered by MacNeilage. Halliday, in his analysis, concentrates on the social and functional aspects of language and in doing so really emphasizes the communicative aspects of language.

2

An Outline of an Investigation into the Special Character of Pictures

Margaret A. Hagen

Boston University

EDITORS' INTRODUCTION

Representational displays, by definition, are examples of stimuli that provide information for alternative percepts: the representations as objects in themselves and the objects that are being represented. Pictures, of course, represent a common type of representational display, and picture perception has been given considerable attention by researchers. There is evidence that both people and animals with little or no exposure to pictures can readily identify pictorially portrayed familiar objects. This would seem to suggest that pictorial object recognition does not involve any special mode of perception. However, the perception of depth and distance relations in pictures does not seem to occur automatically along with the ability to perceive such relations in the real world. Margaret Hagen describes a program of research in which the factors involved in the perception of these pictorial spatial relations are analyzed. One important factor she discusses is the presence of surface information, specifying the flat quality of a picture as an object in itself. While this information conflicts with any pictorial depth information, it can also serve to cue a compensatory pictorial-processing mode.

In the past, I have tried to argue the question of the utility of *mode* as a concept to explain pictorial perception. I argued from a Gibsonian position that mode was indeed a useful concept: It appeared to solve the problems of poor picture perception occurring when: (1) successful perception was hypothesized; and, on the other side of the coin, when (2) successful perception occurred but only poor perception had been expected.

In this chapter I do not discuss the question of pictorial mode per se, but what I call the question of the special character of pictorial perception. Is perceiving pictures much the same as perceiving the ordinary environment, or is there something special going on with pictures? Is there either something special about the information pictures contain, or something special that we do with that information?

To orient the discussion as it was oriented for me chronologically, I must start again with Gibson's theory of pictures. Gibson (1971) has argued: "A picture is a surface so treated that a delimited optic array to a point of observation is made available which contains the same kind of information that is found in the ambient optic arrays of an ordinary environment [p. 31]."

That definition certainly has an elegant simplicity. To represent a particular scene pictorially, all we have to do is fix a point of observation and reproduce the static visual information essential for the identification and location of objects in that scene. What this formula essentially reduces to is the principle of perspective, taken in its broadest sense of the overall regular optical compression with distance of all visible projected surfaces, or projective geometry with special attention to the plane of projection. Leonardo said that:

Perspective is nothing else than seeing a place (or objects) behind a plane of glass, quite transparent, on the surface of which the objects behind that glass are to be drawn. These can be traced in pyramids to the point in the eye, and they are intersected on the glass plane. [Richter & Richter, 1970, p. 53].

The validity of perspective can be demonstrated mathematically and functionally. It is indeed possible to fool the eye with a well-constructed trompe l'oeil painting or photograph. Given such cases it is very difficult to argue against the possibility of capturing essential environmental information in pictures. It also seems rather superfluous to argue for the special character of such captured information. After all, one can even capture it mechanically with a very acultural pinhole camera. If one believes that such perspective information is fundamental to ordinary perception, and, further, that the capture of such information on the picture plane is a logical, optical, geometric necessity, then one is rather firmly committed to the argument that pictorial perception can be, essentially, no different from perception of the ordinary environment.

There is, of course, one caveat that can be introduced here. It may be argued that the information fundamental to ordinary perception is not that from static, monocular perspective, but the information from motion perspective—regular, lawful changes in the perspective of a scene or object generated by motion of the observer or the observed. It may well be that perception of static perspective, or single snapshot views, is related only in a derivative fashion to the case of ordinary perception. Hence the perception of static monocular views, whether pictorial or otherwise, would be an acquired ability. Such a situation, however, would certainly not provide support for the notion of the special static information (but this question is not the subject of this discussion).

In sum, pictures have no special character because they contain within themselves the same kind of information found in the ordinary environment. Hence, no special training or experience should be required to perceive successfully pictured scenes.

There are two bodies of literature in which the question of the character of pictorial perception vis a vis ordinary perception is considered: the cross-cultural literature and the developmental literature. Within these are two content areas: the recognition or identification of pictured objects, and the perception of pictured spatial relations (which is nearly always pictorial depth perception). Object perception does not immediately concern us here, so let me dispense with it by saying that there is almost no evidence in either the developmental or the cross-cultural literature to suggest any inferiority with object recognition in pictures relative to object recognition in the ordinary environment. A distinctive feature analysis of pictorial object perception and production needs to be integrated into a comprehensive informational analysis of the depiction of spatial relations in pictures; but this is not done in this chapter.

There have been few systematic investigations of the ability to perceive depth in pictures. The evidence available suggests that pictorial depth perception is an acquired ability requiring frequent exposure to pictures for its acquisition. Developmental and cross-cultural researchers suggest in particular that pictorial perception of spatial relations develops somewhat later than does the perception of spatial relations in the ordinary environment. Bower (1965, 1966) found that infants maintained size constancy and unitary object perception only in the presence of motion-parallax information and not when pictorial cues alone were available. Babies 40–60 days old were insensitive to linear and texture information for size at a distance in photographic transparencies, while they responded appropriately to similar information in real scenes. In the latter case, however, the static-perspective information was accompanied by both motion-parallax and motion-perspective information. Hudson (1960, 1962, 1967) investigated African pictorial-depth perception, using the Hudson Pictorial Depth Perception Test. Results on the Hudson test suggest that sensitivity to overlapping and to size- and linear-perspective depth cues is dependent on exposure to Western-style pictures and schooling, but there are numerous difficulties both with the instrument and the attendant methodology (Hagen, 1974; Hagen & Johnson, 1977; Kennedy, 1974).

The development of effective use of pictorial cues in Western children was investigated by Wilcox and Teghtsoonian (1971) in three- and nine-year-old children, and adults. The task was to choose the larger of two objects pictured against various backgrounds. They found that with increasing age, response to size was increasingly controlled by the size of the objects on the projection screen. In an extension of Wilcox and Teghtsoonian's work, Yonas and Hagen (1973) compared judgments of relative size in pictures and in Real Scenes by three- and seven-year-old children and adults.

Using transparencies as stimuli, they found sensitivity to texture perspective in three-year-olds, but very limited accuracy in judging relative size at various distances. Even judgment of seven-year-old children was quite poor when the projected size relations of the objects being judged were the reverse of the real size relations. Pictorial perception was consistently inferior to real object controls even for adult viewers. The low level of successful performance persisted despite attempts to diminish extraneous information for the pictures and objects per se.

Following Bower's (1966) argument on the salience of motion parallax information for the very young, and acting on a suggestion from E. J. Gibson (1969), Yonas and Hagen (1973) manipulated the amount of motion-parallax information available to the observer while making size judgments. As Bower (1965, 1966) observed, motion parallax tells the observer the picture plane is a flat object. Thus, for a picture held upright in the frontal–parallel plane, the entire picture translates at the outside edge of the frame across the extrapictorial background as a unit, and there are no differential rates of translation of objects across the background within the picture (no gradients or discontinuities of optical flow). Yonas and Hagen argued that since motion parallax provides the observer with information for the flatness of the picture's surface, it may distract children's attention from the pictorial depth information. This hypothesis was supported. Correct size judgments were made more often in the motion parallax absent condition with monocular view through a peephole. Overall, however, performance on the task was poor, as previously noted, relative to performance with real scenes. Perception of the real three-dimensional scenes was far superior to perception of the two-dimensional pictured scenes even when viewpoint was fixed and monocular at the correct station point. The spatial information present in both cases was that of size, linear, and texture perspective. In the pictorial conditions, both with and without motion parallax, there remained additional surface or flatness information. It appears that with the very few "trompe l'oeil" exceptions, pictures always have this admixture of flatness and depth.

Information about depth may be captured in pictures in a variety of ways. Examples are color, texture gradients, linear perspective, aerial perspective, superposition, relative size, and arrangements of light and shadows. How pictures carry such information for the real world has been discussed extensively elsewhere (Gibson, 1971; Hagen, 1974; Kennedy, 1974). However, there are also a great many other sources of information specifying a picture only as a rather flat, perhaps framed, surface with a pattern of color on it. In addition to motion parallax, steropsis, and texture information for the surface (canvas, paper, and so on) of the plane of projection also tell the observer that the picture is a flat object with a pattern of varying luminosity or pigmentation. The mismatch of lighting between the picture and the surroundings and the mismatch between the surface of the picture and the surrounding surfaces are also sources of information for the flatness of the picture object. This coexistence in pictures of both flatness (or surface) and depth information may create a functional difference between pictorial and ordinary perception, despite and structural equivalence of the information for spatial relations (size, distance, and so on) postulated by Gibson.

Hagen and Glick (1975) undertook a further investigation of the character of this functional difference between pictorial and ordinary perception in a developmental study of sensitivity to size, linear, and texture perspective using both line drawings and real scenes. The line drawings were created from photographs blown up to life size in order to equate both the perspective information and the visual angles in the pictures and the real scenes. View was either monocular through a peephole at the right station point (the center of projection for the perspective information), monocular at a wrong, oblique, station point, or free with head movement through a slot. The task was to match the drawing or scene to another real scene, which was the model for the drawing. The model was in a field of four real scenes with objects of varying sizes at different distances. In all cases, regardless of age or viewing conditions, results were the same. Perception of the real scenes was vastly superior to perception of the drawings, despite the fact that the view was at the right station point, and despite the apparent equation of static, monocular depth information.

In an extension of thie work, Hagen, Glick, and Morse (unpublished manuscript, 1976) studied the effects of pictorial medium on size judgments using both photographic prints and transparencies. Both prints and slides were projected so that perspective and visual angles were identical to that obtaining in the real scene controls. Again, pictorial perception was consistently inferior to the perception of the ordinary real scenes even when view was monocular at the correct station point. No consistent difference between slides and prints was found.

So, three times now we have studied pictorial depth perception with identical real scene controls. Yonas and Hagen (1973) found that perception of slides was inferior to perception of real scenes; Hagen and Glick, *et al.* (1975 and in preparation) found that line drawings were inferior to real scenes, and that photographic prints as well as slides were inferior to real-scene controls. All three studies included observation from the right station point and equation of visual angles between pictures and real scenes. All three tasks demanded the perception of depicted objective size and distance together for every judgment. In all three studies the perception of such spatial relations was inferior to that obtained with the real scene controls. Thus, we concluded in line with the argument advanced by E. J. Gibson (1969), that the environmental or three-dimensional information in a picture must be suppressed by, or in conflict with, the flatness or surface information occasioned by the plane of projection for the pictures. Within the confines of this explanation, there is no conflict with Gibson's argument for structural equivalence between pictures and their corresponding real scenes; and a special character for pictorial perception need be argued only in the most trivial sense of the term. That is, it may be argued that picture perception has a special character because one must learn to ignore the flatness information for the plane of projection and attend to the depth information within the scene. Such a conclusion is of interest but is not of great significance theoretically.

However, before we can reach this conclusion, we must consider a critical corollary issue put forth by Pirenne (1970), on the interactive effects of surface and depth information in pictures. Pirenne argues that ordinary pictures create a very special kind of illusion. As previously noted, they provide information for both flatness and depth. In Pirenne's opinion, successful perception of the depth relations in a picture depends not upon ignoring of the flatness information, as here hypothesized, but upon an explicit awareness of the picture's flat surface.

Pirenne (1970) has observed that when most ordinary pictures are viewed, they are observed from the wrong station point, from a point of view different from the correct center of projection for the picture. In such cases, the perspective information contained in the picture is no longer equivalent to the information in the light coming to the eye from a similar real scene. If successful perception of the spatial relations within a picture depends upon the pickup of such presumably equivalent information, then, in its absence, one would expect serious disruption of the perception of such spatial relations in pictures. However, when most observers view most ordinary pictures, the predicted perspective distortion does not occur. Following a suggestion from Albert Einstein, Pirenne (1970, p. 99) argues for an "intuitive process of psychological compensation" to account for this lack of distortion. He suggests that the intuitive process of psychological compensation is based on the spectator's perception of a representative event, both on the spectator's awareness of the flat surface of the picture and on the spectator's preconceived ideas about its internal components.

Since Pirenne argues that the ability to compensate for distortion is a product of education and experience with pictures, Hagen (1976) tested this argument developmentally. The investigation was designed to test the effects of varying surface information and station point on the ability to utilize information for surface relations, specifically, perspective information for distance. Judgments of the real size of portrayed objects (as opposed to projective size) were used as an index of distance perception since the correct perception of real size relations depends on correctly localizing the objects in depth. The scaling of surface information available was confined to a comparison between ordinary photographic prints and back projected transparencies. To test station-point sensitivity, the test displays were viewed both from the correct station point on the normal to the picture plane; and from an incorrect one, 40° to the left of the correct station point at the same distance from the surface of the print or projection screen.

It was hypothesized that observation of ordinary pictures from the wrong view point would facilitate the accurate pickup of information for surface relations for adults and diminish the accuracy of young children in the same situation. These predictions rested on the hypothesized existence of a mechanism of compensation for perspective distortion, developed through education and experience with pictures. The data were strongly supportive of the hypothesized operation of such a compensation mechanism. The three-way interaction of age with type of surface and station point over all types of stimuli used was suggestive both of its operation for adults and of developmental change in picture perception contingent on its acquisition. Subsequent separate analyses for each of the three types of stimuli used provided further evidence of the operation in adults of compensation mechanism dependent on both obvious picture surface and oblique view.

It seemed clear from the data that adults need adequate surface or flatness information to compensate for the perspective distortion obtaining at the wrong station point. It was also clear that the perception of ordinary prints from the *wrong* station point was superior to perception at the *right* station point. This is consistent with E. J. Gibson's (1969) argument that the flatness and depth information conflict in such situations. At the wrong station point, the depth information is distorted and the flatness information is rendered even more apparent. Thus it may be argued that observation of pictures from the wrong station point—which is, after all, the ordinary case for picture viewing—trips the observer into a pictorial mode, a mode of compensation for both surface information and perspective distortion. However, it is also clear from the data that, even with compensation, perception of size—distance relations in prints is not as accurate as perception of these relations in back-projected transparencies observed monocularly at the correct station point. In the latter case, the display acquires a near trompe l'oeil character with minimal surface information. In all other non-trompe l'oeil cases of prints, paintings, and drawings, the pictures retain the characteristic mixture of flatness and depth information. This mixture continues to depress the level of accuracy of judgments of spatial relations in pictures, even with the aid of compensation normally operating.

So, in terms of arguing for a special character for picture perception, this type of research is much more promising than a simple conflict hypothesis for a mixture of flatness and depth peculiar to pictures. A compensation mechanism, triggered by surface information and operating during the normal conditions of picture viewing, certainly suggests a special character for picture perception. This is true despite the fact that it may be argued that much pictorial information, like texture gradients and occlusion, is preserved across station point transformations, since perception of pictures at the wrong station point is superior to perception at the right station point (where it may be argued that such information is even better preserved).

To recapitulate briefly:

1. The notion that the information in pictures is just like its equivalent in the ordinary nonpictorial world.

2. As E. J. Gibson (1969) has also postulated, the flatness or surface information in pictures somehow interferes with the pickup of the static depth information.

3. Then, as Pirenne (1970) hypothesized, whereas surface information certainly does depress accurate depth responding in pictures, it is also necessary to compensate for the distorting effects of observation from the wrong, but normal, station point.

4. With this information we attempted to investigate more precisely the consequences of this mixture of surface and depth information in pictures. You will recall that in the Hagen and Glick (1975) study, we found that picture perception was vastly inferior to real-scene perception.

Almost no one, of any age, ever chose the real scenes that matched the pictorial stimuli in size and distance of objects. Nearly every subject, child and adult, made matches that indicated that the degree of perspective convergence or size diminution in the pictures was too great to look "natural." In interviews following the experiment, subjects would often comment that although they knew perfectly well that more distant objects look small in pictures, in our pictures the distant objects looked *too* small. In other words, the degree of perspective convergence appeared too great in the line drawings despite the fact that the degree of convergence was identical to that obtained in ordinary real-world natural perspective, having been determined both mathematically and mechanically.

To us this meant that the perspective information in geometrically correct pictures simply does not look "natural" to the average Western picture viewer whether child or adult. This point of view has been argued without a solid data base by Pirenne (1970), Goodman (1968), and Reggini (1975). Hence it is a logical and necessary step to consider what *does* look natural to the ordinary observer.

Artists since the Renaissance have consistently modified perspective to correct the too sudden convergence or foreshortening observed by our subjects. Artistic modification of perspective, however, relies on the artist's intuition of what looks pleasing and natural. In neither the discipline of art nor psychology has a systematic investigation of the modification of perspective necessary to achieve pictures which look natural to the ordinary observer been undertaken.

However, in the service of architectural design, an engineer from Argentina has written a computer program that systematically modifies perspective. Reggini

FIGURE 1 Size perspective in ordinary conical convergence. (From Hagen and Glick, 1975).

(1975) has devised a system for the generation of pictures varying in degree of perspective convergence from conical (traditional linear perspective) to axonometric (parallel) projection. For a given object of fixed dimension observed from a fixed station point, a family of perspective views may be generated by the fixing of values for an index number which may vary from $i = 0$, conical perspective, to $i = 1$, parallel perspective. The derivation of Reggini's (1975) system from Thouless' (1931a, 1931b) early work and its computer application are fully described.

Using Reggini's system, Elliott and Hagen generated 7 sets of 6 pictures. Index values of $i = 0$, .2, .4, .6, .8, and 1.0 were chosen for the 6 pictures in all 7 sets. Two picture sets were pictures of cubes; the other sets were pictures of pentagonal solids (see Figure 2). The 7 sets were each viewed successively by subjects from a distance of 35.6 cm. For one group of subjects the line of sight was on the normal to the center of the pictorial image (90°); for the other the line of sight was oblique, at a 45° angle to the center of the image. View was monocular through a peephole. Following participation in the experiments, subjects sorted the picture sets in a free-view condition. All subjects were shown the three-dimensional objects that served as models for the pictures prior to participation.

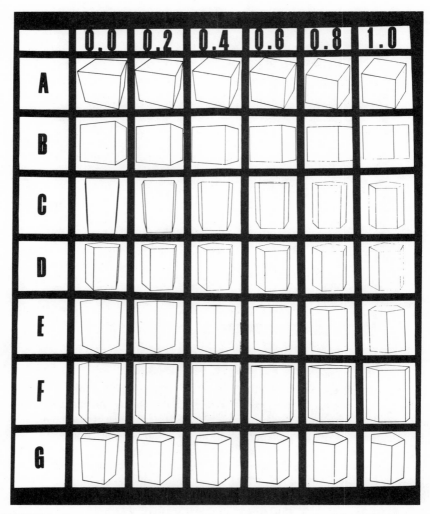

FIGURE 2 Computer-generated pictures of cubes and pentagonal solids varying in convergence from conical (0.0) to axonometric (1.0) perspective.

A subject's task was to order the 6 pictures in each set from the most natural and realistic looking to the least realistic looking. The subject was presented with the first picture set ordered from conical to parallel perspective. The subject was told to observe the pictures carefully as each picture was exposed for approximately 2 sec. The pictures were then randomly recorded and presented again. The subject was told this time to assign a rank number to each of the pictures with 1 indicating the most natural and realistic looking picture in the set and 6 the least. This procedure was repeated with each picture set. Afterwards, the subjects were asked to sort the sets in a completely free situation, again from the most natural and realistic looking picture to the least natural and realistic looking. Subjects were free to rearrange the order until satisfied.

Results were subjected to a two-way analysis of variance for picture set and degree of perspective convergence, and to a linear trend analysis. The dependent variable was the rank number assigned to each of the six degrees of convergence. Separate analyses were performed for each of the viewing conditions. The main effects for picture set were not significant. The main effects for degree of perspective convergence were highly significant. Similarly, the linear trends were also highly significant, indicating that traditional linear perspective was ranked as the least natural and realistic looking degree of perspective. Axonometric, or parallel, perspective was ranked as the most natural, realistic looking, in all three viewing conditions.

In subsequent experiments, the pictures were observed under a greater variety of viewing conditions: (1) each set was viewed at the correct station point for that set; (2) each set was freely sorted without previous experience with the pictures; and (3) the instruction "choose the most accurate drawing" was compared to "choose the most natural and realistic picture." In all cases, regardless of station point or instructions, the results were the same. The linear trend was always highly significant, reflecting the tendency to order the stimuli from most to least natural–realistic in line with the degree of convergence series from parallel perspective to conical. (Sets *B* and *b* show a somewhat different pattern, not discussed here; see Hagen & Elliott, 1976.)

How can these data be interpreted? As can be seen from Table 1, an index number of 1.0 means parallel convergence, that is, no convergence of projected surface size with increasing distance. On the average, parallel perspective was preferred by our Western-reared adult subjects 52% of the time. The mean degree of convergence occasioned by an index number of .8 is approximately 7%. (This is only an estimate subject to reproduction and measurement error.) A

TABLE 1

Index Numbers in Terms of Degree of Convergence and Percentage of Time Preferred

Index numbers	Mean (%) convergence	Mean time preferred (%)
1.0	0	52
.8	7	21
.6	14	9
.4	19	8
.2	24	4
0	28	6

7% degree of perspective convergence was preferred by our subjects, on the average, 21% of the time. (All of the other index numbers fall below chance preference rates.) Thus, 73% of the time subjects chose as natural and realistic looking, pictures with a degree of convergence of not more than 7%.

It should, of course, be kept in mind that 7% is, at best, a rough estimate averaged over multiple ratios of back faces to front faces, far edges to near, across many different station points, with a range from approximately 3 to 10% convergence. Observation of Figure 3 allows for a fixing of the looser estimate of 10% for preferred convergence in terms of distance relative to object size. As can be seen from Figure 3, a 10% front-to-back convergence is obtained for cubes when the object is placed with the front face at a distance approximately equal to 10 times its size. Similarly, a 10% convergence is obtained for the pentagonal solids when the edge of any face is placed at such a distance. (In these cases, the size of the object refers to its greatest front–back dimension.) The objects we

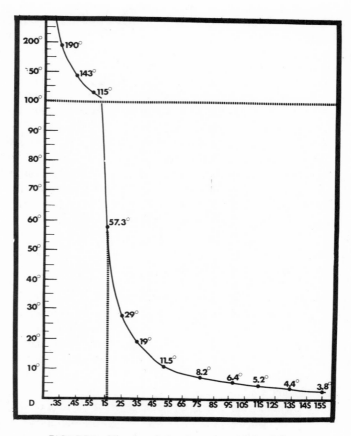

FIGURE 3 Visual angle by size as a multiple of distance.

have tested are regular, symmetric, geometrical solids, so it is too early to generalize to irregularly sized objects or to objects whose near–far dimension is much greater than the left–right dimension, like fountain pens. Ideally, we would like to argue that all objects have a sort of rough size, computed as the mean of their various dimensions along a generalized near–far axis, and that any picture, if it is to look natural, must be taken, painted, or drawn at a distance at least 10 times this mean size. As previously noted, we do not yet know if this preference for minimal perspective, which we have termed the *Zoom effect,* will hold for irregularly shaped objects. It is also not yet known if the preference will hold for environmental container objects like hallways and roadways. We do know, however, that the Zoom effect of preferring as natural a station point at least 10 times as far away as the object is large does hold for pictures of regular geometric solids. The fact that this is true may well alter our conception of the role of the station point in picture perception.

From this work, it is clear that this effect occurs regardless of the station point used in viewing. Also observers refused to accept the realism of geometrically correct perspective, despite the fact that observation was from the right station point (Hagen & Glick, 1975). If they were assuming that the near object was some 10 times its size away, then it is obvious that the 33% reduction in visual angle that we caused to occur over a distance smaller than the object size simply could not have occurred over such a distance. A 33% reduction in visual angle relative to a distance of 10 times the size of the object would have required a distance between far and near objects much greater than that actually present. Subjects, working from such a set of assumptions about distance of the objects, would be perfectly correct in choosing, as they did, to match the pictures to real scenes with far objects truly smaller than the near ones.

The independence for this Zoom effect of the observer's position at the right or the wrong station point, in my opinion, provides support for another interesting aspect of the role of surface information in picture perception. It may be that awareness of the surface of the plane of projection frees the observer from any station point, right or wrong, and allows him or her to assume a pictorial station point, that is, a point of observation at a distance at least 10 times as great as the object size. The evidence presented here certainly supports the hypothesis that such a Zoom effect takes place; thus far, however, investigation has been confined to pictures of regular geometric solids generated with fairly large visual angles in the absence of any contextual information. For more complex stimuli, the effect may not hold, although the results from Hagen and Glick (1975) suggest that it will. Similarly, decreasing visual angle will simply increase distance and build the Zoom effect into the stimuli themselves, that is, in pictures where the distance is great relative to the size of the objects, convergence is already minimal.

The existence of the Zoom effect is really rather an old idea outside psychology. Artists since the Renaissance, and subsequently photographers, have modified correct perspective in order to make it look natural. The correction of extreme foreshortening by alteration of the proportions of near and far object parts is an intuitive application of the Zoom effect. Dürer effected such modifications scientifically rather than intuitively. Photographers consistently step back from their subjects to avoid extreme foreshortening. When they fail to do so, the extreme foreshortening appears distorted. We know now that it will continue to look distorted even under monocular observation from the correct station point.

SUMMARY AND FUTURE DIRECTIONS

Pictorial perception has a very special character in need of elucidation because such perception appears to involve: (1) the pickup of static derivative monocular information; (2) the pickup of surface information for the plane of projection; (3) the employment of such surface information to trigger compensation for oblique view; (4) the freeing of the observer from his or her real and present station point wherever it might be; and (5) the assumption of a station point at a distance at least 10 times as great as the size of the object.

The directions that may be followed in pursuit of elucidation of this special type of perception are multiple and interrelated. If one argues that surface information is the critical difference between real scenes and pictures of those scenes, then one can manipulate surface information to test this hypothesis. One can interpose surface information between observers and real scenes and one can subtract surface information from pictures. Preliminary work on the addition of surface information has shown that viewing a real scene through a piece of window glass doubled the number of errors in a size-judgment task. Observers were unaware of the presence of the glass during the task. Viewing through a window screen only slightly disrupted performance, but the screen was more visually apparent than the glass. When the real scenes were viewed through a 50-mm single lens reflex camera, the error rate increased 2.5 times. In this case, the impact size was reduced, but all size proportions of parts of the image remained the same. It should be possible through such addition and subtraction of surface information to render the perception of real scenes and the perception of pictures of those scenes equivalent. This preliminary work has succeeded in narrowing the gap between the two, but the pictorial error rate is still considerably higher than obtained when viewing real scenes through any of the tested surfaces.

In addition to the role of surface information, another area of exploration that should prove fruitful is the attempt to classify types of pictures with respect to ideal convergence and to explore the relation between ground plane compression and object convergence (which may or may not covary). These attempts require the generation of far more complex stimuli than any tried up to now. Similarly more sensitive measures of perception are needed than those thus far employed, particularly if one wishes to explore that exact character of the information carried by ordinary two-dimensional displays. One should not move too quickly to modification of perspective without understanding the consequences of observing ordinary traditional perspective. One of those consequences, of course, is that of compensation for oblique view observed by Perkins (1973) and Hagen (1975). Observation of anamorphic pictures indicates that there are clearly limits to the amount of compensation one can perform. A specification of those limits and an investigation into the relation between compensation and modified perspective is needed. Last, but important, the investigation here outlined must also be undertaken developmentally. Pictorial perception appears to have a very special character but much of this special character may well be dependent on culture or experience with particular types of pictures. Hagen (1975) found evidence for developmental change in the acquisition of a mechanism of compensation for oblique view and it seems likely that developmental change will also be seen to take place in preference for degree of perspective convergence in the acquisition of the Zoom effect.

REFERENCES

Bower, T. G. R. Stimulus variables determining space perception in infants. *Science,* 1965, *149,* 88–89.

Bower, T. G. R. The visual world of infants. *Scientific American,* 1966, *215,* 80–92.

Gibson, E. J. *Principles of perceptual learning and development.* New York: Appleton-Century-Crofts, 1969.

Gibson, J. J. The information available in pictures. *Leonardo,* 1971, *4,* 27–35.

Goodman, N. *Languages of art: An approach to a theory of symbols.* Indianapolis: Bobbs-Merrill, 1968.

Hagen, M. A. Picture perception: Toward a theoretical model. *Psychological Bulletin,* 1974, *81,* 471–497.

Hagen, M. A. The influence of picture surface and station point on the ability to compensate for oblique view in pictorial perception. *Developmental Psychology,* 1976, *12*(No. 1), 57–63.

Hagen, M. A., & Elliott, H. B. An investigation of the relationship between viewing condition and preference for true and modified perspective in adults. *Journal of Experimental Psychology,* 1976, *2*(No. 4), 479–490.

Hagen, M. A., & Glick, R. Pictorial Perspective: The development of sensitivity to size, linear and texture perspective in children and adults. Paper read at meeting of Eastern Psychological Association, April, 1975.

Hagen, M. A., Glick, R., and Morse, B. The role of two dimensional surface characteristics in pictorial depth perception. Unpublished manuscript.

Hagen, M. A., & Johnson, M. M. Hudson pictorial depth perception test: Cultural content and question with a Western sample. *Journal of Social Psychology,* 1977, *101,* 3–11.

Hudson, W. Pictorial depth perception in subcultural groups in Africa. *Journal of Social Psychology,* 1960, *52,* 183–208.

Hudson, W. Cultural problems in pictorial perception. *South African Journal of Science,* 1962, *58,* 189–195.

Hudson, W. The study of the problem of pictorial perception among unacculturated groups. *International Journal of Psychology,* 1967, *2,* 89–107.

Kennedy, J. M. *A psychology of picture perception: Information and images.* San Francisco: Jossey-Bass, 1974.

Perkins, D. N. Compensating for distortion in viewing pictures obliquely. *Perception and Psychophysics,* 1973, *14,* 13–18.

Pirenne, M. *Optics, painting and photography.* Cambridge, England: Cambridge University Press, 1970.

Reggini, H. C. Perspective using curved projection rays and its computer application, *Leonardo,* 1975, *8,* 307–312.

Richter, J. P., & Richter, I. A. (Eds.). *The literary works of Leonardo da Vinci compiled and edited from the original manuscripts.* London: Phaidon, 1970.

Thouless, R. H. Phenomenal regression to the real object. I. *British Journal of Psychology 21,* 337 (1931a).

Thouless, R. H. Phenomenal regression to the real object, II. *British Journal of Psychology, 22,* 1 (1931b).

Wilcox, B. L., & Teghtsoonian, M. The control of relative size by pictorial depth cues in children and adults. *Journal of Experimental Child Psychology,* 1971, *11,* 413–429.

Yonas, A., & Hagen, M. A. Effects of static and kinetic depth information on the perception of size in children and adults. *Journal of Experimental Child Psychology,* 1973, *15,* 254–265.

3

A Dual Coding Approach
to Perception and Cognition

Allan Paivio

The University of Western Ontario

EDITORS' INTRODUCTION

Language may be thought of as a kind of representational stimulation. The general issue of whether language actually functions representationally, and if so, how this is accomplished is a complex philosophical one. Nevertheless, certain uses are clearly representational. Allan Paivio makes a sharp distinction between perceptual and cognitive processing of verbal and nonverbal information. Non-verbal information is thought to be represented in a more analogue-like fashion and is, in fact, specifically associated with imagery. Paivio describes a program of research that supports his distinction and demonstrates that representations of these two sorts of information can be differentially accessed depending on the task.

It was suggested, as a theme, that we address two general types of information: communicative and environmental. This categorization seems particularly appropriate from my viewpoint, since here I discuss a dual-coding approach that involves a combination of communicative and environmental information processing. First, I review the theoretical assumptions briefly, pointing out their relevance to the environmental–communicative distinction. Then I consider their empirical implications in the context of some recent research.

The major assumption is that two distinct symbolic systems are involved in perception, memory, language, and thought. One system is specialized for processing nonverbal information. Since a prominent part of that information processing includes the interpretation of scenes and the generation of images, it is convenient to refer to it as the imagery system. The other system is specialized for processing linguistic information, that is, interpreting language and generating speech. It is meaningful, therefore, to call it the verbal system. I use the term "system" roughly in the dictionary sense, as a set of connected things or parts forming a complex or unitary whole. The nonverbal system presumably includes processes capable of integrating nonverbal environmental information involving different sensory modalities. Similarly, the verbal system must include visual—motor and haptic components, although it may be predominantly auditory—motor as a functional system for normal individuals. This suggests that sensory and symbolic modalities may be orthogonal, in the manner suggested by Table 1. The table illustrates the categories of stimulus information that result from the crossing of sensory modality with the verbal—nonverbal distinction. Thus visual stimuli can be verbal, as in the case of printed words; or nonverbal, as in the case of visually experienced concrete objects and events. In the auditory modality, we have speech stimuli as compared to environmental sounds associated with concrete objects and events, and so on, for other modalities.

The important assumption here is that the symbolic systems are differentiated along analogous lines, in terms of separate processing systems for dealing with verbal and nonverbal stimulus information in the various sensory modalities. Of course, the verbal—nonverbal dichotomy may not be so clear in the case of some stimuli (like social gestures), but much of the perceptual world is so divided in a fairly unambiguous manner. At any rate, we have used it as a strong working assumption within the framework of dual-coding theory; and this dual-coding theory generated the research described subsequently. Readers can draw their own conclusions regarding the heuristic and explanatory power of the approach on the basis of the evidence.

The relation of the approach to the environmental—communicative distinction should be immediately apparent: the nonverbal system is specialized for representing and processing environmental information, whereas the verbal system is by definition specialized for communication. However, the communicative function of the latter obviously cannot go on in isolation but depends, instead, on

TABLE 1

Examples of Stimulus Input Corresponding to Orthogonal Sensory and Symbolic Modalities

Sensory modality	Symbolic modality	
	Verbal	Nonverbal
Visual	Printed words	Pictures or objects
Auditory	Speech sounds	Environmental sounds
Tactual	Braille	Feelable objects
Kinesthetic	Motor feedback from writing	Motor feedback from haptic exploration of objects

communication between the verbal and the image-generating system, since the latter presumably contains much of the semantic information (knowledge of the world) about which we communicate.

This leads to the next major assumption, namely, that the two systems are functionally independent but partly interconnected. The independence assumption means that one system can be active without the other, or both can be active concurrently without interference. Note that it is possible to question this assumption. Being in a speech mode might preclude being in a nonspeech mode. Again it is possible that competition could arise between spatial and linguistic processing. My view is that the two modes are neither mutually exclusive nor competitive, but independent.

A good deal of evidence does exist in support of independence, but I will not summarize all of that evidence here. One kind of evidence will suffice. I can monitor the events in this room at the same time that I am talking about something completely unrelated to contents of the room, without the two activities interfering with each other. Conversely, I can listen to someone else speaking while at the same time imagining the events that they are describing, or while letting my eyes roam around the room. In both cases, the two modes are active concurrently, I cannot, however, monitor the events in this room with any accuracy and at the same time imagine my cottage or any other visual memory scene. These are common sense examples, but anyone who wants hard evidence on the issue need only refer to the work of Brooks (1967) and others (Byrne, 1974; Segal, 1971). They have studied interference effects that occur when a perceptual task and a concurrent memory task involve the same modality; and they have also studied the absence of such effects when different symbolic modalities are involved. For example, Brooks (1967) found that a conflict occurs when a person *reads* a message that describes a spatial relation while at the same time attempting to visualize the relations being described. The conflict is absent when the subject *listens* to the same messages while visualizing.

It must be assumed at the same time that the two systems are interconnected; otherwise such a model could not explain how we can describe perceptual events or generate images, or draw pictures, or attend selectively to environmental objects and events described by someone else. My assumption is that the two systems are interconnected in the sense that activity in one system can activate the other in a nonrandom fashion. This implies a partial mapping of one system onto the other, so that there is communication at particular points. It is unnecessary for the purposes of this chapter to conceptualize those interconnections in any particular way, be it psychological or neuropsychological. It might help simply to say, however, that the evidence suggests that the interconnections are most direct between representations corresponding to concrete objects on the one hand, and their corresponding names on the other.

Another major assumptions is that long-term memory and perception use the same systems. In other words, perception and memory are continuous. This means that the functional representations of the nonverbal system (as expressed in drawings, imagery, and so on), are analogous and continuous in nature, and are highly isomorphic with perceptual information. Stated in terms of the distinction that Pick and Saltzman made (Chapter 1, this volume), this means that environmental information is represented in long-term memory basically in a perceptual form. Knowledge of the environment is perceptual in the sense that perceptual properties and distinctions along perceptual dimensions such as size, color, and shape are represented in a relatively fine-grained fashion in perceptual memory. This statement concerning an isomorphism between perceptual and memory information is, of course, an inference based on behavioral isomorphism between patterns of reactions to perceptual information on the one hand and reactions to analogous memory representations in the absence of the perceptual objects and events on the other.

I will leave it to linguists and psycholinguists to propose what the nature of the verbal or linguistic representational system is like. For my purposes it is sufficient to suggest that the units of the verbal system are discrete linguistic entities which are arbitrarily related to perceptual information. Elsewhere, I have speculated about the way such units are organized into higher order representational structures and in what way they are reorganized or transformed (Paivio, 1971, 1975a), but I do not include that in this chapter. The important point here is that the linguistic system per se does not contain the perceptual or semantic information that corresponds to our knowledge of the world, or as Pick puts it, "environmental information." Instead, the verbal system can retrieve such information only by probing the nonverbal representational system.

Next, it is implicit in most of what I have said that the nonverbal system is accessed or, more appropriately, activated more directly by nonverbal objects and events than by linguistic stimuli. Conversely, the verbal system is activated more directly by spoken or written language. Moreover, although it is not crucial for these studies, I assume that nonverbal output, such as the generation of a drawing, is a function of the nonverbal system, whereas the generation of speech or writing is controlled by the verbal system.

Finally, the perceptual information in long-term memory can be used for various purposes, depending on task demands. These uses include simple *descriptions* of the environment, *making inferences,* and active *transformations* of the symbolic information. For example, my image of my house permits me to count the number of windows, rooms, pieces of furniture, and so on; it allows me to describe the colors, shapes, sizes, and so on of the objects in it, ad infinitum. This is possible with perceptual information because the facts required to answer such questions are present in the environment. To the extent that we can do so in detail from memory must mean that the memory information is analogous to the perceptual information in a fine-grained way. Transformability means that we can reshape the perceptual information in long-term memory indefinitely. Such abilities have long been documented by spatial manipulation tests, and more recently by experimental work on such transformations by Piaget and Inhelder (1966), and Shepard and his collaborators (e.g., Cooper & Shepard, 1973). Piaget and others assume that this functional characteristic originates from actions toward things. This is my view as well. The symbolic system must include something analogous to responses, that is, it must include or be interfaced with response-control systems. This is relevant to the active–passive distinction also raised by Pick and Saltzman (Chapter 1, this volume). The environmental information in the nonverbal symbolic system is continuous with perceptual information, not only in the passive sense, but also in the sense that it can be actively restructured in much the same way as one can manipulate the real perceptual world; this is true, at least in principle.

The dual coding approach I have outlined contrasts with another popular contemporary view—that both kinds of information are represented in the same symbolic format in a common memory system. Examples are the long-term memory models presented by Norman and Rumelhart (1975), and Anderson and Bower (1973). In principle, Anderson and Bower's (1973, p. 214) human associative memory (HAM) would transform a scene into an abstract propositional representation in long-term memory. Linguistic descriptions of such scenes would be represented in the same kind of abstract format. Conversely, the propositional network would be used to generate images or descriptions. This kind of an approach has a number of difficulties that I have discussed in some detail elsewhere (Paivio, 1974, 1977). One relevant difficulty, given the present context, is that those approaches cannot account for differences in memory reactions to pictures and words, since they assume that both kinds of information are transformed into a common representational format in long-term memory. Another difficulty is that of accounting for perceptual memory transformations of the kind that Cooper and Shepard had investigated, and the kind of perceptual memory comparisons that I have studied.

EMPIRICAL EVIDENCE

I discuss briefly my recent research on the problem (see Paivio, 1975b, for more detailed discussion), and summarize the main findings and weave in some recent extensions as I go along.

Size Comparisons with Names as Stimuli

The first fact—established by Robert Moyer (1973) with pairs of animal names differing in size, and extended by me to include comparisons across animate and inanimate objects from various categories—is that comparison time is an inverse function of the memory-size difference. That is, it takes longer to indicate the larger member of a pair such as *cat–toaster,* in which the real-life difference is

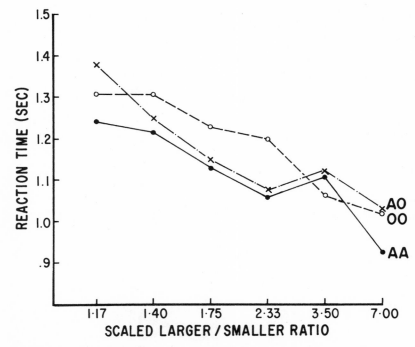

FIGURE 1 Mean reaction time for size comparisons of animal–animal (AA), object–(OO), and animal–object (AO) pairs as a function of scaled ratio size difference. (From Paivio, 1975b.)

relatively small, than a pair such as *mouse–toaster,* in which the difference is large. The general function from my research is shown in Figure 1. This finding in itself suggests that the comparisons are based on analogue representations containing rather precise relative-size information.

Picture–Word Comparisons

The next series of studies involved comparisons of pictures and words in the same task. An obvious prediction from the dual-coding model is that size comparisons will be faster when the items are presented as pictures than when they are presented as words, even when the pictures contain no perceptual size information. This follows from the assumption that pictures have more direct access to the representations in the image system, which presumably contain the relative-size information.

One experiment, not reported in the "Perceptual Comparisons" paper (Paivio, 1975b), involved four size differences based on samples of items drawn from our normative list of items that have been scaled for size. The reaction time functions are shown in Figure 2. Two features are apparent: (1) both pictures and words show the inverse function relating reaction time to the magnitude of the size difference; and (2) the reaction time is generally faster for pictures than words, as predicted. The data are based on repeated measures on different sets of pictures and words, obtained a week apart, with half the subjects getting the picture condition first and the other half, the word condition first. Another experiment with independent groups and a different set of pairs showed essentially the same general pattern except that the picture and word scores converged at the smallest size difference. Ignoring the interaction, which I cannot explain, the results are generally consistent with the prediction from dual coding theory and inconsistent with verbal coding and propositional theories. If it is assumed that information is stored with the names themselves, then it would be predicted that comparisons would be faster with words than with pictures. Theorists who assume that size information is represented in some abstract form

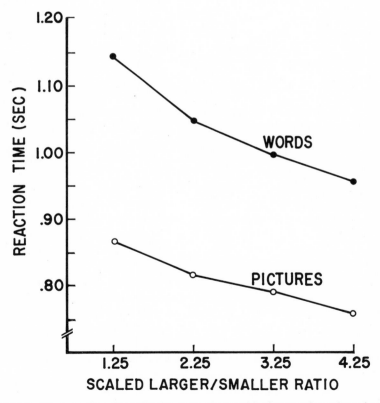

FIGURE 2   Mean reaction times for size comparisons with picture pairs and word pairs as a function of ratio-size difference.

that is distinct from both perceptual information and language would predict no difference in reaction time to the pictures and words.

Individual differences in imagery ability were added to the design of the picture–word experiments recently. After the experimental task, subjects completed spatial-ability tests, including Thurstone's Space Relations test and the Minnesota Paper Form Board, together with a questionnaire asking how they solved the Minnesota Paper Form Board problems (whether by imagery or other means). The subjects were divided into high- and low-imagery groups on the basis of their composite score on all tests following the procedure used in earlier research (e.g., Paivio & Ernest, 1971). The average reaction times for size comparisons involving pictures and words showed the same general interaction in three different experiments, although in no single instance was it significant. That is, the picture–word difference tended to be greater for high-imagery than for low-imagery subjects. High imagers were especially fast in their size comparisons with pictures as stimuli. This makes sense if we assume that such subjects have efficient imagery systems, as their test scores suggest. Of course, we need a more precise theoretical statement on the nature of such differences and more reliable data before detailed discussion is warranted. In the meantime, these data provide additional suggestive support for the dual-coding distinction.

Another striking picture–word difference is a Stroop-like conflict that occurs when picture-size information conflicts with the long-term memory information. The details of the experiment are reported elsewhere (Paivio, 1975b), so I simply summarize the study here. The subject is presented with a pair of pictures or words, so that the two represented objects differ in real-life (memory) size. Sometimes the two are also shown with one member of the pair physically larger than the other, and when this is the case the relation is either congruent or incongruent with real-life size. Thus, the pair *mouse–toaster* would be presented so that the mouse is depicted as smaller than the toaster in the congruent case and larger than the toaster in the incongruent case. In other instances the two are shown as being approximately equal in size. The object names are treated similarly by varying the relative size of the printed words. It was predicted and confirmed that reaction time for choosing the larger member of a pair would be longer in the incongruent case than in the congruent case when the items are presented as pictures. This follows from the argument that the pictures access the image system relatively directly, so that perceptual and memory information concerning objects would conflict when the two are incongruent. The same Stroop-type conflict was not expected when analogous manipulations were done with printed words as stimuli; the words would have to be read before the corresponding conceptual representations were activated in the image system, and print size would be irrelevant. This expectation was also confirmed. The main point is that these results provide especially strong support for the idea that the size information is represented in a nonverbal visual long-term memory system, and that it is continuous with the system that processes perceptual information more directly. No one has yet been able to suggest to me how the interaction would be predicted from, or explained by, abstract representational theories.

Distance Comparisons

Other studies have involved comparisons on dimensions other than size. Relative distance judgments of pairs of pictured objects are particularly interesting for a number of reasons. First, in the absence of perspective or other distance cues, the judgments must be based on not only the relative-size information contained in the pictures, but also on remembered-size information. Second, the task is a classical perceptual one, in the sense that subjects are asked about the appearance of the pictured objects, that is, which one appears to be father away. This is a reversal of the size-comparison task in that the latter asks about memory-size differences rather than the appearance of objects as pictured. Nonetheless, in both cases the judgments must take account of memory information.

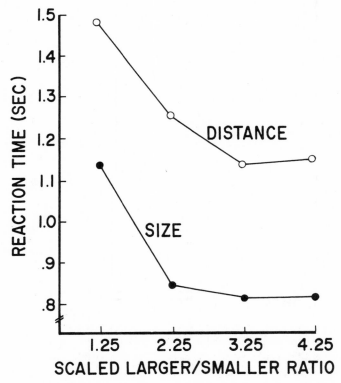

FIGURE 3 Mean reaction times for distance and size comparisons as a function of scaled size difference of pictured pairs.

One expectation is that, with pictures in which the objects are depicted as equal in size, the function relating reaction time to size difference should be the same in the case of distance comparisons as in size comparisons. The two tasks should differ only in that distance comparisons should take longer on the average than size comparisons because the former is a more complex judgment. The results of an initial study on the problem is shown in Figure 3. As demonstrated, the prediction was confirmed.

The more interesting extension to this comparison is described in the "Perceptual Comparisons" paper (Paivio, 1975b). This involved the prediction that the

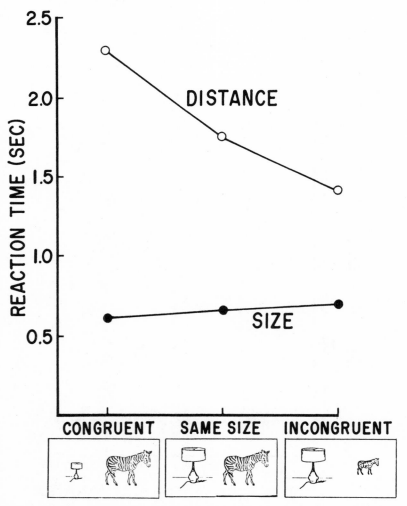

FIGURE 4 Comparison time for relative-distance and relative-size judgments as a function of picture size–memory size congruency. (From Paivio, 1975b.)

Stroop-type conflict I described for size comparisons would be reversed when subjects are asked to judge relative distance. Now the incongruent case (in which the relatively larger member of a pair of objects is pictured smaller than its partner should yield faster reaction times than the congruent case (in which the conceptually larger member is also pictured as larger than its partner). The confirming results are shown in Figure 4, together with the contrasting results for size comparisons. It can also be seen that the predicted result—that distance comparisons would take more time than the size comparisons—occurred, as expected.

These results are interesting again because they demonstrate (1) the continuity between perception and long-term perceptual memory; and (2) that the same memory representations can be used for different ends, depending on the particular task.

Comparisons Based on Verbal Information

Another experiment (Paivio, 1975b, Experiment 4) was based on the idea that picture—word comparisons would yield a completely different pattern of results when subjects are required to compare items on attributes which are presumably represented directly in the verbal system, rather than the image system. An obvious example is the pronounceability of the names of objects. In this case, the information should be accessed more directly when the items are presented as printed words than when they are presented as pictures. This is not a startling prediction because it is already known that it takes longer to name pictures than

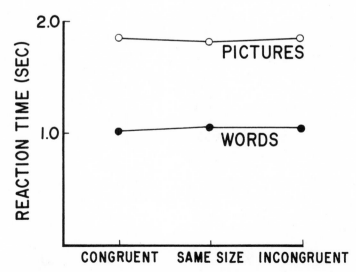

FIGURE 5   Comparison time for relative pronounceability of pairs of pictures and words as a function of physical size—memory size congruency. (Based on data from Paivio, 1975b.)

to read words; but it is important in this context in order to establish a direct contrast with the findings for size comparisons. In addition, physical-size differences in the pictured objects or printed words, whether congruent or incongruent with real-life size, should have no effect whatever on pronounceability comparison time. The experiment on the problem confirmed both predictions in detail: (1) pronounceability comparisons were faster with words than pictures; and (2) pictured or printed size had absolutely no effect on comparison time (see Figure 5).

EXTENSIONS AND SPECULATIONS

The patterns of results from the different experiments I have described provide strong support for a dual-coding theory and, at least in these tasks, they rule out verbal coding and abstract representational theories as they are of present formulated. It remains possible, of course, that some kind of common-coding system must be postulated in addition to verbal and imaginal codes in order to account for other performance data. Some comparison studies now being planned will explore such possibilities. For example, my colleagues and I have obtained pleasantness ratings on our pool of items and these data will be used to construct pairs that differ in varying degree in pleasantness. I expect that comparison time will vary inversely with the pleasantness difference, but I am uncertain about picture–word differences in this task. Pleasantness is a more abstract attribute than is size, and it might well be that such information is stored in a semantic system separate from linguistics or concrete perceptual information. Osgood's semantic differential factors (Osgood, Suci, & Tannenbaum, 1957) suggest that this might be so; that is, evaluative meaning as defined by pleasantness and other related scales, is distinct from other connotative dimensions, which in turn are independent of denotative dimensions such as concreteness (Paivio, 1968). From such facts one might predict that the speed of pleasantness comparisons will not differ for pictures and their noun labels. Indeed, they should be the same for abstract word pairs differing in rated pleasantness. Should the comparison be faster for pictures than words, however, one might wish to argue that pleasantness is more closely associated with the representational substrate of things rather than words.

The issue I have just raised is relevant also to Craik and Lockhart's (1972) depth of coding and Jenkins' (e.g., Walsh & Jenkins, 1973) related semantic approach to memory processes. These are alternatives (not necessarily mutually exclusive ones) to my dual-coding approach, and I have been comparing them in memory studies as well.

Other perceptual memory comparisons now being planned include perceptual attributes other than size. In our laboratory, we have obtained some preliminary norms on judged angularity versus roundness as a first approach to shape representation in long-term memory; and we have also obtained judgments on active–passive and brightness dimensions. These will be used in the kinds of chronometric tasks I have described as well as in extensions in which I hope to determine the extent to which one can access different perceptual-memory dimensions in parallel.

ACKNOWLEDGMENTS

The author's research reported in this paper was supported by a grant (A0087) from the National Research Council of Canada.

REFERENCES

Anderson, J. R., & Bower, G. H. *Human associative memory.* Washington, D.C.: Winston, 1973.

Brooks, L. R. The suppression of visualization by reading. *The Quarterly Journal of Experimental Psychology,* 1967, *19,* 289–299.

Byrne, B. Item concreteness vs spatial organization as predictors of visual imagery. *Memory & Cognition,* 1974, *2,* 53–59.

Cooper, L. A., & Shepard, R. N. Chronometric studies of the rotation of mental images. In W. G. Chase (Ed.), *Visual information processing.* New York: Academic Press, 1973.

Craik, F. I. M., & Lockhart, R. S. Levels of processing: A framework for memory research. *Journal of Verbal Learning and Verbal Behavior,* 1972, *11,* 671–684.

Moyer, R. S. Comparing objects in memory: Evidence suggesting an internal psychophysics. *Perception & Psychophysics,* 1973, *13,* 180–184.

Norman, D. A., & Rumelhart, D. E. *Explorations in cognition.* San Francisco: Freeman, 1975.

Osgood, C. E., Suci, G. J., & Tannenbaum, P. H. *The measurement of meaning.* Urbana, Ill.: University of Illinois Press, 1957.

Paivio, A. A factor-analytic study of word attributes and verbal learning. *Journal of Verbal Learning and Verbal Behavior,* 1968, *7,* 41–49.

Paivio, A. *Imagery and verbal processes.* New York: Holt, Rinehart, & Winston, 1971.

Paivio, A. Language and knowledge of the world. *Educational Researcher,* 1974, *3,* 5–12.

Paivio, A. Imagery and synchronic thinking. *Canadian Psychological Review,* 1975, *16,* 147–163. (a)

Paivio, A. Perceptual comparisons through the mind's eye. *Memory & Cognition,* 1975, *3,* 635–647. (b)

Paivio, A. Images, propositions, and knowledge. In J. M. Nicholas (Ed.), *Images, perception, and knowledge* (The Western Ontario Series in the Philosophy of Science). Dordrecht: Reidel, 1977.

Paivio, A., & Ernest, C. Imagery ability and visual perception of verbal and nonverbal stimuli. *Perception & Psychophysics,* 1971, *10,* 429–432.

Piaget, J., & Inhelder, B. *L'image mentale chez l'enfant.* Paris: Presses Universitaires de France, 1966.

Segal, S. J. Processing of the stimulus in imagery and perception. In S. Segal (Ed.), *Imagery: Current cognitive approaches.* New York: Academic Press, 1971.

Walsh, D. A., & Jenkins, J. J. Effects of orienting tasks on free recall in incidental learning: "Difficulty," "effort," and "process" explanations. *Journal of Verbal Learning and Verbal Behavior,* 1973, *12,* 481–488.

4
Is the Speaker-Hearer a Special Hearer?

Peter F. MacNeilage

The University of Texas at Austin

EDITORS' INTRODUCTION

In Chapter 3, Paivio distinguished between processing verbal and nonverbal information primarily on the basis of visual materials. A similar distinction has been made for verbal and nonverbal auditory information. Speech perception has been thought to be prototypic of perception in a particular mode. Such a concept was derived partially from a view of speech perception as occcuring with a special relation to speech production; this concept has been referred to as the motor theory of speech perception.

A central issue was whether speech perception could be adequately described in terms of traditional detection and discrimination experiments of psychoacoustics, or whether speech perception demanded analysis in terms of phonetic units more relevant to speech production. The speech signal in that sense is ambiguous. That is, it can be described in completely spectral terms or it can be described as a series of phonetic elements. Peter MacNeilage provides a critical analysis of the evidence for a motor theory of speech perception. It should be kept in mind that even if it could be shown that speech perception is specially mediated by reference to production, the pattern-recognition problem must still be solved. The pattern of acoustical energy must somehow implicate the appropriate production elements.

The possibility that speech perception is achieved partly by the listener's reference to stored information about his or her speech production has been and, presumably will continue to be, a recurring theme in speech research. The viability of this theme is probably due mainly to feelings such as that expressed by Lashley (1951) that "the processes of comprehension and production of speech have too much in common to depend on wholly different mechanisms [p. 120]." A number of efforts have been made to give substance to claims of production-related influences on speech perception. The claims have referred specifically to the process of decoding the acoustic signal into segmental and suprasegmental linguistic categories. The segmental categories have been *phoneme* and *distinctive feature*; and the suprasegmental categories have been *stress* and *intonation*. The relevant production information has been that involved in producing the aspects of the acoustic signal used to perceive these categories. The purpose of this chapter is to review and evaluate these claims, with the hope that future theories will benefit from their history.

MOTOR THEORIES OF SEGMENTAL SPEECH PERCEPTION

The Motor Theory of Speech Perception

The main theory stressing that motor factors play a role in speech perception has been presented in a series of papers by the Haskins Laboratories group (Cooper, Liberman, Harris, & Grubb, 1958; Liberman, 1957; Liberman, Cooper, Harris, & MacNeilage, 1962; Liberman, Cooper, Harris, MacNeilage, & Studdert-Kennedy, 1967; Liberman, Cooper, Shankweiler, & Studdert-Kennedy, 1967).[1]

The problem they addressed was that a number of aspects of performance on perceptual experiments did not seem to be explicable in terms of the characteristics of the acoustic stimuli, but did seem intelligible in terms of properties of the speech production system. The main difficulty was that acoustic stimuli for particular stop consonants varied considerably as a function of the speech segments that abutted them, and there did not appear to be any invariant acoustic characteristic underlying the single phonemic response by the listener. Some illustrations of the results of perceptual experiments conducted by the Haskins group must be considered here in order to show, in detail, the basis for their claim.

Studies at Haskins Laboratories have shown that a very important cue for

---

[1] The titles of these papers suggest a curvilinear trend in the confidence that the group had in the theory over the 10-year period. The titles, in order, were: *Some results of research on speech perception, Some input-output relations observed in experiments on the perception of speech, A motor theory of speech perception, Some observations on a model for speech perception, Perception of the speech code.*

perception of the place of articulation of stop consonants is the second formant transition. This is a very rapid change in the frequency of the second lowest resonance of the vocal tract, produced by a rapid change in the position of speech articulators (tongue, lips, and so on) as they move towards or away from the point of occlusion of the tract for the stop consonant. It was also found that the main cues for the identification of particular vowels in careful speech derived from the frequencies of the first three formants (resonances). As the second formant frequencies are different from different vowels, it follows that the second formant transitions for consonants in the environment of different vowels must differ with the identity of the vowel. Using a speech synthesizer it is possible to construct a series of consonant–vowel syllables in which the vowel is always the same, but the second formant transition for the consonant varies in a series of 14 or so equal steps ranging from one typical of the consonant /b/ through one typical of /d/ to one typical of /g/. A listener on hearing this series of stimuli in order will identify the phoneme /b/ in the first few syllables and then abruptly switch the identification response to /d/. After a few /d/ responses, the listener again abruptly switches the response to /g/ for the last few stimuli. If a large number of stimuli are played to the subject in random order, almost all stimuli are placed consistently in one of the three categories, and in the process, stimuli differing considerably in acoustic properties are identified as the same phoneme. Furthermore, if subjects are asked to *discriminate* between two stimuli placed in the same category, their performance is scarcely better than chance. On the other hand, if the two stimuli were placed in different categories, even if they were adjacent stimuli in the series, the level of discrimination between them is very high.

The set of performances described here for stop-consonantal stimuli has come to be known as *categorical perception*. These performances include (1) virtually unanimous identification within phoneme categories; (2) sharp crossovers in identification at phoneme boundaries; (3) near chance-level discrimination between stimuli within categories; but (4) peaks of discrimination between stimuli in different phoneme categories.

Another important example of categorical perception of stop consonants occurs in the case of perception of the voicing characteristics. It has been shown by Lisker and Abramson (1964) that an important cue for distinguishing the voicing characteristic of consonants is what they have called *voice onset time*, the time relation between the release of the stop, signified by a burst of noise, and the beginning of vocal-fold vibration (voicing). If a stimulus series is constructed in which this time relation is varied in small steps in consonant–vowel syllables, stimuli in which voicing leads release or follows it by less than about 20 msec will be identified as voiced consonants (/b/, /d/, or /g/). Stimuli in which voicing follows release by about 30 msec or more will be identified as voiceless consonants (/p/, /t/, or /k/). Again the crossover in judgements from one category to another is quite sharp. And again discrimination between stimuli within categories is near the chance level; but discrimination between stimuli that straddle the boundary between categories is very high.

Perception of vowels presented in isolation was found to be different from that of stop consonants in consonant–vowel syllables (Fry, Abramson, Eimas, & Liberman, 1962). Stimuli for vowel experiments consisted of series of steady-state representations of the first three formants in which formant frequencies were varied in small steps. There was found to be less unanimity in identification of vowels within categories, and more gradual crossovers in identification from one category to the next. Discrimination was considerably above chance levels within categories but was only slightly higher in the region of phoneme boundaries than within categories. Vowel perception was thus described as *continuous,* in contrast to the categorical perception of stop consonants.

In the examples of consonant perception given here, acoustically different stimuli are considered as examples of the same phoneme when within a phonemic category; but stimuli with equal-sized acoustic differences between them are considered to be examples of different phonemes when they occur on opposite sides of the phoneme boundary. It was particularly these properties of consonant perception that led researchers to the motor theory of speech perception. It was argued that dissimilar stimuli that were categorized as one phoneme are produced by the same motor command from the central nervous system, and reference to this motor command by the listener enabled him or her to categorize the dissimilar stimuli as the same phoneme. The existance of context determined differences in formant transitions associated with a given phoneme was attributed primarily to structural constraints of the vocal apparatus in moving from one articulatory position to another: "Because of the interactions and constraints inherent in the mechanism of the vocal tract, the encoding of motor commands into shapes and movements is often a complex transformation. The motor commands operate ahead of these complications, and so escape this kind of encoding [Liberman, *et al.,* 1962, p. 8]." The consonantal commands were considered to be not only invariant but quite distinctive from each other in articulatory terms. For example, the consonant /b/ is made with the lips; /d/ with the tongue tip; and /g/ with the tongue body.

The lack of categorical perception for vowels was considered to result from a lack of distinct invariant motor commands for their production. "From an articulatory standpoint the vowels are different from the stops and some of the other consonants in that the articulators can more continuously from one vowel phoneme to another [Liberman, *et al.,* 1962, p. 5.]."

Thus the motor theory of speech perception applied specifically to stop consonants and depended on the specificty of categorical perception to stop consonants, since categorical perception was the result of articulatory reference, and single invariant articulatory commands only existed for stop consonants.

Three lines of evidence have led to the refutation of the motor theory of speech perception outlined here. First, listeners without normal ability to speak, who are thus presumed not to possess invariant motor commands for stop consonants, are able to perceive stop consonants. An oft cited paper is that of Lenneberg (1962), who showed quite convincingly that a 6-year-old child who did not talk was, nevertheless, able to understand a speaker producing a variety of linguistic forms including commands, questions, and stories. In my opinion, these particular findings are not nearly as damaging to the motor theory of speech perception as has been widely assumed. The motor theory of speech perception was formulated to account for categorical perception of stop consonants, and the fact that a six-year-old can "understand" speech does not necessarily entail the fact that he perceives stop consonants categorically. A more appropriate test of the motor theory in subjects without normal articulatory abilities would involve administration of the perceptual tests that gave rise to the findings that the motor theory was constructed to explain. Such a test has been conducted on a 16-year-old girl with normal hearing and intelligence (and good language comprehension), but without the ability to closely approximate normal segmental articulation (MacNeilage, Rootes, & Chase, 1967). It has been shown that this subject behaved in a manner similar to normal subjects in virtually all respects. Crossovers between one identification category and another were sharper for stop consonants than for vowels. Discrimination peaks were sharper at consonant boundaries than at vowel boundaries and discrimination levels were lower for consonants within categories (approaching chance levels) than for vowels. These findings considerably weaken the motor theory of speech perception by forcing the conclusion that invariant motor commands are not necessary for categorical perception of stop consonants.

A second form of evidence against the motor theory pertains to the claim that there are invariant motor commands for stop consonants in normal subjects. The claim was that the invariance may lie in the actual commands to the muscles; and therefore, electromyograms of the muscle activity associated with a stop consonant should show a pattern independent of segmental context. In a number of electromyographic studies it has been shown that muscle-action patterns associated with stop consonants (and with vowels) are typically affected by both the preceding and the following segmental context (Fromkin, 1966; Lubker, 1968; MacNeilage & DeClerk, 1969; Ohman, 1967; Tatham & Morton, 1968).

In retrospect it is easy to see why muscle activity patterns associated with a given phoneme would be dependent at least on prior segmental context. Different commands must be necessary in order to approximate the same position for a stop consonant following different vowels. The consideration of motor commands for stop consonants did not lead to a conclusion that motor control was different from perception in possessing an invariance, which was absent in the perceptual process, at the final command stage (the neuromuscular level). Rather, it was concluded that motor control involved the same kind of problem as did perception, namely, the equivalence problem (MacNeilage, 1970). The motor theory of speech perception was an attempt to solve the stimulus equivalence problem, the problem of defining the essential property or properties of the set of acoustic stimuli that gave rise to the single-phonemic percept. The proposed solution was that invariance lay not directly in the stimulus but in the final neural command stage of motor control. Investigation of this stage resulted not in the solution of the stimulus-equivalence problem but in the unearthing of the analogous problem of motor equivalence—the problem of defining the essential properties of a set of *different* neuromuscular events which lead to a single end result.

The third and most damaging form of evidence against the motor theory of speech perception is presented by a third group of researchers (summarized in Studdert-Kennedy, 1976; and Darwin, 1976), who suggest that the phenomena of categorical and continuous perception can be accounted for in terms of properties of the auditory-perception process. Some of these investigators appear to effectively rule out motor influences on speech perception of the type claimed by the motor theory. They demonstrate that the various perceptual effects associated with categorical perception can be obtained with nonspeech stimuli, and that some of the effects can even be obtained in subhuman species.

Basic to most of these studies is the assumption that the process of perceptual categorization is assisted by the operation of a short-term memory store which has a limited capacity and is subject to information loss as a function of time (Fujisaki & Kawashima, 1969). In brief, the differences between stop consonants and vowels in the earlier experiments have been attributed to the tendency towards an inverse relation between the amount of use that can be made of information in short-term memory and the amount of reliance on linguistic-categorization operations in perceptual experiments. Consonantal stimuli have been considered to place constraints on short-term memory because of the relatively short duration during which the crucial acoustic information is present. Consequently, consonantal decisions in identification and discrimination experiments are considered to be made more on the basis of absolute linguistic categorization. In contrast, vowel decisions are considered to be based on comparative auditory judgments that are made possible by the availability of comparative information in short-term memory. Consistent with this hypothesis, perception of consonantal stimuli can be made more continuous, and perception of vowel stimuli can be made more categorical by manipulating the availability of the stimuli in short-term memory. For example, short-duration vowel stimuli tend to be perceived more categorically than do long stimuli (Fujisaki & Kawashima, 1969). In addition, consonantal-discrimination functions become more continuous if two pairs of stimuli are presented, with members of one pair being the same but members of the other pair being different (House Lazarus, and Pisoni, 1972). Darwin (1976) has presented evidence that the extent to which categorical or continuous perception will occur is related to the amount of acoustic distinctiveness possessed by members of the stimulus subset; and such distinctiveness is present less for the standard series of stop consonantal stimuli than for the vowel series.

With respect to nonspeech stimuli, Cutting, Rosner, and Foard (1975) have shown that all the criteria of categorical perception can be obtained in the perception of a set of musical stimuli arranged along a pluck-bow dimension. Ades (1977) has also shown a number of the characteristics of categorical perception in experiments with a nonspeech analogue of the voice onset time dimension.

Evidence of categorical perception has also been demonstrated in subhuman listeners. Kuhl and Miller (1975) have found identification functions for the voice-onset-time continuum to be virtually identical in humans and chinchillas.

Two conclusions seem possible from these studies:

1. It now seems unlikely that the phenomena of categorical perception have anything to do with the listener's use of information related to the mechanism of *production* to stop consonants.

2. Evidence of categorical perception of speech apparently cannot even be used to make a somewhat less specific claim, relevant to the present volume; that there is a special perceptual processor for speech-, distinct from nonspeech-perception processes. (Liberman, Mattingly, Turvey, 1972).

A Motor Theory Based on Shadowing Experiments

Chistovich and her colleagues (Chistovich, Klaas, & Kuzmin, 1962; Kozhevnikov & Chistovich, 1965) have argued that there is motor involvement in segmental perception. In these studies a subject is presented with recordings of vowel–consonant-vowel sequences and is required to repeat the sequences aloud as soon as possible. On some occasions the beginning of production of features of the consonant occurred with reaction times as short as 100 msec from the presentation of the appropriate stimulus. It should be noted that this latency is considerably shorter than 140 msec which is typically cited as the minimum in simple auditory reaction-time studies. In addition, production of some aspects of the consonant were sometimes begun before all the information necessary for phonemic categorization was available.

Chistovich and her colleagues hypothesized that the process that must be involved in these experiments, namely, a short latency articulatory synthesis based on acoustic information in the incoming signal, is part of the normal process of speech perception. But, as Fant has pointed out, the results are also compatible with the view that in the shadowing experiments "the distinctive sound features are first recognized and then translated to the equivalent motor patterns causing innervation of the speech organs [Fant, 1967, p. 116]."

Evidence for Motor Involvement Based on Adaptation Studies

A third very recent claim that there can be motor effects on segmental speech perception has been made by Cooper, Blumstein, and Nigro (1975). The claim was based on an adaptation experiment[2] in which subjects were required to identify speech stimuli immediately after a 1-min period in which they repeatedly uttered a sequence of syllables. The syllable sequence consisted of 3 consonants involving labial articulations, each followed by the vowel /æ/ ([bæ], [mæ], [væ]). Subjects were required to identify synthetic stimuli on the [bæ], [dæ], [gæ] continuum. There were 2 articulation conditions:

1. Subjects received normal auditory feedback during production.
2. Subjects whispered their responses under a white noise masking condition.

Under both conditions a group of 3 subjects showed a nonsignificant shift of their [b]−[d] phonetic boundary towards the bilabial consonant [b]; this suggests that the subjects adapted to the bilabial category, although they showed no shift in the [d]−[g] boundary. In addition, it was noted that subjects who showed boundary shifts under both of these conditions tended to be those who showed the largest boundary shifts under the standard perceptual adaptation conditions in which repeated *listening* to stimuli is followed by identification tests.

In another study, Cooper and Nager (1975) have shown that these adaptation effects can also be obtained in the opposite direction; namely, repetitive listening to synthetic acoustic stimuli can result in changes in the values of articulatory parameters of subsequent speech production. In both the Cooper *et al.* (1975) and Cooper and Nager (1975) studies, it is postulated that there is a common processing site for speech perception as well as speech production; and this common processing site is involved in both the perceptual–motor and the motor–perceptual results.

As the authors themselves point out, the evidence for the effects of speech production on speech perception is at present inconclusive. In addition, no speculation is presented as to the relevance of these results for the normal speech perception process (although one might readily imagine a mechanism for setting phonetic boundaries common to input and output processing). Nevertheless, the results of the whisper–noise condition, in particular, are not readily explained in terms of purely perceptual factors; and might yet form the basis for a new motor theory of segmental speech perception.

---

[2] Reviews of adaptation studies are provided by Darwin (1976) and Studdert-Kennedy (1976).

MOTOR THEORIES OF SUPRASEGMENTAL PERCEPTION

In motor theories of suprasegmental perception it is hypothesized that perceptual decisions are made on the basis of the listener's direct knowledge of the amount of *physiological effort* involved in producing the speech waveform. Claims have been made about perception of intonation and stress.

Intonation

The intonation contour of utterances, considered to consist mainly of the overall pattern of changes in fundamental frequency, (F_0) provides information about certain grammatical properties. For example, in the English sentence, "The boy hit the ball," a relatively constant F_0 during most of the utterance, followed by a terminal fall in F_0, signifies a simple declarative sentence. On the other hand, a terminal rise in a sentence with the same lexical items signifies a question. It is well accepted that in sentences of these types, a terminal increase in F_0 involves more physiological effort than a terminal fall, taking the form of an increase in tension of the vocal folds (Lieberman, 1967). Hadding-Koch and Studdert-Kennedy (1964) investigated in detail listener's use of terminal-contour information in deciding whether sentences were statements or questions. Stimulus material consisted of 42 versions of the utterance "for Jane," identical except for the possession of a different intonation contour. All contours started at an F_0 of 250 Hz. This frequency was maintained for 140 msec over the word "for." The contours then rose to peaks at 370 or 310 Hz. They then fell to one of three "turning points" at 130, 175, or 220 Hz. The period of the rise and fall totaled 300 msec. The contours then proceeded to one of 7 "end points" between 130 and 370 Hz in 200 msec. In two separate sessions, subjects were asked: (1) Is it a question or a statement? [linguistic judgment] and; (2) Does it end in a rise or a fall [psychophysical judgment]?

One particular aspect of the subject's responses to these stimuli led Lieberman (1967) to postulate a motor component in perception of intonation. It was found that when the peak of the turning point of the stimulus was relatively high, a smaller terminal rise was necessary in order for the utterance to be perceived as a question or as a terminal rise. Lieberman pointed out that preterminal rises in F_0 in natural speech are typically associated with the phenomenon of *sentence prominence* or major sentence stress. Lieberman presented evidence that F_0 increase in prominence was a result of a transient increase in subglottal pressure. He argued that such an increment in subglottal pressure during the utterance would reduce the amount of respiratory drive that remained available to sustain rate of vocal fold vibration at the termination of the utterance. As a result, a given increment in tension of the vocal folds to produce the terminal F_0 increase for a question would result in a lower final F_0 level than would otherwise be the case. Lieberman contended that because a speaker–hearer "knows" this, as a result of his/her own physiological maneuvers in producing such a contour, he/she accepts lower terminal F_0 levels as signifying questions when higher preterminal F_0 levels have preceded them.

Results of a subsequent study by Studdert-Kennedy and Hadding (1971) suggest that Lieberman's (1967) interpretation of these results is not correct. In their study a similar analysis was made of a set of intonation contours associated with the word "November." In addition, a nonspeech control condition was included in which subjects reported on whether the terminal portion of pure-tone facsimilies of the intonation contours were rising or falling. Studdert-Kennedy and Hadding found that the previously observed effects of the frequency of the turning point on terminal judgments was observed for pure-tone stimuli, thus ruling out a speech motor explanation of the performance. In addition, the effects of the peak frequency were observed in the linguistic judgments but not in the speech-psychophysical judgments. This result was also contrary to a motor-based explanation that requires that the effects appear in speech-psychophysical judgments, though it leaves unresolved the discrepancy between the speech-psychophysical results of the two studies.

The effects of the peak frequency on linguistic judgments may be explicable in terms of the listener's linguistic knowledge. There is some agreement in analyses of intonation that it is the last accented syllable in a sentence that gets the major pitch-contour superimposed on it (Ohala, 1970, p. 99), and would thus receive a pitch rise in a question. If unaccented syllables follow this peak, the tone remains high. Thus, in the absence of a definite down turn in pitch following the accented syllable, subjects might be expected to judge stimuli with high preterminal peaks as questions, on the basis of their knowledge of the language.

Stress (Amplitude)

Amplitude of the acoustic signal, perceived as loudness, appears to be a relatively minor cue to the perception of stress in English (Fry, 1958) and in real-life situations is only one of four cues to stress. The others are fundamental frequency, duration, and vowel quality. It has been suggested that loudness judgments of speech stimuli to some extent may be made on the basis of the physiological effort required to produce them.

Two versions of this hypothesis exist. The first is an attempt to account for differences in the perception of loudness of different vowels. If a subject produces a number of different vowels at the same level of subjective effort or respiratory drive (as indicated by subglottal air pressure), then the amplitude of the vowels produced will vary over a range of about 5 dB (Lehiste & Peterson, 1959). High vowels have lower amplitudes than low vowels. But despite these amplitude differences which would be well above threshold for perceived differences in the same vowel, subjects report that the vowels are approximately equally loud. In addition, if a set of vowels is recorded at a uniform sound-pressure level (which involves more vocal effort for high than for low vowels), high vowels in the set are considered to be louder than low vowels. The motor-based explanation of these results, according to Lehiste (1970), is that perhaps "listeners were not reacting to the actual intensity differences but were in fact responding to differences in effort, whatever the cues may have been that were present in the sound waves to indicate the relative amount of effort the speaker had used in producing the vowels [p. 118]." Lehiste considers these results to be evidence for a motor theory of speech perception. But the critical question from this chapter's standpoint is whether one needs to have had experience in *speaking* the language in order to make use of the effort cues. An alternative possibility is that from experience in listening to vowel sequences on many occasions when they are produced with relatively uniform effort, and thus unequal amplitudes, a listener learns to apply an equalizing correction factor to vowel amplitudes.

The second version of the hypothesis arises from experiments in which listeners make relative-loudness judgments of speech samples presented with a wide variety of different amplitudes, and overall functions relating loudness judgments to amplitudes are obtained. There is some agreement that for pure tones, and for a number of other stimuli, including vowels and consonants produced in isolation, perceived loudness increases in proportion to the .6–.8 power of the second pressure level (Mendel, Sussman, Merson, Naeser, & Minifie, 1969). On the other hand, with consonant–vowel–consonant monosyllables and other material analogous to real speech, a larger exponent is found with a modal value around 1.2. This has led a number of researchers to conclude that loudness judgments of speech in lifelike situations differ from those of other acoustic stimuli. Ladefoged and McKinney (1963) found that an index of work done by the respiratory component[3] of a subject producing monosyllables was, as in their speech loudness judgments, proportional to the 1.2 power of the sound-pressure level. This led them to conclude that the listeners were judging loudness by "assessing the amount of effort they themselves would have to make in order to produce corresponding sounds [cited in Ladefoged, 1967, p. 40]."

Again, it would appear that Mendel *et al.*'s (1969) alternative explanation remains possible. "It appears to us that there are sufficient variations in the acoustic signal that result from increasing the effort level during production that listeners may make loudness judgments primarily on the basis of acoustic cues (Mendel *et al.*, 1969), p. 1560).

As a footnote, a more refined analytical approach has been made by Allen (1971), who points out that exponential functions may be of limited value because they only relate loudness and one other variable. If that variable and others are highly correlated, as they may well be in the speech signal, then the

---

[3] Work was defined as "proportional to the product of subglottal pressure and volume velocity of air through the glottis" (Ladefoged, 1967, p. 30).

exponent is conveying a very limited amount of information. Allen showed, by means of partial correlation analysis, that subjects appear to make use of both acoustic cues, as measured by peak sound-pressure level; and vocal effort cues, as measured by subglottal pressure of the speaker. The relative dependence on each of the two types of cues is different for different listeners. This suggests that even if the motor theory is true, the extent to which it is appropriate varies from subject to subject.

CONCLUSION

In all the work reviewed here, with the possible exception of the preliminary findings of Cooper *et al.* there has been no result that strongly implicates motor information in the hearer's perceptual response process. With that exception, processes of direct analysis of the acoustic stimulus appear to always provide at least the potential for an alternative explanation of all of the results. Thus, it has not yet been shown that the speaker—hearer is a special hearer in the sense that any motor information possibly gained from producing speech helps in perceiving it. Nevertheless, the intimacy with which perception and production must cooperate in learning speech will no doubt continue to encourage the belief that the speaker's production capabilities contribute more to perception than just an acoustic signal. Perhaps this is only a quantitative matter. We may never perceive speech quite as well if we did not go through all the target-matching operations involved in learning to speak. If there is a qualitative dividend to speech perception, arising from our having learned to produce speech, it has not yet been isolated, and arguments in the literature to the effect that it exists, other than those reviewed here, are extremely indirect.

ACKNOWLEDGEMENTS

I would like to thank Harvey Sussman for his comments on the manuscript.

REFERENCES

Ades, A. Categorical perception and the speech mode. *Cognition,* in press.
Allen, G. C. Acoustic level and vocal effort as cues for the loudness of speech. *Journal of the Acoustical Society America,* 1971, *49,* 1831–1841.
Chistovich, L. A., Klaas, I. A., & Kuzmin, I. I. [The process of speech sound discrimination.] *Voprosy psikhologii* 1962, *6,* 26–39.
Cooper, F. S., Liberman, A. M., Harris, K. S., & Grubb, P. M. Some input—output relations observed in experiments on the perception of speech. *Proceedings of the Second International Congress of Cybernetics* Association Internationale de Cybernetique, Pp. 930–941. Namur, Belgium: (1958).

Cooper, W. E., Blumstein, S. E., & Nigro, G. Articulatory effects on speech perception: A preliminary report. *Journal of Phonetics*, 1975, *3*, 87–98.

Cooper, W. E., & Nager, R. M. Perceptuo-motor adaptation to speech: An analysis of bisyllabic utterances and a neural model. *Journal of the Acoustical Society of America*, 1975, *58*, 256–265.

Cutting, J. E., Rosner, B. S., & Foard, C. F. Rise time in nonlinguistic sounds and models of speech perception. *Haskins Laboratories Status Report on Speech Research, SR-14*, 1975, 71–93.

Darwin, C. J. The perception of speech. In E. C. Carterette & M. P. Friedman (Eds.), *Handbook of perception* (Vol. 7). New York: Academic Press. Pp. 175–226.

Fant, C. G. M. Auditory patterns of speech. In W. Wathen-Dunn (Ed.), *Models of the perception of speech and visual form*. Cambridge, Mass.: M.I.T. Press, 1967, Pp. 111–125.

Fromkin, V. A. Neuromuscular specification of linguistic units. *Language and Speech*, 1966, *9*, 170–199.

Fry, D. B. Experiments in the perception of stress. *Language and Speech*, 1958, *1*, 126–152.

Fry, D. B., Abramson, A. S., Eimas, P. D., & Liberman, A. M. The identification and discrimination of synthetic vowels. *Language and Speech*, 1962, *5*, 171–189.

Fujisaki, H., & Kawashima, T. [Normalization and recognition of vowels] (Annual Report No. 1). Tokyo: Division of Electrical Engineering, Engineering Research Institute, University of Tokyo, 1969.

Hadding-Koch, K., & Studdert-Kennedy, M. G. An experimental study of some intonation contours. *Phonetica*, 1964, *11*, 175–185.

House Lazarus, J., & Pisoni, D. B. Categorical and noncategorical modes of speech perception along the voice onset time continuum. Paper presented at the 84th meeting of the Acoustical Society of America Miami Beach, Florida 1972.

Kozhevnikov, V. A., & Chistovich, L. A. 1965. [Speech: articulation and perception.] (*Joint Publication Research Service 30*, 1965, 543.)

Kuhl, P. K., & Miller, J. D. Speech perception by the chinchilla: Voiced–voiceless distinction in alveolar plosives. *Science*, 1975, *190*, 69–72.

Ladefoged, P. *Three areas of experimental phonetics*. London: Oxford University Press, 1967.

Ladefoged, P., & McKinney, N. Loudness, sound pressure and subglottal pressure in speech. *Journal of the Acoustical Society of America* 1963, *35*, 454–460.

Lashley, K. S. The problems of serial order in behavior. In L. A. Jeffress (Ed.), *Cerebral mechanisms in behavior*. New York: Wiley, 1951. Pp. 112–136.

Lehiste, I. *Suprasegmentals*. Cambridge, Mass.: M.I.T. Press, 1970.

Lehiste, I., & Peterson, G. E. Vowel amplitude and phonemic stress in American English. *Journal of the Acoustical Society of America* 1959, *31*, 428–435.

Lenneberg, E. Understanding language without ability to speak: a case report. *Journal of Abnormal Social Psychology* 1962, *65*, 419–425.

Liberman, A. M. Some results of research on speech perception. *Journal of the Acoustical Society of America* 1957, *29*, 117–123.

Liberman, A. M., Cooper, F. S., Harris, K. S., & MacNeilage, P. F. A motor theory of speech perception. In *Proceedings of the speech communication seminar*. Stockholm: Royal Institute of Technology, 1962.

Liberman, A. M., Cooper, F. S., Harris, K. S., MacNeilage, P. F., & Studdert-Kennedy, M. G. Some observations on a model for speech perception. In W. Wathen-Dunn (Ed.), *Models for the perception of speech and visual form*. Cambridge, Mass.: M.I.T. Press, 1967.

Liberman, A. M., Cooper, F. S., Shankweiler, D. P., & Studdert-Kennedy, M. G. Perception of the speech code. *Psychological Review*, 1967, *74*, 431–461.

Liberman, A. M., Mattingly, I. G., & Turvey, M. T. Language codes and memory codes. In

A. W. Melton and E. Martin (Eds.), *Coding processes in human memory,* (New York: Wiley), 1972, Pp. 307–334.

Lieberman, P. *Intonation, perception and language.* Cambridge, Mass.: M.I.T. Press, 1967.

Lisker, L., & Abramson, A. S. A cross-language study of voicing in initial stops: Acoustical measurements. *Word,* 1964, *20,* 384–422.

Lubker, J. F. An electromyographic-cinefluorographic investigation of velar function during normal speech production. *The Cleft Palate Journal,* 1968, *5,* 1–17.

MacNeilage, P. F. Motor control of serial ordering of speech. *Psychological Review,* 1970, *77,* 182–196.

MacNeilage, P. F., & DeClerk, J. L. On the motor control of coarticulation in CVC monosyllables. *Journal of the Acoustical Society of America,* 1969, *45,* 1217–1233.

MacNeilage, P. F., Rootes, T. P., and Chase, R. A. Speech production and perception in a patient with severe impairment of somesthetic perception and motor control. *Journal of Speech and Hearing Research,* 1967, *10,* 449–467.

Mendel, M. I., Sussman, H. M., Merson, R. M., Naeser, M. A., & Minifie, F. D. Loudness judgments of speech and nonspeech sounds. *Journal of the Acoustical Society of America,* 1969, *46,* 1556–1561.

Ohala, J. Aspects of the control and production of speech. *U.C.L.A. Working Papers in Phonetics,* 1970, No. *15.*

Ohman, S. E. G. *Peripheral motor commands in labial articulation.* (STL-QPST 4/1967). Stockholm, Sweden: Royal Institute of Technology, 1967.

Studdert-Kennedy, M. G. Speech Perception. In N. J. Lass (Ed.), *Contemporary issues in experimental phonetics.* Springfield, Illinois: C. C Thomas. Pp. 243–294.

Studdert-Kennedy, M. G., & Hadding, K. Further experimental studies of fundamental frequency contours. In A. Rigault & R. Charbonneau (Eds.), *Proceedings of the 7th International Congress of Phonetic Sciences.* The Hague: Mouton, 1971. Pp. 1024–1031.

Tatham, M. A. A., & Morton, K. Some electromyographic data towards a model of speech production. *Occasional papers* No. 1). Essex, England: University of Essex Language Center, 1968.

5
Meaning and The Construction of Reality in Early Childhood

M. A. K. Halliday
University of Sydney

EDITORS' INTRODUCTION

How language develops is an interesting and vitally important inquiry in its own right. It also can provide a means of telling how a child perceives and structures the world. One approach of this sort is to examine the order in which certain physical distinctions are reflected in the child's understanding and use of language. That sort of approach, perhaps exemplified by some of the work of Eve and Herbert Clark, emphasizes the referential aspect of language. Michael Halliday here uses a description of language development to reflect the child's perception and construction of reality taking a somewhat different approach. In Halliday's analysis, it is the functional aspects of language that reflects the child's perception and cognition. In particular, by 10 months of age the child's protolanguage manifests at least a self–other distinction and a social–physical object distinction. These are two of the modal distinctions considered in the introductory chapter (page 68). When these distinctions are viewed in relation to the child's further language development, the functional aspects of the protolanguage become especially important. These include reflective and action oriented uses of language with specific personal, interactional, regulatory, and instrumental functions. Halliday interprets the meanings communicated on the basis of a language reflecting this world view as arising out of the social or inter-subjective interaction of a child with significant others.

FUNCTIONAL SEMANTICS OF LANGUAGE DEVELOPMENT

The Concept of the Protolanguage

Long before a child begins to speak in his mother tongue, he is engaging in acts of meaning.

The meanings may be expressed in various ways. The child may use either of the two modes, vocal or gestural; and, in the vocal mode, in which the expression is a complex pattern of intonation and articulation, he may either create new patterns of his own, or attempt to imitate sounds he hears in the speech of others. Most children probably use some combination of all three kinds of expression, though many show a preference for one particular kind. I made an intensive study of one child, Nigel, from birth to 3½ years (Halliday, 1975); Nigel showed a clear preference for the vocal mode, and for inventing sounds rather than imitating them, though he did use some gestures and vocal imitations as well. All three are variants of a single, more general mode of expression, that of bodily postures and movements, with which a child constructs his *Protolanguage.* The essential ingredient of the protolanguage is not the form of the output but the nature of the act of meaning itself.

An *Act of Meaning* is a communicative act that is intentional and symbolic. A cry of hunger is a communicative act; and so, for that matter, is clamping on to the mother's breast. Both convey a message—that the child is hungry. But neither of these acts embodies the intention to communicate; they are not symbolic acts. A symbolic act is one of which the meaning and success criteria do not reside in its own performance.

The outward form of a symbolic act is sometimes iconic. If I hit you because I'm angry with you, that is not an act of meaning. If I hit you to show that I'm angry with you, that is an act of meaning, but it is one in which the expression is related to the meaning in a nonarbitrary fashion: the symbol is an iconic one. The distinction between iconic and noniconic symbols is, needless to say, a matter of degree; the expression may be more or less iconic, and it may be both iconic and noniconic at the same time. At eight months Nigel had a small repertory of gestures, one of which was that of grasping an object firmly, without pulling it towards him, and then letting go. The meaning was "I want that." (See page 84). This was a partially iconic gesture, but the act was clearly a symbolic one—it did not itself constitute an attempt at realizing the desire. Nigel was not acting directly on the object. The gesture was an act of meaning, addressed to the other person taking part in the situation.

Acts of meaning, in this specific sense, take place early in a child's life; much earlier than the time at which language development studies have usually been begun, and long before the child has anything that is recognizable as a "language"—if language is defined by the presence of adultlike linguistic structures or words. As far as I was aware, Nigel's earliest act that was unambiguously an act of meaning took place just before six months, when for the first time he produced a sound—a very short and rather quiet nasal squeak, on a high rising note—the meaning of "What's going on?" On the other hand I was not prepared for acts of meaning at this early age, and I may have failed to notice earlier instances. Perhaps the sad tale that he told at the age of two months, after having his first injections, should be thought of as an act of meaning, given the very clear contrast between this and his usual cheerful narrative (see page 85).

By the age of nine months, Nigel had a *System* of acts of meaning—a "meaning potential"—which marked the beginning of his protolanguage. At this stage the protolanguage consisted of five meanings. Three, which were expressed gesturally, were in the more active mode: "I want that," "I don't want that," and "Do that (again)." The other two, which were expressed vocally, were in the more reflective mode: "Let's be together" and "Look—that's interesting." At that time, therefore, Nigel showed a correlation between the two modes of expression, vocal and gestural, and the two modes of meaning, reflective and active: reflective meanings were expressed vocally and active ones gesturally. Within four to six weeks, however, he abandoned the gestural mode almost entirely (the exception being the demand for music, expressed by "beating time"), and settled for vocal symbols in the expression of meanings of all kinds.

Systematic and Social Character of Acts of Meaning

An act of meaning is systematic in a dual sense. First, the act itself is an act of choice, of selection within a meaning potential; and the selection is nonrandom, in that it is coherently related to the context of situation—the semiotic structure of whatever portion of the child's reality construct constitutes the relevant environment in the given instance.

Secondly, the meaning potential is also systematic. It is a resource, a network of options each one of which can be interpreted by reference to the child's total model of reality and of his own place in it. The reality, and hence the meaning potential, is constantly under construction, being added to, differentiated within, and modified.

Between the ages of 9 and 16 months, Nigel's protolanguage grew from a system of five to a system of about fifty different meanings. For example, whereas at the start he had had just one meaning of an *interactional* kind, a generalized signal of participation, exchanging attention with another person through the conversational process, he now had a resource of about fifteen. These included: (1) *greetings*, where he distinguished among the different persons that he exchanged meanings with, and between initiating and responding; (2) *sharings*, with which he distinguished between shared attention and shared regret; and (3) *responses*, to specific invitations to mean. All these were coded in the system as recognizably distinct symbolic acts.

The term "act" is however semantically loaded; it suggests something purely subjective. But an act of meaning is a social act, again in the same dual sense as previously discussed. First, the act itself is shared, between the actor and the attender. It is shared not merely in the sense that the one is acting and the other is attending at the same time (the one "giving" meanings and the other "receiving" them), but that both are taking part in an exchange of meanings and that there is no act of meaning in isolation from such exchange. The process is one of conversation; the act becomes meaningful only when the other (who is a "significant other" by virtue of taking part in the conversational process) joins in and so gives value to the child's symbolic intent.

Secondly, the act of meaning is social also in the general sense, that the meaning potential from which it derives is a social construct. The semantic system, in which the child encodes his subjective reality, must be shared between the child and the significant others if his acts of meaning are to be successful. Experience may be private, but the symbolic coding of experience is social; there can be no private symbols, in this sense. But the child is not yet approximating the others' semantic system; he is creating one of his own. To say that the creation of a semantic system is a social process means, therefore, at this stage, that the others must be approximating the child's semantic system, and this is precisely what they do. It is clear from the observations of Nigel's conversation that the others not only understood him but actively understood him; they played the conversational game according to his rules. Here is an example at 18 months (see page 82):

Nigel set himself to eating his lunch. Some fish fell off the fork.
"Ooh!" It was another very high pitched squeak.
"Ooh you lost a bit then," said Anna. "Where did it go?"
"Byebye." Nigel looked up at Anna, inviting her to share a memory. "'yebye, byebye," he said.
"Yes, all the trains went away, and you said "byebye," didn't you?"
"Byebye," said Nigel sadly, waving his hand. He finished his lunch. "Nomore. No-more."
"Where has it all gone?" Anna asked him.

It is obvious that Anna is, quite spontaneously, interpreting what Nigel says as relevant participation in the dialogue. At the same time, the semantic approximation is not a one-way process; it has its own natural dialectic. Anna responds with meanings of her own; and she interprets Nigel's meanings in terms of what is coded in her own semantic system—or (since she is an imaginative person) in terms of what is not necessarily coded but is at least codable. This, in fact, is the role of the others in the conversational process: to interpret and to respond with their own meanings. So the means exist whereby the child, even at the protolinguistic phase, has access to adult meanings in a context in which they can modify and feed into his own meaning potential.

Semantic Continuity

A child's earliest protolanguage can perhaps best be interpreted by reference to a small set of extralinguistically defined semantic functions. At 10 months Nigel's acts of meaning fell into four functionally defined categories: the *Instrumental* and the *Regulatory,* which are more in the active mode of meaning; and the *Interactional* and the *Personal,* which are more in the reflective mode. These are "extralinguistic" in the sense that they exist as modes of intent independently of being encoded into, or realized through, symbolic acts of meaning.

It seems clear that, with Nigel at least, this functional orientation of the protolanguage is the ontogenetic base of the major functional components (what I have called *metafunctions*) of the adult semantic system, the *Interpersonal* or active component and the *Ideational* or reflective component (Halliday, 1973).

The functional organization and functional continuity are thus properties of the system. In order to represent them we express the system as a potential—as a resource, not as a set of rules. Hence in representing Nigel's protolanguage I have used an "or"-based, not an "and"-based, model of language—one in which the underlying relation is the *paradigmatic* one (system) rather than the *syntagmatic* one (structure). A system, in this technical sense, is any set of options, or range of alternatives, together with its condition of entry.

If we follow closely Nigel's development from a protolanguage (Phase 1) through a transitional stage (Phase 2) to the adult linguistic system (Phase 3), a striking pattern of semantic continuity emerges. The "self"-oriented systems, the interactional and the personal, at first define meanings such as "Let's be together," "Here I am," "That's pleasing," "That's interesting." These then evolve, through the intermediary senses of "Let's attend to this together" and "Now you say its name," to the naming of things, beginning with persons, objects and processes; and thence through observation, recall, and prediction into the narrative mode and the ideational component of the adult semantics. This seemed to be Nigel's way in to the reflective mode of meaning.

The "other"-oriented systems, the instrumental and the regulatory, at first define meanings such as "Give me that," "Do that," and "Do that again." These then evolve, through intermediary senses such as "You do that," "Let's do that," and "Let me do that" (command, suggestion, and request for permission), into the exchanging of things, giving, demanding, and giving on demand; and thence through the exchange of information into the dialogue mode and the interpersonal component of the adult semantics. This was Nigel's way in to the active mode of meaning.

Central to this process of the evolution of the functional modes or components of meaning is the evolution in the concept of *Function* itself. Nigel's earliest system of meaning potential, the Phase 1 protolanguage, is "functional" in the sense that each element in the system, and therefore each act of meaning, realizes an intent in respect of just one of a small set of extralinguistic functions (those that we identified as instrumental, regulatory, interactional, and personal, and the one or two that are added later). Nigel's conversation is meaningful in relation to his domains of social action, those of: (1) achieving material ends; (2) controlling the behavior of the "others"; (3) establishing and maintaining contact with them; or (4) expressing his own selfhood in the form of cognitive and affective states. These are the social contexts of his acts of meaning—parts that he can play in the symbolic interaction. If we call these the "functions" of his protolanguage, then in this context 'function' is equivalent to 'use.'

For some months (9 months to 16–17 months) this system continues to expand. The meaning potential is considerably enlarged; but it remains a system of the same kind. Then, towards the middle of the second year, the system undergoes a qualitative change. Hitherto, it has been a coding system with just two levels, a level of content (the meaning) and a level of expression (the sound or gesture); the elements of the system have been individual signs, content-expression pairs. Elements like "è - e - eh,": 'Here I am!'; or "ùh": 'Do that some more'; or "dòh": 'Nice to see you, and shall we look at this picture together?,' are meanings coded directly into sounds, without any intervening organization. (Needless to say, the glosses need not be taken literally as statements of meaning; they are intended as an aid to understanding. But they also serve to bring out the fact that the meanings of Nigel's protolanguage are typically not meanings that are fully coded in the adult semantic.)

Just before the middle of his second year, however (though there have been previews of what was to come), Nigel introduces a third level of coding intermediate between the content and the expression, a level of formal organization consisting of words and structures. In other words, he adds a grammar—or more accurately, a lexicogrammar. The elements of the system are no longer individual signs, but configurations at three different levels, semantic, lexicogrammatical, and phonological, which are related to each other by realization. The meanings are "first" realized as (encoded into) wordings and "then" realized as (recoded into) sounds. This is the way the adult language is organized.

By taking this step, Nigel made it possible for himself to combine meanings into a single complex act; and he exploited this possibility by means of a functional strategy of his own devising, by which he distinguished all acts of meaning into two broad types, the *Pragmatic* and the *Mathetic*. The former have a "doing" function, and require a response from the person addressed: at first a nonverbal response, such as giving something or doing something, but later on these acts increasingly call for a verbal response, such as an answer to his question. The latter require no response and serve what we may interpret as a "learning" function. This distinction has arisen directly by generalization out of the functions of the protolanguage; but it means that Nigel can now converse in new ways, adopting and assigning roles in the conversational process (dialogue) and ranging freely over time and space beyond the confines of the here and now (narrative).

Because he has a grammar, which allows meanings to be split up and their components combined and recombined in indefinitely many ways, Nigel is able to make this distinction explicit; and he does so in an interesting way. The meaning "pragmatic" is expressed by the use of a rising tone, and the meaning "mathetic" is expressed by the use of a falling tone. In other words the functional distinction has itself now been coded, as an opposition between two "macrofunctions"; Nigel creates this pattern more or less overnight, at 19 months, and it remains his dominant semiotic strategy throughout the rest of Phase 2, the transition to an adultlike language, and into Phase 3. "Function" is now no longer synonymous with "use"; it has to be reinterpreted in the sense of "mode of meaning."

The significant others with whom Nigel exchanges meanings respond to this new language as understandingly, and as unconsciously, as they did to his protolanguage. When the tone rises, they respond with goods and services, or, gradually, with new meanings—that is, they offer something in exchange. When the tone falls they listen, if they are there, but they feel no need to respond; and if they do respond, it is typically not with any new meaning but with an echo of what Nigel has said, though coded in adult words and structures, or with a prompt, inviting him to continue. Nigel, in turn, makes it clear that such responses are appropriate. This is not to imply, of course, that he always gets the response he wants; but he does get it in enough instances for the system to work. It should be noted that this semantic opposition is not at all the same as the meaning of the contrast between rising and falling tone in adult English. The two are, ultimately, related, but many of Nigel's wordings come out with what is, for the adult, the "wrong" tone. For example, all his commands and "wh"- questions rise in tone, since they require a response; while his dependent clauses (when he begins to develop them) fall, since they do not.

In this transitional phase, however, the two modes of meaning, pragmatic and mathetic, are still alternatives: an act of meaning is always either one or the other. For example, *more méat* means 'more meat' + 'do something' (pragmatic), that is, 'Give me some more meat'; *chuffa stúck* means 'train stuck' + 'do something', that is, "Get it out for me'; *high wáll* means 'high place' + 'do something', that is, 'I'm going to jump—catch me!' On the other hand, *green càr* means 'green car' + 'I'm taking note,' 'I'm learning' (mathetic), that is, 'I see (or saw, or will see) a green car'; likewise *loud mùsic* means 'That's loud music'; *chuffa stòp* means 'The train's stopped'. Nigel's next move, already implicit however in this scheme of things, is to combine these two modes of meaning so that every act of meaning is both one and the other. This means reinterpreting the concept of function yet again.

By the end of Phase 2, near the end of his second year, Nigel's grammatical resources have developed to the extent that he can map grammatical structures one on to another the way the adult language does. For example, he can select the categories "transitive" (in the transitivity system) and "interrogative" (in the mood system) and produce the expression *did you drop the green pen* which encodes both these selections simultaneously. He still does not use this sentence in the adult sense, as a question, because his semantic system is not yet that of the adult language; but he has successfully combined in it an interpersonal meaning, represented by the interrogative structure, and an ideational meaning, represented by the transitivity structure. (The sentence, of course, contains much else besides these two selections.)

The macrofunctions have now become what we might call metafunctions. They are no longer just generalizations of the earlier functional categories but reinterpretations of them at another level. They have now become the functional components of the semantic system; and each has its own systems of meaning potential, having as output some specific contribution to the total lexicogrammatical coding. The adult language is structured around these two components of meaning: the ideational and the interpersonal (together with a third, the textual, which I omit from the discussion here for the sake of brevity). They represent the twin themes of reflection and action in the adult semiotic: language as a means of reflecting on reality, and language as a means of acting on reality. The really striking fact about a human infant is that these two modes of meaning are present from the start. In his earliest acts of meaning we find Nigel already engaged in an ongoing conversational process in which the exchange takes these two primary symbolic forms.

The Context of an Act of Meaning

It is a mistake to suppose that a child's language is ever fully context-bound or that an adult's is ever fully context-free. The principle of semantic continuity and functional evolution means that: (1) an act of meaning always has a context; while (2) the way in which an act of meaning is related to its context changes in the course of development. Equally, the system as a whole (the meaning potential) has a context, and this too changes in the developmental process.

The context for the *Meaning System* is the *Social System*, as it exists as a semiotic construct for the child at the given time. The context for an *Act of Meaning* is the *Situation*, which is also a semiotic construct, a recognizable configuration of features from the social system. The situation consists essentially of a *Field* of social process, and *Tenor* of social relationships, together with a third element, a *Mode* of symbolic action—that is, the specific part that is assigned to acts of meaning in the particular context.

Much of the speech a child hears around him is, typically, relatable to its context of situation in recognizable and systematic ways. (It is also, despite a common belief to the contrary, richly structured, grammatically well formed, and fluent.) The meanings reflect the field, tenor, and mode of the situation in which they are expressed; and they do so in a rather systematic way. Typically, ideational meanings, realized in thing-names, transitivity structures and the like, represent the "field," the nature of the social process—what is going on at the time. Interpersonal meanings, realized in moods and modalities, expressions of comment, attitude and so on, represent the "tenor," the social relationships in the situation—who-all are taking part. Textual meanings, realized as patterns of cohesion and the organization of discourse, represent the "mode," the symbolic or rhetorical channel—what part the exchange of meanings is playing in the total unfolding scene. In much adult speech, whether backyard gossip or deliberations in committee, the actual components of the situation are fictions that are construed out of the meanings that are being exchanged: persons and objects are being talked about, and even acted upon, that are not there outside of the talk. But when the child himself is part of the interactive process, the situation is typically such that its features are made manifest to him: the feelings and attitudes of the participants and the objects and actions referred to can be seen or felt or heard.

The child's own acts of meaning relate likewise to his own social constructs. At first, in Phase 1, as we have seen, the relation is one in which meaning is goal directed ('Do this,' 'I want that,' 'Let's be together'); the context *is* the goal, and the act of meaning is successful if the goal is achieved. (We should remember that right from the start there are also purely reflexive acts of meaning: 'That's pleasing,' 'That's interesting.') But this relationship changes, by the natural dialectic of development. Nigel's own ability to mean allows him to construe acts of meaning in others, in their relation to the context; but the nature of this relation in adult conversation—or rather in conversation in the Phase 3 system—is such that the process of understanding it changes the contextual basis of the child's own acts of meaning. Hence what happens in Phase 2, when the child makes the transition to the adult system, is that meaning no longer consists in aiming a shaft at a preexisting target; now, it also involves defining the target. Success criteria here are of two kinds, and with Nigel, as we saw, each act was clearly marked for one or the other. Either success is external (pragmatic acts—rising tone), where Nigel is, or is not, satisfied with the other's response; or it is internal (mathetic acts—falling tone), where Nigel is, or is not, satisfied with his own achievement. In neither case is success a foregone conclusion. It is obvious that, with a pragmatic utterance, such as *more méat,* Nigel may not get an acceptable response: he may get no response at all, or a response that does not accede. But it is just as often the case that, with a mathetic utterance, Nigel recognizes failures of meaning; as he did for example when, holding a toy bus in one hand and a train in the other, he was trying to encode the situation, saying *two ... two chùffa ... two ... two ...*—finally he admitted defeat and gave up. But in both cases the act of meaning here consists in more than merely specifying a function in context, it involves making explicit the context in which that function is relevant. Nigel has now taken the critical step towards freeing his conversation from the limitations of his immediate surroundings—within which, however, it was never totally confined. Not only can he ask for toast when the toast is not in front of him; he can also recall, or predict, seeing a bus when the bus is no longer, or not yet, in sight.

Functional Continuity and the Construction of Subjective Reality

The functional-semantic continuity not only enables a child to construct a language; it also enables him, at the same time that he is constructing it, to use the language in the construction of a reality.

When Nigel takes the major step of converting his protolanguage into a language, by adding a grammar, which is a new level of coding intermediate between the meanings and the sounds, this is the one major discontinuity in the development of his linguistic system. He takes it against a background of clearly recognizable continuity in the functional-semantic evolution. From his earliest acts of meaning to the complex configurations that mark his entry into the adult mode, there is an unbroken line of development in which the twin themes of action and reflection provide the central thread.

It is this same continuity that allows Nigel to construct a reality, of which the language is both a realization and a part. This is not so much because reality construction is necessarily a continuous process—whether it is or is not is likely to depend on whether or not there are discontinuities in the reality itself. Rather, it is because the continuity of meanings proclaims and symbolizes the permanence of what is "in here" and what is "out there": of the self, and of the social system that defines the self, and of the relation that subsists between the two. The act of meaning, above all others, is what creates and maintains our identity in fact of the chaos of things. It is as if, having become self-conscious through learning to mean, we have to go on meaning to keep the self in suspension.

At the very outset of Phase 1, around 9—10½ months, Nigel has developed a picture of how things are. We know this, because only with some such picture could he mean in the ways he does; we can see the structure of his thinking through our interpretation of the structure of his meaning. By 10 months of age Nigel has constructed a subjective reality that we could interpret as being based on the separation of himself from the continuum of things. Given this interpretation, in order to explain the protolanguage that we find him using at that time, we would have to postulate that, at the least, he has constructed a schema of the kind shown in Figure 1. On this same basis, the schema that Nigel has developed by the end of Phase 1, six months later, may be represented in Figure 2. (For the data underlying the interpretations in Figures 1 and 2, see Figures 1 and 5 in Halliday, 1975.) Again, this schema is one which we can recover from

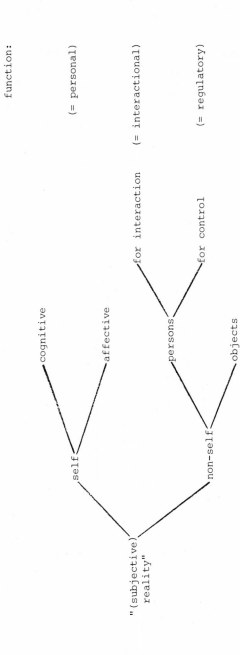

FIGURE 1 Nigel at 9–10½ months.

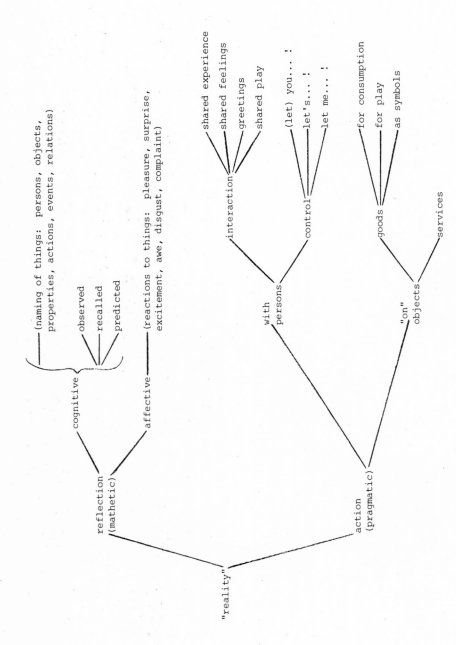

FIGURE 2 Nigel at 15–16½ months.

observations of Nigel's semantic system; it is implicit in what he is able to mean at the time.

With any such representation, we are always in fact *behind* the time. These are the minimal structures that we have to recognize as the basis of what Nigel himself can mean—what he can encode in his own speech. Since his understanding is always further developed than his powers of expression, we are seeing things long after they actually happen; as far as his model of reality is concerned, listening to Nigel speak is like observing the light rays from a distant star. And yet we have to be careful here: Nigel has got where he is not by being inducted into adult ways of thinking but by following his own route. Hence, while *his* understanding of what is meant by others (and if we continue to use the word "mean" in this rather un-English way it is because we are talking not about what is said but about what is meant; saying is merely the outward sign and channel of meaning) shows that he knows more than he himself can mean, we cannot represent what he knows simply by describing what he must know in order to understand the meanings that are addressed to him. This is because we can only express these meanings in the terms of the adult semantic.

When Nigel moved into Phase 2, the transition from protolanguage to (adult-like) language, his key functional strategy was, as we saw it, the development of an explicit opposition of pragmatic versus mathetic. It is important to stress at this point that both these modes of meaning are fundamental to the reality-constructing process. Reality, as mediated through a child's semantic system, has a twofold property, namely that it is at once both good to think and good to eat. Just as, when we observe a child using vocal or gestural signs to demand what he wants we have to remember that he has other signs too, signs that express his pleasure in and curiosity about the surroundings, so also when we are focusing on the child's subjective reality we should not forget that it is something that is acted on as well as thought about. And this is what the pragmatic—mathetic opposition signifies. When Nigel uses a rising tone, he is acting on reality; when he uses a falling tone, he is reflecting on reality; and both action and reflection are mediated by the act of meaning. He achieves by meaning to others, and he learns by meaning to himself. It is the potential to mean—that is, by now, language—that integrates and synthesizes the two modes. Reality can be acted on and reflected on because it can be talked about; and the exchange of talk, *Conversation,* is what makes it one reality not two. When Nigel enters Phase 2, a word or a structure belongs to just one mode or the other; by the time he leaves Phase 2, each word, and each structure, functions in both. Hence in the transition to the adult mode of meaning we can see rather clearly displayed the empirical foundations of Nigel's theory of what it is all about.

To illustrate the argument, here are a number of short narratives of Nigel's interaction, starting at two and a half years and going back to the first two weeks of life.

EXAMPLES OF CONVERSATIONS

Two Years, Six Months

"We broke the cot in Mrs. Lampeter's house and you licked it and pressed it dòwn," said Nigel. *You* at this stage meant 'I': 'I licked it and pressed it down'.

We have broken the cot—that is, dismantled it for packing. But I didn't remember Nigel licking it. "What did you lick?" I asked.

"The st— . . . the paper—"

"Oh, the label," I guessed. But I was wrong.

"The paper tàpe," he said. I had stuck strips of gummed paper around it, and Nigel had been given some of the pieces to stick on by himself.

Nigel's mother came in.

She had a large sheet of paper in her hand, and a pencil, with which she proceeded to draw an outline of Nigel's foot, explaining that she was going to get a pair of sandals made for him. Nigel recalled the incident later.

"Mummy draw round your fòot," he said.

"Yes, Mummy drew round your foot."

"She didn't draw a lĭon."

"No, she didn't draw a lion."

"She drew a line."

"Yes, she drew a line."

"Aràilway line."

"Oh, I didn't know it was a railway line!"

"And then you got off the letter and sat on Daddy's knèe." The piece of paper now had marks on it, so it had become a *letter*.

Two Years, Three Months

Nigel was sticking pictures in his scrapbook. He could now put the gum on by himself, turn the picture over, and stick it where he wanted it. He had learnt to put the gum on the *back* of the picture; this was difficult, because there was often a picture there too and you had to decide which picture you wanted to be seen and then turn it over, without letting yourself be distracted by the one on the back. He called this the 'second side,' as it was like turning over a gramophone record.

"You did put the gum on the sècond side," he said proudly, "but not on the ùnderground train picture."

"That's very good," I said.

"You can put the gum on the bàck of the fast electric underground train pícture," he explained, "but not on the bàck of the fast electric underground train picture." In other words, you can turn it over once to put the gum on, but you have to be careful not to turn it over again.

Another time, we came to a picture of a train that had been stuck in upside down. I pointed to it and looked at Nigel inquiringly.

"Did you stick it wrong way up because it doesn't stìck that wáy," he said. "You stuck it wrong way up because it doesn't stìck that wáy."

I looked puzzled.

"No the tràin is not wrong way úp," he explained. "It's the picture that's wrong way up. The picture won't fall off the scrápbook."

In other words: it looks as if the train is going to fall off the rails. But it won't, because the train is really right way up. The picture is wrong way up. But being wrong way up doesn't make the picture fall off the scrapbook. And I stuck it wrong way up because there wasn't room for it to go in right way up.

One Year, Eleven Months

"Daddy coming to look at that train has gòne," said Nigel. "It already gone whòosh."

I came to look. It was the picture in his "Trains" book, showing a train which had just sped through a station without stopping. 'Whoosh' (pronounced "whoo' ") was the noise the train made as it rushed past when you were standing on the station platform—this being one of Nigel's favourite pasttimes.

"Thàt train alrèady gone whoosh," Nigel explained. "Thāt train has alrèady gone whoosh."

A week later, we were in a train, on our way to visit friends for the day.

"There no bùmblebee in thís train," said Nigel. "There was a bumblebee in the wĕt train." This was a reference to a train journey he had made three months previously; it had been raining, and a bee had got inside the train where he was sitting.

Nigel spent the time looking out of the window and talking about what he saw.

"This not an ùnderground train," he said. "Ooh there's a bi-i-ig cràne! There's anòther railway line thére; we're not going on thăt railway line. It not líon," he corrected himself with a growl. "It line . . . Fast weel ('diesel') tràin. It gòing nów. But it not say whòosh . . . but . . . but it not say whòosh . . . whòosh . . . whòosh," he repeated many times over, thoughtfully to himself.

He was puzzling over a problem. If you were standing on the platform, and the train rushed past you, it made a tremendous noise. Why was it that, when you were inside the train, it didn't make the same noise?

One Year, Nine Months

We had finished a meal, and were sitting talking about nothing in particular. Nigel was in his high chair.

"eat chúffa," he said.

"You can't eat trains!" I said.

"can't eat blue chùffa"

"No, you can't eat the blue train."

"can't eat rèd chuffa"

"No, you can't eat the red train."

Nigel looked at the little wooden man from his cart. "can't eat màn," he said.

"No, you can't eat the man."

Nigel looked at his book. "can't eat that bòok"

"No, you can't eat that book. You can't eat any book!"

Nigel looked at Pauline. "can't eat Pàuline book"

"No, you can't eat Pauline's book."

Nigel looked thoughtfully at Pauline's hair. "Pauline got èar," he said.

"Yes," I said, moving Pauline's hair aside. "Pauline's got an ear, though you can't usually see it."

Nigel touched his wooden Pinocchio doll. " 'nocchio got funny nòse," he said.

"Yes, Pinocchio's got a funny nose, like a—"

"càrrot," Nigel finished off for me.

"Yes, like a carrot."

Some days earlier, Pinocchio's foot had come off, and I had had to mend him. Nigel recalled the incident.

"scrèwdriver," he said. "mend 'nocchio fòot"

One Year, Six Months

Nigel was waiting for his lunch. He picked up his fork, and tried the prongs on the palm of his hand. "oôh," he said in a low, breathy voice. It meant 'ooh, it's sharp.'

He dropped the fork on the table. "ōo" It was a short, high-pitched squeak.

"Ooh, dropped it," I said. "Is it sharp?"

Anna came in, with lunch.

"Do you know what it is?" said Anna. "You're having fish."

"lù'," said Nigel. "lù' "

"Lunch, yes," said Anna. "It's fish."

"vò" ('fish')

Nigel set himself to eating his lunch. Some fish fell off the fork.

"ōo" It was another very high pitched squeak.

"Ooh you lost a big bit then," said Anna. "Where did it go?"

"bâiba" Nigel looked up at Anna, inviting her to share a memory. "âiba . . . bâiba," he said.

"Yes, all the trains went away, and you said "byebye," didn't you?" she said.

"bâiba," said Nigel sadly, waving his hand.

He finished off his lunch. "nōumò . . . nōumò"

"Where has it all gone?" Anna asked him.

Nigel turned his attention to the salt. "adīdà," he asked.

"That's salt," said Anna. "Salt and pepper."

"ùh . . . ùh" ('I want it')

Anna passed it to him. "That's salt."

Nigel poked the hole in the top with his finger. "lôu! lôu!" ('a hole!')

"Yes, it has a hole in it," she said.

"adīdà"

"It's salt."

"lò"

"Salt."

"lò"

One Year, Three Months

Nigel was in his high chair; his mother gave him a piece of toast.

"There you are, Bootie," she said. "Toast."

"dòu," said Nigel, picking it up. "dòu"

He looked over at my piece. "dòu," he said again.

"Yes, I've got a piece of toast as well."

Nigel finished his piece.

"dòu," he said firmly.

"Do you want some more?"

"n̄" It was a short, very high pitched squeak, with lips spread, meaning 'yes I do' or 'yes do,' in answer to an offer of goods or services.

His mother started to butter another finger of toast. Nigel watched her with growing impatience.

"ùh . . . ùh . . . mǹg!" ('I want it, I want it. Give it to me!')

"All right, it's coming! You want some butter on it, don't you? See? that's butter."

"bàta"

There was a plop and a miaow, and the neighbor's cat appeared at Nigel's side. She was a regular visitor.

"abâe . . . abâe"

It was a greeting to the cat. Apart from Anna, his mother and me, the cat was the one other being with whom Nigel exchanged meanings. They spoke the same kind of language.

Twelve Months

Nigel and I were looking at his book together.

Nigel took hold of my finger, and pressed it lightly against one of the pictures. "èya," he said.

The meaning was clear: 'You say its name.' "It's a ball," I said.

"è — e — eh" Nigel gave his long drawn out sigh, meaning 'yes, that's what I wanted you to do.' He was pleased that his meaning had been successful, and he repeated the procedure throughout the book.

Later he was looking at it all by himself.

"dò . . . èya . . . vèu"

This was Nigel's first complex utterance, and the only one for many months to come. But it made excellent sense. He had picked up the picture book, opened it at the ball page, and pointed it at the picture. It was just as if he had said, in so many words, 'Look, a picture! what is it? a ball!'

Ten and One-Half Months

Nigel was sitting on my knee. On the table in front of us was a fruit bowl with an orange in it. Nigel struggled to reach it."

"nà nà nà nà," he said. It meant 'I want it,' 'Give it to me.'

I gave him the orange. He made it roll on the table; it fell off.

"nà nà nà nà," he said again.

When the game was over, he got down, crawled away and disappeared along the passage, going boomp-boomp-boomp as he went. Then silence. His mother began to wonder where he was.

"Nigel!" she called.

"è — e — eh" It was his special response to a call: 'Here I am.'

"Where is he?" said his mother. "Nigel!"

She went to look for him. He was standing, precariously, by the divan, looking at his picture cards that were hanging on the wall.

"dòh," he said as she came in. It meant 'Hullo—shall we look at these pictures together?' "dòh . . . dòh"

"Are you looking at your pictures?" his mother asked him.

"dòh . . . dòh"

Nine Months

Nigel had just learnt to sit up on his own, and was now ready to start meaning in earnest.

He had a little floppy rabbit; I was holding it on my hand and stroking it, then making it jump in the air. When I stopped, Nigel put out his hand, and touched the rabbit, firmly but without pushing it. It was a gesture which meant 'Go on, do that again'—the same meaning that he was later to express vocally as "ùh."

He had two other gestures. If he meant that he wanted something, he would grasp it firmly in his fist, without pulling it towards him, and then let go. If he meant he did not want it, he would touch it very lightly and momentarily with the tip of his finger.

These gestures were true acts of meaning. Nigel was not acting directly on the objects; he was addressing the other person, enjoining him to act.

In addition to the three meanings conveyed by gesture, Nigel had two other meanings which he expressed vocally. The two expressions were almost the same: one was "èu," the other, slightly higher pitched at its starting point, was "èu." The first meant 'Let's be together,' and was used in conversation: "Nigel!" "èu" "*There's* a woozy woozy woozy" "èu," and so on ad lib. The other meant 'Look—a commotion,' and was the successor to "'", the tiny high-pitched squeak. Nigel used it to express interest in his surroundings, especially that part of the surroundings that went into violent movement, like a flock of birds taking off.

This was the opening scene of Nigel's language.

Six Months

We were in the park. Nigel was in his pram, and was lying in his usual posture, on his tummy.

Some pigeons scattered noisily as we went by. Nigel lifted his head.

"'", he said, making a tiny squeak on a very high note. It meant 'What's that?' 'What's happening?'

"Those are birds," we told him. "Big birds; pigeons. They flew away."

This was Nigel's first act of meaning, the first time he had used a symbolic expression to communicate with someone. It was a soft high-pitched squeak with what sounded like a note of query in it.

Nigel said this frequently during the next three or four weeks, always with the same meaning. Then he abandoned it. It was as if he had established the principle that he could start the conversation and be responded to. For the moment he was satisfied with that.

Two Months

Nigel greeted me when I came home from work. He gave a long gurgling account of the day's events, always in a cheerful tone, his face breaking into huge smiles. Then he listened while I told him my news.

One day I came into the flat and heard him cooing away with his mother as usual. But as soon as he saw me, his whole expression changed. His face frowned, his tone became mournful, and he was almost starting to cry.

"What happened today?" I asked his mother.

"He had his first injections," she said.

Twelve Days

Nigel had just come home from the hospital, and seemed pleased at the move. But one day he was crying miserably, and his mother was in distress.

The time came to bath him. As she undressed him she noticed a nasty looking boil in the crook of his elbow.

She called to me. "Look at this," she said.

As soon as she drew attention to it, Nigel stopped crying. The boil must have gone on hurting; it had had nothing done to it. But his mother had found what was wrong, and Nigel didn't cry any more.

THE SOCIAL CONSTRUCTION OF LANGUAGE, AND OF REALITY

The Subjective Angle: A Summary

After a short preview at 5 months, Nigel's acts of meaning began in earnest at 8 months; and by 10½ months his conversational powers were organized into a system of meaning potential that we have referred to as a protolanguage. Unlike adult language, which is a three-level system (meaning, wording, sound), the protolanguage is a two-level system (meaning, sound), the elements of which are content–expression pairs, corresponding to the classical Saussurean notion of the "sign." These elements have meaning within a small range of semiotic functions; initially we can identify four: an instrumental, a regulatory, an interactional, and a personal. These are distinct in two respects: (1) in orientation, towards persons or objects, and (2) in the type of mediation that is involved. In the instrumental function ('I want'), the child is acting on objects through the mediation of other persons; in the regulatory ('do as I say'), the child is acting directly on other persons; in the interactional ('me and you'), the child is interacting with other persons, but through the mediation of shared attention to objects; and in the personal ('here I come'), the child is becoming a self through active attention to, or rejection of, his environment.

From 8 to 17 months, that is, throughout what is referred to as Phase 1, Nigel expanded his protolanguage, enlarging his conversational powers until he had a meaning potential of some 50 elements; they were still largely within the same four functions, though a fifth one had been added. This was the imaginative ('let's pretend') function, in which meaning is a mode of play. But up to this point the language had remained a two-level coding system; and, as such, it was subject to certain constraints. The "signs" of such a system are elementary particles, which can be strung together like beads but cannot be dispersed and recombined. Hence Nigel could never mean two things at once.

For this a three-level system is needed, one with an abstract level of "wording" intervening between the meanings and the sounds. This intermediate level (a lexicogrammar, in linguistic terms) is what makes it possible to name, and so to separate meaning as observation of reality from meaning as intrusion into reality. In a two-level system, such as Nigel's protolanguage, it is impossible to name something independently of acting on it. Once given a lexicogrammar, naming something and acting on it become distinct symbolic acts.

Why should Nigel want to separate these two modes of meaning? Because only in this way can conversation evolve along the lines of narrative and dialogue. Narrative and dialogue are the two cornerstones of conversation, prerequisites to the effective functioning of language in the construction of reality.

By the term *narrative* we understand the ability to make meanings context-free: to bring within the scope of conversation things that lie outside the perceptual field—processes in time past and future, states of consciousness, abstract entities, and other nondeictic aspects of subjective reality. To mean '(I see) sticks and stones' is not necessarily a narrative act; it need not imply naming, nor does it require a lexicogrammar in the system. But to mean 'I saw sticks and stones' is a narrative act, one that cannot be performed with a grammarless language; not because it requires grammatical structure (that comes later), but because it requires that the thing-name 'stick' is coded separately from any meaning such as 'I want' or 'I like.' From the moment the child has introduced this intermediate level of coding, his conversation becomes independent of the context of situation. It took Nigel about 3 weeks (at 17 months) to move from '(I see) sticks and stones' to 'I saw sticks and stones'; and about another 3 weeks after that to get to 'I will see sticks and stones' (for example, in answer to "Nigel we're going out for a walk"). The form of the utterance did not change—it was simply "stick, stone" in each case—but it now had a different significance as an act of meaning.

By the term *dialogue* we understand conversation of a particular kind, in which the interactants not only exchange meanings but also engage in dynamic role play, each in turn both adopting a role for himself and assigning a role, or rather a role choice, to the other. Nigel made the discovery that the symbolic system he was constructing for himself as a means of *Realizing* a world of meaning simultaneously *Created* a world of meaning of its own, a semiotic of social roles and social acts. Since the system creates information, it can be used to exchange this information (that is, to ask and to tell) as well as to exchange goods and services in the way the protolanguage does. This in turn means that conversation becomes not merely a symbolic reflection of the sharing of experience but an actual alternative to it. Up to this point, when Nigel's mother suggested he should "tell Daddy what happened" it had made no sense to him. He could tell Mummy, because she had shared the experience, but how could he tell Daddy, when Daddy hadn't been there? Now he adds an "informative" function to his functional repertoire—and at once becomes its prisoner for life.

Like other major forward leaps in development, this too had had its preview. It was at 15 months that Nigel took his first steps in grammar, when he came to separate the *Name–Choice* of the three people he conversed with from the *Act–Choice* of seeking versus finding. The former he expressed by articulation, the latter by intonation. In this way he was able to combine the two systems, so that each name, *ama* ('mummy'), *dada, anna,* could be used with either sense, 'Where are you? I want you' (mid level + high level) or 'Hullo! There you are!' (high falling + mid level). But it is in Phase 2, the transition to the adult language, that this distinction between naming and acting becomes his primary semiotic strategy. Naming, as we have seen, is too narrow a concept here, if it is taken to mean merely the creation of a lexicosemantic taxonomy; we are talking about the whole ideational aspect of meaning, of which the assignment of thing-names is only a part. What Nigel did was to generalize, from his Phase 1 functional repertory, a simple opposition between conversation as a means of learning (a mathetic mode as we called it) and conversation as a means of doing (a pragmatic mode). So fundamental is this opposition to Nigel's construction of reality that at 19 months he took the step of encoding it systematically in prosodic form: from then on, all pragmatic acts of meaning—all utterances of a dialoguic nature, demanding a response—were performed with a rising tone, and all mathetic acts—those of a narrative kind, demanding no response—were performed with a falling tone. In this way Nigel made explicit the fundamental distinction between meaning as reflection and meaning as action, a distinction that lies at the heart of the adult semantic system.

Nigel maintained this opposition intact for about six months; it was the major strategy whereby the concrete functions of his protolanguage were to evolve into the abstract functional components which are the basis of the adult semantic. At the same time, it was more than a strategy of transition; it was itself a form of the schematization of reality. By making this distinction, Nigel represented reality to himself as existing on two planes: as material to be quarried, and as terrain to be explored. Not only objects but also persons figure in this dual role; through dialogue, one person "acts on" the other, and in fact it is only through the intermediary of a person that an act of meaning can be directed onto an object, since objects are not, in principle, affected by symbolic acts.

But from the moment of its inception, Nigel's bimodal strategy, in which each act of meaning is either pragmatic or mathetic, is already breaking down. As soon as the language in which he converses has a lexicogrammar, every utterance in it is inevitably both pragmatic and mathetic at the same time. The cost of being able to mean two things at once is that it becomes impossible not to, except in very limited ways. The intonation signals what continues to be the dominant mode: response demanded (rising tone), or response not demanded (falling tone). But as Nigel moves through Phase 2, the other mode becomes more and more prominent as a submotif; until by about 23 months all acts of meaning are in equal measure both pragmatic and mathetic. But in the process, these concepts have changed once again. The original functions first become macrofunctions and then metafunctions.

The pragmatic component is now, more often than not, a demand for a verbal response: giving and requesting goods and services has been superseded, as the favorite act of meaning, by giving and requesting information. Other elements have been added, including some that would subsequently disappear, such as the very useful distinction Nigel makes, from around 21 months, between telling listeners something he knows they already know and telling them something he knows they do not know. At this point the pragmatic function has evolved into the full interpersonal (sometimes called "socioexpressive") component in the adult semantic system; while the mathetic, meaning as a way of learning, has evolved into the ideational component. Every one of Nigel's conversational acts is now simultaneously both a reflection on and an action on reality.

But Nigel has never lost the essential links between meaning and social context that are what enabled him to make the transition from his own protolanguage to a mother tongue in the first place. Interpersonal meanings—those expressed in the grammar as mood, modality, person, key, and the like—reflect the role relationships in the communication process. Ideational meanings—expressed in transitivity, time and place, lexical taxonomies, and so on—reflect the goings-on around, the phenomenal world of processes and their participants and attendant circumstances.

This is not to say that an act of meaning typically relates directly to its immediate social context; most of them do not. We have already noted that, from the beginning of Phase 2, thanks to the introduction of a lexicogrammar, Nigel's conversation has been effectively context-free, not constrained by the situation of speaking. But the meaning potential underlying his acts of meaning has its ultimate frame of reference in Nigel's experience, including, of course, his experience of his own states of consciousness; and it is a fundamental characteristic of acts of meaning that they create their own context out of this past experience. More particularly, what underlies the conversational process is not just the individual's experience of things; it is things as phenomena of inter-subjective reality, as bearers of social meaning and social value. Nor is it just the face-to-face interaction of the participants in the dialogue; it is their entire function in the child's social system. Nigel has, after all, been busying himself with all this from birth. The social context of an act of meaning is far more than is made manifest in the sights and sounds around.

The Intersubjective Angle

A child's construction of language is at once both a part of, and a means of, his construction of reality; and it is natural to Western thinking to view both these processes largely from the standpoint of the individual. We tend implicitly to define the aim of the investigation as that of explaining what happens to a child in his development from infancy to maturity.

This preoccupation is embodied in and reinforced by prevailing metaphors such as "language acquisition" and "primary socialization." The former suggests that a child takes possession of a new commodity, that of language; and the latter that he is transformed into a new state, that of being social. In either case he is seen as an individual serving as the locus of external processes; and while we should not make too much of the metaphors themselves, they do perhaps reflect a tendency to think of a child as acquiring language and the rest of reality from somewhere "out there,"—as if he was a preexisting individual who, by a process of learning the rules, achieves conformity with a preexisting scheme.

Sociolinguistic theorists of language development have attempted to place the developing child in a social context; they have removed the "nativist versus environmentalist" controversy from the agenda and offered instead some version of an "interactionist" approach. A number of investigators have suggested an interpretation in terms of the notion of communicative competence. This leads to what is essentially a socialization model of language development, according to which the child has to master, in addition to the 'rules of language,' a set of socially accepted norms of language use. It is open to the objection that learning to mean cannot be reduced to a matter of learning how to behave properly in the contexts in which meanings are exchanged. A more recent interpretation is one based on the notion of the speech act, the speech act being put forward as the structural unit which a child acquires as the simultaneous representation of his conceptual, communicative, and grammatical skills (Dore, 1974, 1976). But the speech act is a subjective, not an intersubjective, construct; it is supposed to take account of the fact that people talk to each other, but it represents this fact in terms of the knowledge, the belief structures, and the behavior patterns of the individual. The consequence of this is that the theory fails to account for the dynamics of dialogue, the ongoing exchange of speech roles through which conversation becomes a reality-generating process.

I think we need to interpret language development more in terms of a conception of social or intersubjective creativity. Learning to mean is a process of creation, whereby a child constructs, in interaction with those around, a semiotic potential that gives access to the edifice of meanings that constitute social reality.

There is ample evidence that children engage in communicative interaction from birth. A newborn infant's orientation towards persons is quite distinct from his orientation towards the objects in his environment; he is aware of being addressed, and can respond. He exchanges attention with the persons who are the "others" in his social system (Bruner, 1975; France, 1975; Trevarthen, 1974b).

In these intersubjective processes lie the foundations of the construction of reality. Reality is created through the exchange of meanings—in other words, through conversation. The exchange of attention which begins at birth already has some of the features of conversation; it has been described by Bateson (1975) as "protoconversation."

But protoconversation does not yet involve an exchange of meanings. If we adopt the distinction made previously in this chapter between an "act of meaning" and other communicative acts, then conversation proper is an exchange of acts of meaning—or, simply, an exchange of meanings; whereas protoconversation consists of communicative exchanges which do not yet take the form of acts of meaning. Protoconversation begins at birth; conversation begins some months later. It begins, in fact, with the beginning of the protolanguage.

At this point it may be helpful to offer a tentative schematic account of the development of a child's powers of conversation (see Figure 3).

The central concept here is that of intersubjectivity (Trevarthen, 1974a). The construction of reality depends on conversation—on the exchange of meanings. But the foundations are laid in the protoconversational period when the child is already engaging in intersubjective acts. A child is not born endowed with language. But he is born with the ability to recognize and respond to address; and to communicate with someone who is communicating with him. He even engages, from the age of a few weeks, in what Trevarthen calls "prespeech,": the manipulation of the expressive resources that will be put to use in the protolanguage, and eventually in language itself. (It is important to distinguish between prespeech and protolanguage. Prespeech is expression only, whereas protolanguage is expression and content. There is no semantic component in prespeech. But it is significant that it typically accompanies communicative acts of this protoconversational kind.)

Patterns of intersubjective activity are thus well established by the time the child takes the crucial step of starting to mean. An act of meaning is inherently an intersubjective act, one which makes possible the exchange of meanings and hence the construction of reality. Berger and Luckmann (1966) speak in very clear terms of "the reality-generating power of conversation;" and although, as they remark, conversation usually implies language, we have stressed all along that true conversation already begins in the protolanguage. The protolanguage—if Nigel is at all typical—is not organized the way the adult language is, with a grammar and a vocabulary; but it is nevertheless a language in which conversation can and does take place.

The crucial property of conversation in Berger and Luckmann's account is that

proto-	conversation						
	proto-	language					
		proto-	narrative and dialogue				
			proto-	discourse			
				proto-	turn taking		
					proto-	variation	
0–¾	¾–1½	1½–2	2–5	5–9	9–13	13–	

FIGURE 3   The development of powers of conversation.
0–¾, communicative acts (protoconversation), prespeech;
¾–1½, acts of meaning (functional protolanguage);
1½–2, transition to language, macrofunctions mathetic/pragmatic;
2–5, narrative and dialogue, elementary lexicogrammar;
5–9, discourse, intermediate lexicogrammar;
9–13, turn taking, advanced lexicogrammar;
13(–18), variation, register and social dialect.

it is casual. It does not consist of explanations. Nobody instructs the child in the mysteries of things; he would not understand them if they did. Conversation consists of ongoing contextualized chatter. Out of this a child builds an order of things and events, including his own part in them and attitudes towards them.

What makes it possible for the child to do this is the relation of an act of meaning to its context (discussed on pages 74–76). *How* he does it is a different matter. Typically, he organizes his conversation around a limited number of generalized semantic strategies, ways of meaning that are the ontogenetic analogue to, and anticipation of, the speech functions and rhetorical modes of the adult language. Here is a small example from 23 months:

> Nigel's mother and I were planning a visit to the aquarium. Nigel did not know what an aquarium was, but he heard us discussing it.
>
> "We're not going to see a rào ['lion']," he said to himself. "Vòpa ['fishes']. There will be some wàter."
>
> In other words, it was not a zoo, but it was something of the same kind, with fishes (and water for them to live in) instead of lions.

The principle of contrast—of seeing things as "same but different"—is a favorite strategy for the representation of experience at this stage. These strategies are not the same as those of an adult, nor can they be understood as unsuccessful approximations to those that an adult employs. A child uses language in different ways; not because he is trying to do what an adult does and failing, but because he is a different person engaged in a different set of tasks.

It is tempting to think of a child's construction of reality as simply his construction of a model of the outside world: of things and their properties, and how they relate and interact. This is, certainly, one important aspect of what he is doing. But it is not the whole story. The child is constructing a social semiotic, a reality in which things are because people are, and people construe them in certain ways. To say that people "construe" things means that they act on them, value them, and interpret them; and it is this construction that is shared through intersubjective acts of meaning. When the child sees things interact, typically he is seeing how people act on them; when he apprehends their significance, typically he is finding out how people value them; and when he builds them into his meaning potential, typically he is learning how people interpret them. He is not taking over a meaning potential, or a reality, that is ready made for him 'out there'; on the contrary, as the interpretation of Nigel's protolanguage makes clear, a child is *Creating* meanings, not imitating those he finds around him. But this process of creation is an interactive process, in which the meanings are created in the course of being exchanged between the child and the significant others. The exchange takes place in the context of, and in interpenetration with, the reality that is "out there;" but what is "out there" is a social construct—not a pile of sticks and stones, but a house.

As was said earlier, an act of meaning is a social act, not only in the simple sense that it is a form of interaction between people each of whom is producing meanings of his own and tracking those of others, but also in the deeper sense that the meaning potential from which these meanings derive is itself a social construct; and so is the reality beyond it. The meanings that are embodied in conversation in the protolanguage are, obviously, not very sophisticated; but they are already such that we can see them as the realization of some higher order semiotic—of a social reality, in fact. Nigel's reality is a social reality and its construction is a social process. It is shared between Nigel and those with whom he exchanges meanings: the significant others, who are significant precisely for this reason, that they are the ones with whom meanings are exchanged.

One of the most remarkable features of the interaction that takes place between a child and his mother—or anyone else with whom the child regularly exchanges meanings—is the extent to which the mother (or other person) knows at each point in time what the child will and what he will not understand. This can be seen (or rather heard) not only in the way in which the mother converses with the child but also in the way in which she tells him stories and modifies or explains for him anything she is reading aloud. (And we notice it with a shock when we come across someone we feel should have this knowledge and find they have not. One major problem for a child who is cared for in an institution is the lack of anyone who shares his language and his reality.) The phenomenon is all the more astonishing when one takes account of the fact that what the child understands is changing day by day. The mother keeps pace with this development to such an exact degree that it is not unreasonable to say that she is simultaneously building up the same language and the same reality. (I do not mean that she imitates the child's sounds. On the contrary, imitating the sounds a child makes and repeating them back to him nearly always in my experience covers up a failure to track his language adequately; it is an attempt to "con" him into thinking that one is with him in an exchange of meanings. He is never deceived, and usually rejects the attempt as insulting.) Essentially the mother is going through the processes of mental development all over again, but this time in the child's persona; under impetus from the child, the mother is creating a world of meanings along with him. It is for this reason that we call the process an *intersubjective* one.

If one was to attempt to characterize language development in the most general terms, it would be as the process of the intersubjective creation of meanings, and hence of a meaning potential that is a mode of the representation of reality. A child constructs, in interaction with others, a reality that has two parts to it, since it includes within itself a symbolic system—language—through which the rest is mediated. The two parts, language and nonlanguage, are essentially continuous, each influencing and modifying the other. Hence the symbolic system through which reality is mediated is not only a part of reality but is also, to a certain extent, a determinant of the other part.

The schemata illustrated in Figures 1 and 2 represent reality as apprehended through our understanding of Nigel's protolanguage. There is a direct continuity between the infant's intersubjective experiences of mutual address, shared atten-

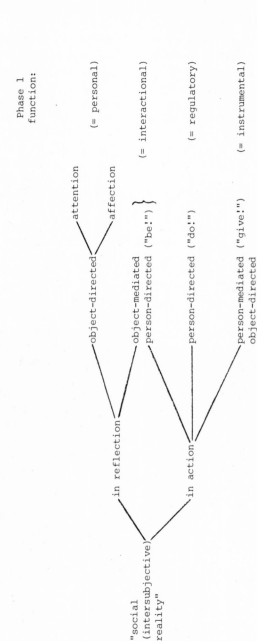

FIGURE 4 Nigel at 9–10½ months (another interpretation).

tion and protoconversation, on the one hand, and the social construction of reality through the natural rhetoric and natural logic of conversation on the other. In Figure 1 we know, from Nigel's ability to mean in the various modes at the outset of the protolanguage, that his subjective reality must contain certain conceptual discontinuities: at the very least, (1) reality distinguished into "out there" (nonself) and "not out there" (self); (2) non-self distinguished into persons and objects; and (3) persons distinguished into two roles, (i) for interaction and (ii) for control. The reality is an intersubjective reality, not only constructed through intersubjective acts of meaning (conversation) but also held in common with the significant others. It is a joint construction; otherwise it could not get built. The self thus lies, in Meadian fashion, at the intersection of various dimensions of social process—including, critically, processes of a symbolic or *Sociosemiotic* kind.

If we then look back at our representation of Nigel's model of reality at 10 months we find in it the same preoccupation with the child as individual that was referred to at the beginning of this section. Reinterpreting in the light of what turned out to be Nigel's primary transition strategy as he moved from protolanguage to language and began to construct an adultlike semantic system, we might arrive at something more like Figure 4 (see pages 86–89 above). This schema, suggesting an alternative interpretation of Nigel's meaning potential at 10 months in terms of the ordering of persons and objects, brings out more clearly the continuity of his transition to the adult language (see Figure 2).

I have tried to outline the nature of the reality that is shared between a child and those with whom he exchanges meanings, with particular attention to the period between nine months and two years. The facts have been taken from the study of Nigel's language, and the results of this study have been used in an interpretation of the language development process. The organizing concept is that of shared meanings. At any one moment, the child has a meaning potential, a semantic system that is shared between himself and the significant others. It has been developed by an ongoing process in which the others first track the child by participating in his acts of meaning, and then reinforce, extend and modify the child's meaning system through the effects of their own responsive acts.

Note: In transcriptions of Nigel's speech, the following symbols are used to indicate intonation:

   ` falling
   ´ rising
   ˇ falling-rising
   ˆ rising-falling
   ¯ mid level
   = high-level

REFERENCES

Bateson, M. C. Mother-infant exchanges: The epigenesis of conversational interaction. In D. Aaronson and R. W. Rieber (Eds.) *Developmental psycholinguistics and communication disorders.* New York: (*Annals of the New York Academy of Sciences 263*). 1975.

Berger, P. L., & Luckmann, T. *The social construction of reality: A treatise in the sociology of knowledge.* New York: Doubleday, 1966.

Bruner, J. The ontogenesis of speech acts. *Journal of Child Language,*1975, 1–19.

Dore, J. A pragmatic approach to early language development. *Journal of Psycholinguistic Research* 1974, *4,* 343–350.

Dore, J. Conditions on the acquisition of speech acts. In I. Markova (Ed.), *The social context of language.* New York: Wiley, 1976.

France, M. *The generation of the self: A study of the construction of categories in infancy.* Unpublished doctoral dissertation, University of Essex, 1975.

Halliday, M. A. K. *Explorations in the functions of language.* London: Edward Arnold, 1973.

Halliday, M. A. K. *Learning how to mean: Explorations in the development of language.* London: Edward Arnold, 1975.

Trevarthen, C. Conversations with a two-month-old. *New Scientist,* 1974, *62,* (2 May).   (a)

Trevarthen, C. The psychobiology of speech development. In E. H. Lenneberg (Ed.), *Language and brain: Developmental aspects (Neurosciences Research Program Bulletin 12).* 1974.   (b)

Part II

SPACE AND EVENT PERCEPTION

The following section deals with perception of physical events in the world around us, whether they be in a well-instrumented psychological laboratory or in a grassy field after a rainstorm. The scope of this section is quite broad. However, there are several recurring themes that implicate possibly distinctive modes of perceiving.

One primary modal distinction is between the perception of object existence and essence, to use the phrasing of Shaw and Pittenger. An object's existence can be perceived in terms of its occupying a position in space or tracing a trajectory through space. Such spatial properties, however, are not essential to the perception of an object's essence or identity which instead depends on such attributes of the object as its shape, sound, or smell, Thus, this distinction is not unlike that of Trevarthen's neural–behavioral distinction between ambient and focal visual processing. Posner, Nissen, and Ogden also make a distinction that can be interpreted in a similar manner. They describe the development of attentional set for a target's sense modality as opposed to its spatial location.

A second recurrent theme consists of the perception of spatial information specifically. Two general types of spatial information are considered. One is information about the layout or position of objects in the environment. The other is information about the position of the perceiver him/herself or the relative position of parts of his/her body. Lee, for example, distinguishes between exteroception, perception of the layout of the environment without reference to the perceiver, and proprioception, perception of the relation of parts of the body to each other without reference to the environment. However, perception of environmental spatial information is more complex, and perception of environmental spatial information may explicitly take into account aspects of the body position of the perceiver. This leads Mack, for example, to distinguish between object-relative constancy judgments and subject-relative constancy judgments. Analogously, the processing of body spatial information is more complex, as it often is filtered through aspects of the environmental layout. This leads Lee to distinguish proprioception from exproprioception.

The final recurring theme in the following chapters is first a concern for conscious and attended versus unconscious and automatic modes of processing perceptual information, and then a resulting curiosity about interactions between them. Posner has specifically focused much of his research in this area, as is evident in his chapter here as well as in much of his past work. Mack's involvement is more indirect, however, as she has discovered that the types of perceptual information that will contribute to a viewer's awareness will depend on the visual mode by which the information is being processed. More specifically, she has found that perceptual judgments in the subject-relative constancy mode will depend in part on the use of body and body part spatial information, while such body-related information will not contribute to perceptual awareness if the viewer is operating in the object-relative constancy mode. Lee's interests, too, have led him to investigate not only ways in which vision can be used to consciously "teach" the body new skills, but also to investigate ways in which vision can automatically and unconsciously affect one's posture with respect to gravity.

6
Modes of Perceiving and Modes of Acting

Colwyn Trevarthen

University of Edinburgh

EDITORS' INTRODUCTION

Colwyn Trevarthen has a strong psychobiological orientation. He shows many of the same concerns as Halliday in examining the structure and function of early prelinguistic communicative behavior. This behavior is manifest initially in the infant's great sensitivity in distinguishing between physical and social objects. Social objects, that is, other people, elicit distinctive behavior; this in turn elicits further responses from the social objects. Trevarthen, however, is also concerned with how it is that infants are so sensitive to social objects. He suggests that other persons' intentional behavior provides a unique form of stimulation. It is characterized by a steplike, saccadic, and "unprovoked" behavior. The intentionality of the behavior is somehow communicated to the infant on the basis of his or her own ability to intend similar behavior. This theme of action-organizing perception is extended to brain development and to the orienting and performatory behavior of adult organisms. Perception in orienting as compared with performatory behavior is the now well-known distinction between ambient and focal perception. Thus, Trevarthen has discussed both social communicative modes of processing and modes of perceiving the physical world. In doing so, he has emphasized the salient role of action in perception.

MENTAL OR
ECOLOGICAL MODES?

To perceive or to do something is to establish a relation between the world and the mind. It follows that information for perceiving or for acting is not external and independently constituted; it is determined jointly by the psychological demands, and by what the environment affords that is relevant to these demands.

On one side, structure in the world enters into the determination of percepts, and of all acts that are adapted to cause specific effects on the world or on the subject's place in the world. Order in nature outside the brain influences both the evolution and the development of psychological processes. This has been stressed in the ecological perception theories of Brunswik (1956) and Gibson (1966). However, since even the simplest psychological operation is active and self-maintaining to some degree, I would contend that modes of psychological function must all *originate* on the other side, as adaptive properties of the mind. All the perception-granting affordances and all the act-realizing properties of objects that are put in motion by the subject's behavior (though one may choose to regard them as occurring independently of the subject, confused with other physical events in the word) are in reality extensions of programs, strategies, processing routines, intentions, or images in the mind. They are creations of the psychological subject.

Psychological modes of operation in individuals such as intending, perceiving, thinking and communicating change through learning. Developmental adaptation in mankind's intelligence to fit external reality is so powerful and so extensive that the mental representations that govern knowledge and skills seems in their mature form to be entirely the result of learning.

Cognitive psychologists accept only a few basic physical constraints on knowledge in the form of processing, encoding, and channel-switching operations which they hold to be innate. The generative functions they have in mind are essentially nonpsychological, because they do not reflect the predetermined operations of purpose. Social psychologists are still explaining human social behavior by a tacit learning theory, even though most of them don't believe in the theory.

Recent studies of the development of intelligence not only relate well to our knowledge of the reproduction and development of biological systems in general, but also cast doubt on the prevailing psychological theory—the behavioristic theory presented in most text books of psychology. This behavioristic theory is based on experimental studies of perceptual judgments or discrete acts which mature subjects make in response to stimuli that are defined physically, and varied systematically. We should not forget when assessing such experiments that physically defined stimuli are products of scientific tradition and technique; that is, they are artificial. Natural objects of perception and action are "more complex" in the sense that they are "harder to make or to define," but they are not usually harder to perceive or to act upon for a free subject. Most psychological experiments confirm the limitations of adaptation when a subject has a very narrow choice of action. It is not clear from these experiments how choice and self-organization determine which thing a subject will do when there is virtually no limit on the number of things that may be done.

In this chapter I present evidence from three areas of research in psychobiology to support the theory that natural modes of psychological function *originate entirely* in the growing constitution of the mind. In this view, assimilation of experience, though not predetermined in its specific instances, is sanctioned a priori in its general outline as well as in its finest detail. Experience allows for selection from a prepared set of alternative functions, to change the integrative balance between the innate modes. Developments of consciousness and skill, and above all, development of the languages and cultures of mankind, are thus caused epigenetically by the inherent and nonrandom structure of the mind as it grows and develops.

There are great advantages for psychology in this theory. It helps to pull many loose ends together. But it cannot be denied that there are dangers as well. As a committed ecologist, I am opposed to a retreat into nativism. The innate mind is nothing without the world. Moreover, I believe that in the history of psychology, simplistic theories of brain functioning have impoverished and cramped psychology. I consider myself a pupil of those psychologists who rejected the simple notions of reflex associationism so they could understand the natural laws of awareness, volition, and social cooperation.

Now, because of the success of experimental psychology, a great deal is known about the external conditions for perception and about the selective limitations on uptake of externally defined "information". Less is known about the productive or generative "informees" that make sense of the data. In the meantime, problem solving machines have developed prodigiously, increasing the strength of nonmentalistic and impersonal metaphors available to psychologists. Mechanistic analogies incorporating systems theory are so powerful that they threaten to draw attention away from the unique characteristics of natural intelligence which is something more than a technological artifact of man. I believe we need a comprehensive psychobiological theory that is designed to explain natural intelligence and its growth and evolution.

In the following section an attempt is made to outline how a brain mechanism might be formulated to determine adaptive functions of intelligence in anticipation of experience. It establishes some of the fundamentals for a psychobiological theory.

A Design for the Brain of a Subject—Agent

The basic organization of attention and intention. The requirements for locomotor guidance, orientation, and object discrimination for a free-moving animal differ. The resulting division of tasks favored the evolution of complementary basic mechanisms in the brain, each of different morphological design. Let us consider the requirements of each kind of action in turn.

1. (a) For the *guidance* of the displacement of the whole body, a wide coverage of the field and parallel detection of changes in many separate locations is required. It would not be possible for the subject to perceive and monitor a gap in solid surroundings, a surface for support, or a goal for forward movement unless the information in signals from different points in the surroundings were immediately related. Separate signals are related in one "space" that must be the same as the space in relation to which body movement is specified.

This may be regarded as the primary system. On both the motor side, in which separate limbs are coordinated to produce a planned displacement or change of shape of the body, and on the perceptual side, in which separate stimulus events are to be located and measured in one field of space and motion, there is a requirement for a single, coherent, polarized and adequately differentiated nerve net to constitute a field that ties elements together unambiguously.

(b) As a corollary to the unit and anatomical fixity of this field, its different space locations will have transitivity with respect to each other. Not only may Loci A,B,C, etc. have fixed simultaneous relation, but a path from A to B to C one at a time will give the same end result as a path from B to A to C or from A to C.

(c) Efficient guidance of a body through a nonhomogeneous medium requires prediction or modeling of the changing relations between surfaces and boundaries near the body and the locomotor function, because movements cannot be executed or modified instantaneously. The interval of time through which prediction must be cast will be longer for larger, more complex body forms executing more rapid displacements. However, even in primitive swimming vertebrates, the neural field governing locomotor guidance must have a time-generating mechanism or clock that can predict at least one measured interval ahead and calibrate events in relation to the varied power of its motor effort and the course of displacements it will make. Behavior must be specified in time as well as space.

(d) A proprioceptive error-detection function becomes increasingly useful with increase in activity of locomotion because there is a rapidly increasing risk of misjudgment or surprise in the dynamic body mechanics with more elaborate and faster action. Vertebrate brains have developed a mechanism for body-part-on-body-part coordination and assimilation of internal physical consequences of parts acting on one another. Parallel to this development is the development of an exteroceptive mechanism for perceiving paths of action in relation to the masses, surfaces and spaces of the surrounding medium outside the body. (The first mechanism is centered on the cerebellum, the second on the cerebral neocortex.)[1]

---

[1] These two kinds of proprioception, one entirely inside the body the other relating to externals, correspond with David Lee's proprioception and exproprioception.

(e) The above considerations indicate that a form of memory—preferably one capable of taking note of what happens when predictions about behavior prove inaccurate—would be part and parcel of a neural apparatus for guiding the body in locomotion. It would also be needed for keeping the body in some defined state of displacement (including stationarity) relative to surroundings that may be in joint states or in several states of their own motion (Greene, 1972).

2. (a) *Orienting* accomplishes choice of direction or location in surroundings. It must be defined relative to the subject's field of experience and action. Primitive orienting of independently mobile forms consists of rotating the direction in which one specialized part of the body, usually the anterior end, is facing (Fraenkel & Gunn, 1940).

Guidance of progression in a nonhomogeneous medium involves change in direction of movement. If the body is nonspherical and has a preferred direction of displacement, change of direction implies change of orientation. Orienting may also be carried out round an axis through a stationary body. This will change the radial direction of all stimuli in a stationary array with respect to the body, without changing their relative directions.

(b) The resolution of stimulus information in a part of the field is limited by the amount of neural structure given over by the brain to that part in the brain "map". But the apprehension of general relations sufficiently independent of movements so that the subject can be guided in relation to external structures, needs essentially complete coverage for the whole field of behavior with equal representation in all directions. If progression is usually forward, this is qualified by increase in the significance of information from the forward part of the field and reduction in significance of information from the backward part. Nevertheless, guidance may require occasional change of direction even to the extent of an "about face." Species that are harrassed by predators have to keep alert in all directions. There is a conflict between the requirements for alertness and those for discrimination.

(c) Orienting without progression clearly pays off if it is used as a test of hypotheses about potential movement in different directions. Its power for picking up useful information will be increased if a region of high receptor resolution is displaced by measured rotatory steps that are calibrated in relation to the same whole-body field that governs locomotor progression. This principle is incorporated in a variety of complementary receptor systems (like the eyes or ears), each specialized to scan the environment in a different physical domain (light, sound). Each kind of receptor is displaced by a separate orienting motor apparatus. Hence comes the characteristic behavior of intelligent animals: they not only sit, but also look, feel, listen, sniff or taste—and in different directions—before taking action to move in relation to surroundings (Gibson, 1966).

An orienting motor system permits a limited patch of sensory detection to have high density of distinctions in the nerve net, per unit of space, and higher resolving power for discontinuities of matter and their displacements. This narrowed but more intensive detection must be complimented by a motor-scanning operation that itself represents the field as a coherent set of locations. In a simple case—a small window can "cover" the world to inform a perceiving subject only if the subject moves the window systematically and efficiently to scan in different directions. This is the origin of orienting movements. One cannot develop focal analysis based on high resolution of sensory information without also having orienting movements.

(d) The primary neural map that could be employed for primitive taxic locomotor guidance, and that would serve as a wide-scope alerting field for events likely to occur anywhere in the field round the body, is transformed by the orienting process. This process comprises a separate mover of the direction of aim and a separate perception device. Together they allow resolutions of space structure to be made in a limited location centered on the direction in which the receptor is aimed.

The limitations on the representational and discriminatory power of the primary mechanism for locomotor guidance must thus be regarded as the evolutionary cause of the scanning programs essential for those perceptual mechanisms that orient as separate parts of the body (like the eye or hand). Plans for guiding progression of the whole body seem to be naturally adapted for probing surroundings from a safe station by means of what I call *partial orientations* (orienting of parts).

3. (a) Pressure to *identify the forms* of objects, events, and portents of all kinds comes from development of more refined requirements for life. For example, the feeding function can be greatly increased in efficiency if tasty or highly nutritious objects can be sought out, recognized in advance, and then taken by a well-directed movement. Put the other way, emphasizing enterprise rather than necessity, the active principle of orienting frees the receptive principle for evolution of elaborate discriminatory powers.

The space-resolving powers that are a feature of even the most primitive perception could provide the elements for a mechanism that detects much finer space differences. I believe that the now famous "line-segment" or "edge" detectors of the striate cortex of cats and monkeys are microfields with similar anatomical design and the same embryogenic determination in miniature to the whole-body field that is to be seen mapped on the midbrain roof. That is, I believe that each cortical receptor field (a striate pyramidal neurone and its little galaxy of associated neurones) is a minibehavioral field capable of storing, perhaps permanently, a particular configuration of excitations relative to the common somatotopic axis.

Both striate cell receptor field and the field of the whole tectum record the distribution of light-disturbing matter in space. Both are sensitive only to temporary changes in the distribution of excitations over retinal receptor cells and are, in fact, detectors of boundaries of matter. The states of individual retinal receptor cells are not important. It is the configuration of change over an array of receptors that determines if a feature will become active in exciting a cortical "detector" neurone.

(b) In the tectum the array is large and locations or directions in it may be directly related to the whole-body locomotor field, or to the orienting of the head. Each striate minifield is lost without a complementary eye-movement field to keep track of its local sign; and the geometry, direction of displacement, or inclination of the exciting stimulus has motoric significance only if it is integrated with many other fields or if it can direct a very fine scanning movement. Foveal neurones in the striate cortex may govern the scanning function directly, but they do so only after amplification of the information they convey in combination with other units.

It is extremely important to realize that *form vision* is made possible only by the detection of fine boundaries in space and time relative to a larger field of action. Local features must be integrated within the general field of space round the body. It is essential for many such detections by nerve cell groups to be brought together in a coherent neural network that is capable of representing their combination in larger, higher-order compartments of the behavior field. Thus discovery of the receptor fields of the striate cortex has done no more than explain the limits of detection of principal kinds of discontinuity in energy in the light array. This information does not tell us how we see form.

Likewise, binocular stereopstic vision requires coupling of the excitations from correctly located positions in the fields of the two eyes. These positions are held in correspondence by an exceedingly precise motor function that intrinsically couples the displacements of the two eyes. Moreover, absolute detection of local space structure by binocular stereopsis, as in monocular form perception, depends upon a reliable process of reference to the larger visual field.

(c) There must be a generative mechanism capable of anticipating retinal information taken up in different directions towards separate features of an object. This, I presume, would be analogous to the mechanism that plans ahead of locomotion and detects environmental information accordingly. This same mechanism is also capable of generating a set of retinal loci in readiness for detection of fitting signs in the excitation received. As is demonstrated in the following sections of this chapter, this process attains a power to perceive shapes from one instantaneous retinal image. It is also highly independent of movements of verification or commitment, even though it is readily translatable in a given instance into a precisely selected number out of a virtually unlimited potential set of acts.

More Complex Intelligences

From questions of action to questions of knowledge. At the origin of every psychological act is a "question about the world" juxtaposed with a "statement of purpose." The field of information to which the question is addressed may be extensive and relative to the way the whole body is to move or be coordinated by a set of movements; or the question might be restricted to a very small locus with reference to one discrete act of a part of the body. To some uncertain extent the body itself is indeterminate for the brain, that is, it is part of the world to be perceived. The field may thus refer largely to conditions of action *inside* the body, or it may refer almost exclusively to relations among externals considered independent of their spatial and temporal relations with the subject's body.

As we have seen, orienting and attending involve separate movement of a part of the body to facilitate one direction or one kind of question. Thus, attention may be focused in space and may be confined to a single kind (modality) of sensory reception or to a limited set of modalities. Objects may be perceived in different ways, using different physical means (light, sound, chemistry) to discover different properties in them. Acts of attending and of selective focalization in space—or in one modality at a time—greatly increase the efficiency of information uptake by perception. However, they must be made from a single central question-asking system if they are not to lead the subject into multiple and conflicting forms of action.

I believe that this unity of attending is assured by having a single anatomically determined hierarchy of question—statements inherent in all phases of an individual's intelligence. Although there are, for each individual, many kinds of focal questions and in each kind there are many directions in which they may be posed, the full set is related together. That means, for example, that listening to an event at one place is normally quite compatible with seeing a different event at another place, but that to do both at once may be ruled out if the acts of attending in the different ways or different directions are competing for common parts of the hierarchy of "question statements." This will finally depend on how the form of the body and its apparatus of actions are to be implicated.

Experiments concerning the limits of space for attending, or the maximum number of goals to which attention may be distributed, show that, while a very large number of different details may be stored for a short time as potential material for answering questions (perceptual image in short-term memory), the primary statements of direction of interest (choice of response) are limited. Presumably this is because in the end, every direction of orientation has to be translated into a coordination of all body parts for action. Answers to questions at the tips of the branches in the hierarchy cannot be allowed to multiply indefinitely into simultaneous goals for the whole subject.

Awareness maintains a rich array of knowledge in which a coherent set of question-statements is built up and continuously extended. Detailed study of the process of attention that keeps consciousness going, and study of the patterns of action that are produced in consciously perceived conditions, shows that the coordination mechanism has surprisingly few levels of operation. This has emerged, for example, from Bernstein's (1967) analysis of the rhythmical properties of voluntary movements. He finds that the force curves of skilled movements have only three or four Fourrier components. That is, they are coordinated by only three or four clocks. Perceptual uptake (reaction time, refactory periods) and perceptual scan studies reveal a similar economy of times on the afferent side indicating that, indeed, the pace of perception questions is set by the highly organized mechanism that prepares motor statements.

A simple example of the hierarchy of question statements in psychological action comes from studies of attainment of visual targets by arm and hand movements. The locus of a visual stimulus may be reached by a ballistic arm movement in about .25 to .5 sec and without any feedback from vision of the limb and also without information about error. The magnitude of error is within the range of visual angle of the fovea (about $1-2°$). Normally eye and hand move synchronously to a target in a coordinated double orientation (ballistic or open-loop phase) and then final correction of aim is made in the last quarter second or less as the hand comes close to the goal and slows its motion (servo phase). It is a 2-step process. Finer aim involving finger adjustment with a stabilized wrist would impose at least one more stage of aiming.

Ocular fixation to far off-center targets is also usually at least a 2-step process of very regular temporal form. Normally the first large saccade falls short and it is followed by a small correction saccade. Even when the second finer step of orienting appears continuous with the first, as with hand movement, it is probably based on a second discrete "ballistic" question statement following the first one.

Responses to such single-point stimuli (actions ending in arrival at target), however, do not help us understand either form perception or the formulation of complex patterns of skilful movement. In both, apparently continuous series of discrete acts are combined in large numbers with variable intervals of time between them. I feel there is one answer to both Lashley's (1951) famous serial order questions in execution of movements and to the puzzle of form perception. There is in the brain a mechanism of very large capacity which may store arrays of part questions within contexts of large questions. The levels to which these unresolved detailed questions are designated by the brain may be as few as the basic periods within coordinated movement, but the number of combinations they may hold for all purposes is obviously unlimited, at least in the experienced adult mind.

Arrays of potential foci may be set up in two ways as awareness or reasoning progresses. They may be produced as a serial *chain,* each link determining the reference direction to the next, the series building as long as directions can be added without forgetting. Alternatively, the foci may be produced simultaneously and parallel to one another, like a *fan* of directions. Chain and fan schemata for perceptual exploration and for motoric coordination enter into theories of the highest cerebral functions and their anatomical localization in the brain.

In the above outline of a deterministic structure for intelligence, one that combines adaptive prepatterning of movements with pickup of sensory information from inside and outside the body, an evolutionary process can be made out that leads the subject into more and more intricate and effective means of obtaining advanced information for its plans of action. At all stages action and perception remain inseparable. In the end, however, the exploratory functions are so powerful that they image a whole reasoned world of possibilities. A world in which abstract meanings are defined in consciousness as remote goals for projects of activity, in which the actual component movements are undetermined until just before they are to occur. The environment of each evolutionary form of animal is not the creator but the anticipated provider of occasions for intelligence to flourish.

For behavior to be the outcome of such adaptive modes of perception and action as have been described, every facet of the system must be anticipated in the process of growth. In particular, nerve networks of the brain must be innately defined with precision and in great complexity. Psychobiological research begins to reveal how this is achieved.

NERVE CIRCUIT THEORY AND BRAIN EMBRYOGENESIS: HOW THE BRAIN GETS ITS SHAPE

As a student I became familiar with Sperry's somatotopic theory of brain development (Sperry, 1951, 1963, 1965). According to this theory, nerve networks grow exceedingly refined patterns of communication with the body by means of some encoding of affinities for intercellular connection. Sperry considers the encoding to be chemical in nature, interneuronal affinities being derived from the macromolecular mechanisms of cell-cell communication and cell labeling that operate in morphogenesis of the body as a whole. Individual neural elements are tagged chemically in the embryo so that the growth forces of their axons and dendrites will be guided to establish definite synaptic relations: between receptor loci on the surface of the body and brain fields, centrally from one part of the brain to the other, and between organ structures and muscular mechanisms governing movement (Meyer and Sperry, 1976; Trevarthen, 1977d). This theory has been extended by Richard Mark (1974) into a developmental anatomy of memory.

By far the most studied system in this area is the visual-motor field of the midbrain, especially its coupling with the retinas of the eyes via the optic nerves (Gaze, 1970; Jacobson, 1970; Gottlieb, 1976). The eye is a geometric organ, representing by its form an orderly radial space of directions in the external world. Discrimination of rays of sight and of relations between them in the visual field depends on a distinguishing "local sign" for each separate retinal ganglion cell with its constellation of receptors. If it is to have use in directing behavior, this local sign must transmit without degradation through an orderly chain or neurotransmission, excite or modulate impulse patterns to specific muscles, and so, in the end, determine a movement that is correct in direction and magnitude.

Sperry felt that his nerve regeneration experiments with eyes, skin, and vestibular organs of fish and amphibia showed that one scheme of chemical encoding of loci relative to body form was the basis for orienting in all sensory modalities. This would provide the basis for an innate association of modalities within one perceptual field capable of directing movements of all parts of the body. Sperry conducted one of the first experimental studies (1950) of the self-regulatory function of reafference and its essential role in locomotor guidance. He concluded—independently of von Holst and Mittelstaedt (1950)—that a feed-forward process called "corrolary discharge from efference" was required. No self-sensing reafference mechanism could work unless the brain could specify independently of stimuli the directions of goals for action and the sense of displacements of surroundings relative to the body. Gibson's (1966) theory of visual information for guidance of movement depends (more than he acknowledges) on a neural detection field that is congruent with the body, and in which relations between separately detected local events like displacements of features or surfaces may be correlated (for example, to detect pattern of transformation in velocities that exhibits the effects of parallax).

Sperry's method of experimental psychology was a radical departure. Instead of experimenting with stimulus control over responses, he sought to observe the effects on behavior of brain surgery and rearrangement of brain connections. Moreover, he was interested in spontaneous motor coordination, the intimate coupling of object and space perception to motor orientation; and the retention of learned discriminations in relation to the movements made to acquire experience. He concluded that resolution of the mind-brain problem required attention at least as much to the coordination and regulation of movements as to the patterning of stimuli (Sperry, 1952).

Maps of the Behavior Field

Although some of the earliest discoveries of somatotopic fields in the adult brain resulted from surgery or brain injuries, more of our present knowledge comes from mapping with point electrical stimulation and recording. Recently, anatomical mapping by differential silver staining or radioactive tracer methods has become very refined. These methods combined with electrographic mapping provide a fairly complete picture.

Body-shaped maps are found throughout the brain and they all correspond functionally because they are interconnected in correspondence by orderly arrays of nerve axons with highly selective distribution of endings. Segmental relations characteristic of the spinal cord are tied together and overlaid by an integral topography representing the whole-body field. "Higher" levels of the brain replicate this field innumerable times, with a great diversity of affinities for separate modalities of sensory reception in the different parts of the cortex.

Many of the representations of the somatotopic field are not "isometric." Thus, each primary field of the cortex with direct input from one modality shows relative magnification for the center or focus of the particular perceptual apparatus (hand eye, cochlea, and so on) to which it is linked by a specific afferent projection pathway. Privileged regions are established (such as the foveal part of the striate cortex) that have exceptionally high density of neural units per degree of projected behavior space. This magnification was discovered by Adrian (1928), who pointed out its important relation to perceptual acuity as determined by psychophysical tests. By comparison between different species of mammal, Adrian also showed the ecological significance of this anatomical correlate of perception. Primates have very large foveal and hand areas, pigs have a large snout area. Adrian's work has been extended enormously in recent years (Whitteridge, 1973).

On the motor side, the relation between maps of body form in the central nervous system and the differentiation of skill has become increasingly clearer since the famous stimulation experiment of Fritsch and Hitzig (1870) with the dog, by which motor territories were discovered in the cortex. Sherrington, Woolsey, Penfield and many others since have demonstrated magnification of the regions representing body parts that make finer patterns of movement. Recently Brodal, Kuypers and others have described the vertical coherence of motor structures in the brain; they have also noted the remarkable columnar segregation of proximal orienting functions (in medial parts of the neuraxis) from distal functions of refined praxis (in more lateral parts) (Kuypers, 1973). This is a distinction between brain elements which split brain studies (discussed in this chapter) have shown to be of great importance for psychologists.

The modern anatomical view of the brain, though it is not yet interpreted by a unified general theory of teleological type, is beautifully orderly and is applicable throughout the vertebrates. For example, the somatotopy principle permits exceedingly strong inferences about ecological adaptations within phylogenetic series. It also provides an explanation for the phenomenon of attention, for the confluence of modalities in perception of the world, and for the equivalence of movements made by different parts of the motor apparatus of the body. The body-shaped maps of the brain, of embryogenic origin, form no less than the common code of brain function.

Recently, however, direct evidence has been obtained of the selective or molding effect of stimulus information on the form of nerve circuits that mature after birth. Apparently, extensive changes in nerve connections of some parts of the brain may be caused or guided by selection or competing alternatives in response to stimuli. Jacobson (1970) has proposed a theory to incorporate such functional plasticity within an embryogenic framework. He emphasizes the distinction between macroneurones, which establish extensive connections according to the morphogenetic plan of the embryo with little influence from the environment, and microneurones, which appear later in brain development in enormous excess of numbers and which form interstitial short connections. The microneurones permit environmental influences of select particular cells or connections. This theory supports the idea of innate modes of coordinated action built of macroneurones. These modes, in turn, expose prepared assimilatory structures (microneurones) to environmental stimuli in a directed way at critical periods in brain maturation. This theory, like the synapse suppression theory of memory of Mark (1974), lacks direct support and recent findings show that the evaluation of plasticity in developing brain circuits is difficult. The latest evidence suggests that a large part of the refined cortical anatomy that may be changed by extreme environmental manipulations in the newborn is normally formed by self-selection of nerve connections. Patterned stimuli serve to calibrate or refine rather than to create the critical circuits (Trevarthen, 1977d).

Early Embryology of the Behavior Field

The generative aspect of Sperry's (1951; 1963) theory that the origin of brain maps should be traced to the embryo, receives support from experimental studies which show that the bisymmetry and form of the nervous system with antero-posterior axis is a consequence of inductive coupling of the primary central nervous system to adjacent body segments in each part of the embryonic body (Trevarthen, 1973, 1977d). The following correspondences between body configuration and neuroconnective fate seem to give powerful support for the theory:

1. The map of the visual field on the midbrain of all vertebrates is a body action map, independent of the orientation of the eyes in the head (Trevarthen, 1968).

2. The retinal receptor array is physically rotated by growth in the embryo, relative to the body, countering the inverting effect of the lens in the projection of a visual image on the retina (Trevarthen, 1974c, 1977b).

3. Neurones in the spinal-cord segments are organized to map both body shape and its boundaries with external and internal millieux in an orderly array, before nerves grow from the cord to the body (Trevarthen, 1974c).

4. Multiple "parallel" hemisphere maps appear to conform to a simple layout of somatotopies in the early stages (Trevarthen, 1972, 1974c) and the cross-sectional arrangements in the hemispheres are seen by the anatomist Yakovlev (1968) to reiterate the primitive arrangements of the cord.

5. The associative cortex, the neocortical commissures, and the cerebellum grow last and longest of all brain parts. Their relation to the hierarchy of somatotopic maps (most integrative, representing highly differentiated mechanisms of the special sensory and motoric organs in equivalent systems) seems to fit well with their long cycle of development. The cerebellum associates the mechanics of a moving body of many complex mechanical parts. The neocortex associates experiences from many intricate modalities of sense. These structures, too, are intimately related with the integrative reticular system of the brain stem, which also matures slowly. Studies of myelinogenesis indicate that this whole complex goes on differentiating throughout life (Yakovlev & Lecours, 1967).

SURGICAL ANALYSIS OF COMPLEX BRAINS

Separation of Orienting and Focal Action in Split-Brain Monkeys

The structure of a complex voluntary agent has been revealed through the study of the effects of split-brain surgery on cats and monkeys. The most important finding in this research (which, apart from a few scattered surgical experiments by others much earlier, began in Sperry's laboratory at the University of Chicago and at the California Institute of Technology in the 1950s), has been the proof of a single hierarchical organization of brain circuits based on the principle of somatotopy (Sperry, 1961; Trevarthen, 1965, 1968, 1972, 1974d, 1975c, 1977a).

A monkey with cerebral hemispheres disconnected by cutting the corpus callosum has two separate mechanisms of perception and learning, but remains a single agent of activity. Locomotor guidance is unaffected, and large scale orienting functions remain united within one field of action, yet processes of refined and local exploration are divided into two separately-functioning mirror halves. To put it another way, the functions of oculomotor recentering for small changes of fixation are bisected and so are those of predictive hand-shaping on visual criteria, and those of delicate reaction to touch in skilled manipulation of objects.

The effects of this operation on vision, which is unified at one level though divided at another, have given support for a two-visions theory that considers the visual mechanisms of the brain to be laid down anatomically in close correspondence with motor structures (Trevarthen, 1963, 1968, 1974d). As there are two kinds of motor function, there are two modes of seeing. Information for orienting in space at large (ambient vision) and exploration of local structure for identity determination (focal vision) are different. This relates closely to Kuyper's anatomic distinction between proximal (near the trunk) and distal (limb end) motor systems of different function, a distinction that applies to all levels of the brain and spinal cord (Brinkman & Kuypers, 1972, 1973; Kuypers, 1973).

Correspondence between the distal orienting mechanisms of the eyes and of the hands is partly broken down by cerebral commissurotomy. Split-brain monkeys have defects in eye-hand orientation when two contralateral half systems are to be used together (as the left visual-oculomotor field with right arm and hand) (Trevarthen, 1965, 1968, 1977a). This effectively reduces the power of exploration and attention and tends to lead the subject into unilateral biases of movement and perception when the field of motion is restricted. However, since the main axial orienting functions remain bilaterally coordinated, split effects are hidden or compensated for most of the time, and they are not conspicuous, as a rule, in the spontaneous behavior of the operated subjects.

Hemisphere Differences and Higher Modes of Attending and Intending in Man

In 1959, the first of a series of epileptic patients were operated upon by Vogel in an attempt to control their intractable seizures (Bogen & Vogel, 1962). The effects of complete (and more recently of anterior partial neocortical) commissurotomy have been subjected to detailed psychological study by Sperry, Bogen and numerous collaborators (Sperry, 1968, 1970, 1974a; Sperry, Gazzaniga & Bogen, 1969). The tests with this series of patients confirm and greatly extend the findings with monkeys and give us a new perspective on the organization of consciousness. In addition to bringing out a clear dissociation of complementary partial orienting systems for the two halves of space, as with monkeys, psychological tests with the human subjects show one entirely new phenomenon. The cognitive processes of the two separated cerebral hemispheres are found to differ in basic strategy. Left and right halves of the human brain have different consciousnesses and different modes of performance.

This phenomenon of hemispheric lateralization of function, known for more than one hundred years, poses one of the most significant challenges in contemporary psychology. The basis for hemispheric differences in mental process is clearly genetic (Levy, 1976). At the same time all the evidence would support the view that the assymetry of function is acquired slowly in postnatal life and that it is furthered by experience and the exercise of such culturally significant skills as manipulation, speech, and reading.

I believe it is possible to outline a theory of cerebral lateralization of functions in terms of hierarchical somatotopic system revealed by the split-brain monkey work. However, before discussing this I shall review the evidence for a basic hierarchy of visuomotor functions in man like that described for the monkey. The phenomenon of hemispheric duplication of the field of vision and its significance for an anatomical theory of conscious experience is also considered.

Ambient and focal perceptions in man: the central hierarchy.   Sperry and I have studied the ability of commissurotomy patients to cross-integrate visual information directed simultaneously from both sides of the visual field in one percept of space relations (Trevarthen, 1970; Trevarthen & Sperry, 1973). We have also tested the unity of the visual awareness of these patients. We asked them to tell us, presumably using their left hemispheres, about visual experiences in the peripheral left visual field. The left visual field, of course, projects to the striate cortex of the right hemisphere exclusively. However, there are large extrastriate visual projections in man. The tests are designed to explore what the alternate visual route through the midbrain contributes to human awareness. We found that a partially conscious or subconscious perception of space, detecting kinetic transformations within the visual array, remains a unified process in the brains of these subjects. In it left and right visual fields are represented together (Trevarthen, 1972, 1974a, b, d).

Reaching and pointing experiments add further information. A high degree of primary functional unity of movements (that is, not secondarily established through feedback of sensory cues across the midline of the body) is sustained in spite of total disconnection of the hemispheres (Trevarthen, 1974a, d). Obviously these findings help explain the ability of commissurotomy patients to retain well-coordinated general body movements as well as bilateral coordination in orienting. This retained integrity is also made possible by many cross integrations involving transmission of stimuli between two halves of the body surface and thence between the two halves of the brain. "Peripheral cross-cuing" will automatically occur very efficiently because there is a sub-hemispheric unity in control of intention. In ordinary life feedback from a unilateral act will almost always cause disturbances in the environment to send stimuli back to both sides of the peripheral receptor apparatus, and thence to both sides of the brain. Most of the important controls in tests of commissurotomy patients are to reduce or eliminate this feedback over the midline.

When one looks at all the information available—not only evidence from commissurotomy subjects for complete duplication of visual awareness in the two halves of the field and from either side of the point for foveal fixation but also the recent evidence for retained unity of orienting control—the outline of hierarchical organization of the visual mechanism of the brain begins to become clear. Vision of space at large, detected by the whole retina, is mediated through subhemispheric mechanisms; but foveal vision of detail, essential to full conscious perception of the substances of surroundings and of the identities of objects, is mediated by a hemispheric or cerebral cortical mechanism. This cortical mechanism is sharply divided in two parts which correspond to the two halves of visual space—either side of the vertical meridian in the visual field.

In addition to visual processing, perceptual processes by means of touch are also affected in the commissurotomy subjects. The feeling of form by delicate manipulation with the fingers is divided in two; what each hand feels is not known to the other hand. In contrast, detection of the place of immovable surfaces and the massiveness of objects (through pressure and by force detection in proximal proprioceptive systems) is still bilaterally integrated. Digital proprioception is divided but position of the arms or legs is detected by a system that remains unified.

I have discussed the important problem of how the brain articulates the moveable visual field or the hands with respect to the main axis of the body, and with respect to the midplane of the brain. The direction of sight or of reaching with the hand are achieved by a motor function that directs fovea or finger tips in measured steps. These steps are specified in units of the main body-orienting field, thus distal parts are kept in known relation to the central body axis.

Double awareness. Experiments in collaboration with Marcel Kinsbourne (Kinsbourne, 1974; Trevarthen, 1974a, d) indicate that the conscious perceiving of objects, including symbolic objects such as written words, is carried out in a part of the hemisphere which "knows" both the immediately available information from its striate cortex as well as the *potential* existence of other parts of the field to which the fovea may be aimed by eye movements. If one projects a stimulus on the vertical meridian of the visual field, each hemisphere of the observer *receives* striate information only about the contralateral *half* of the object. Nevertheless, one finds that each hemisphere *perceives* a *whole* object extending both sides of the meridian. I have demonstrated this by presenting half objects, and the subjects speak about or draw these as if they were complete objects. There seems to be no evidence that the percept is any weaker in the half field for which no direct striate information is available. This means the percept is not "in" the striate cortex. It also indicates that object perception is related to active plans to use available visual information, rather than related to the contents of that information itself. I do not believe this would be possible by extrapolations of perceived contours or surfaces into a neural void or random net. There must be a predetermined, orderly structure representing space bilaterally in each hemisphere. Pribram (1971) hypothesizes that such representation may take the form of a holograph interference pattern. I think it much more likely that the space structure is morphologically determined in units that are isomorphic with the large-scale somatotopic or behavior field maps that we know in the projection areas of the tectum, cortex, and so on.

Two different minds. Tests of perception with commissurotomy patients (Sperry, 1968, 1970; Sperry, Gazzaniga & Bogen, 1969) have clearly brought out consistent but very complex differences between the hemispheres. The differences are similar to those previously discovered with brain-injured patients. There is no doubt that a fundamental segregation of higher mental functions between the hemispheres exists due to an inherent developmental principle in the brain. Recently experimenters studying normal subjects have shown: (1) that small, but functionally comparable differences in hemispheric processes are part of an everyday mental life; and (2) that these hemispheric processes are also responsible for differences between the intellectual predispositions of individuals, in particular responsible for consistent differences in style of mental function between persons of different sex. We do not know the developmental strategy behind the hemispheric lateralization of function, but there are, on first analysis, tantalising consistencies and correlations between results of very different tests. We can, however, state with more confidence that the principle of hemispheric lateralization is related to the active, generative processes of attention and intention.

Because there are many reviews of the studies done with commissurotomy patients (e.g., Levy, 1974; Milner, 1974; Nebes, 1974; Sperry, 1968, 1970, 1974a; Sperry, Gazzaniga & Bogen, 1969), I shall simply summarize my conclusions concerning the main differences of hemisphere function. To do this I shall rely principally on one series of experiments (Levy, 1974; Levy, Trevarthen & Sperry, 1972; Levy & Trevarthen, 1976, 1977) with stimuli that were designed to offer the subject a free choice of hemispheric strategy for perception and understanding. The stimuli were double and presented in such a manner so that in each trial the subject had potentially two different conscious images to choose from, one seen by each hemisphere. We also performed a test in which each stimulus half could be seen in one of two ways, depending on the mental task set the subject (Levy & Trevarthen, 1976).

Given these conditions, the right hemisphere showed a spontaneous dominance over the left for recognition of faces, nameless shapes, familiar pictures, indeed for any visual recognition that required perception and memorizing of appearance. The left hemisphere was strongly dominant for any task involving naming of the objects, whether this naming was overt (spoken) or covert (like the silent matching of rhyming names). The left hemisphere was also inclined to assume direction of responses in which analysis of meaning or of combination of interchangeable features was required. For example, if the subject was asked to match objects by their functional association (like gloves with hat or bird with nest) rather than with their immediate or superficial appearance (like a pair of gloves, and a bird drawn to look very similar to the gloves in overall form), then the left hemisphere became dominant even though no overt naming was required. Visual recognition of patterns of color (like butterflies with wing color A and spots of color B on them to be distinguished from butterflies of color B with spots of A) also seemed to attract the processes of the left hemisphere (Trevarthen & Levy, unpublished).

These results lead me to conclude that: (1) an attentional processing difference in vision lies at the basis of hemispheric differences; and (2) that superiority of the left hemisphere for production of language is initially a consequence rather than a cause of hemispheric lateralization of function (Trevarthen, 1974a).

Studies by Bogen (1969), Gazzaniga (1970), Levy (1974), Milner (1974), Nebes (1974), D. Zaidel (1974) and E. Zaidel (1976) with Sperry have shown that commissurotomy patients are better at several tasks when using the right hemisphere. These tasks include such things as copying outline drawings of three-dimensional shapes, feeling the layout of features on an object, or recognizing the overall form of incomplete or shattered shapes. The left hemisphere is better at calculation as well as detection or isolated features. These findings, which correlate well with those obtained from patients with unilateral cortical lesions, suggest that simultaneous combination of features in relations is perceived better by the right hemisphere; however, separation and systematic recombination of features or elements in productive strategies is more easily mastered by the left hemisphere.

An orientation-program theory of hemispheric functional difference. One may gain a simpler view of the distinction by considering the two ways in which successive foci of visual attention may be determined in looking for meaning. Whenever vision is fixed on one part of the world, the relations between the foveal part of the field (seen clearly) and the surroundings (seen less clearly) are of two possible kinds. There are two kinds of scan: (1) novel features may appear in the periphery and *attract* further attention as stimuli; or (2) features may be inferred from knowledge already available, causing attention to be *projected* to where the features were thought or imagined to be. The two kinds of scan must occur in each hemisphere alternately whenever a commissurotomy subject looks across the visual field, for if the fovea is displaced to the right it will be sent to a location for which there is immediately prior visual information only in the left hemisphere. If the eye movement is to the left, then the left hemisphere must receive entirely new input on arrival.

Both hemispheres may direct the two eyes conjugately to left or right (Trevarthen, 1974a; 1975c). That is, either hemisphere may perform an *attracted scan* to look more closely at a signal detected as interesting in extrafoveal vision; or either hemisphere may make a *projected scan* to see if something imagined to be at a place off center is indeed that thing and at that place. Both kinds of integration of ambient and focal visual information (or foveal and parafoveal information) must be going on in consciousness all the time.

I would suggest that in more complex instances the hemispheres may differ in their scanning tendency. The right hemisphere (of the majority of persons) may be more attentive to immediate circumstances and the situation of the subject in the array of surroundings (a fan) while the left hemisphere may be more concerned with expression of expectations and specific outcomes of action (a chain). Normally the former processes must be present to provide a context for the specifications of the latter. In this way we may attempt to relate higher modes of intelligence to the theory of behavioral control for a subject-agent.

Observe the characteristic differences in style of movement in, for example, movement of the left and right hands in skilled manipulation, in gesticulation and, especially when writing. There seems to be an anatomical differentiation of strategies: the foci of intention are defined (for right-handers) in the left hemisphere within the larger scale patterns of orientation and coordination that are concurrently being organized in the right hemisphere.

Reading may represent a particular case of an asymmetry in oculomotor function which has much more general application. For it is perfectly possible that normal, untrained visual consciousness is maintained by asymmetric strategies of scan—inspection displaced leftward forming a frame for rightward displacements that seek out defining criteria. Admittedly there is no definite evidence for this in scan paths so far described. The only exception is the initial direction of glance of a visually disengaged subject occupied with a task favoring left or right hemisphere activity (Kinsbourne, 1972). I have data (Trevarthen, 1974a) indicating that a commissurotomy subject looks left and right with different latencies after a stimulus has appeared; and I have also found that reading, which involves the two kinds of looking in close combination is severely disrupted in these subjects (Trevarthen, unpublished).

A note on extensions of two-brain theory. The few unfortunate epileptics who have taught us so much about hemisphere functions have also set free wild speculation about the nature of man and consciousness. I share Sperry's (1974b) belief that the tests that have been done prove the positive, organizing, and highly differentiated role of an innately determined consciousness in regulating all brain functions. They also prove that the right hemisphere, though deficient in serial reasoning, is capable of the most elaborate consciousness in which nonpresent information is rapidly adduced to fill out meaning in experience of an intricate world. For example, the right hemisphere may readily substitute between modalities for perception of an object, may generalize in a class of object between different instances, may associate attributes, which though namable (like color) are not necessarily named, and may even treat the name of a thing as one of its inherent attributes. This rules out, or renders highly improbable, the traditional view that consciousness and thought are wholly based on speech and language, for the right hemisphere can usually not speak even a part of a word and neither can it create word images for unspoken comparisons (Zaidel, 1976; Levy and Trevarthen, 1977).

In spite of these exciting discoveries, I am not happy with further speculation (e.g. Ornstein, 1972) that the right hemisphere is artistic, feminine, visionary, insightful, human and affectionate, spontaneous, mystical, while the left is calculating, rational, logical, machinelike and dispassionate, bound to concrete events, scientific, and masculine. These categories cut in other ways across human nature. I believe that in each of them the kind of process that is separately developed in the two hemispheres is combined in culturally regulated forms of whole-mind activity. Unfortunately we do not know nearly enough about the anatomical foundations of human cooperative intelligence, though work with very young humans, discussed below, shows that no part of our mental nature is more fundamental.

Modes of memory and modes of culture. If the visual consciousness of the hemispheres differ in the way I think they do then their memories will differ likewise, because memory is an aspect of the generation of consciousness. The right hemisphere will have a memory of patterns, constructions, and panoramic configurations of relation in context. The left will have a memory of instances itemized and held together by their definite functional systems of relation. It is possible that written, elaborated scientific memory is developed only in the advanced neural differentiations of the left hemisphere, and if this is so then we may suppose that the attainment of full developmental differentiations is achieved in the left hemisphere rather later than in the right hemisphere. The left may be an outgrowth of the right in this respect.

However, the mature hemispheres must certainly act together in complementary ways—the left does not replace or supersede the right in any sense. Without a right hemisphere the left "chatters" and lacks sense of proportion, just like the discipline of science does when divorced from cultural perspective and the humanities. Note also that the right hemisphere does not attain its functional specialization fully until the left has developed its own—it is possible that the specialization of the right hemisphere is, in part, an inductive or reactive effect of the growth of an analytic mental process in the left (cf. Levy, 1969).

There is a fascinating parallel between the newly clarified picture of the subdivision of mental functions in the hemispheres of the human brain and theories of cultural evolution. It is obvious that cultures differ in the degree to which they depend upon systematic understanding of the properties of things, and in their dependence on written language. Even highly developed cultures with a store of knowledge in elaborate written texts differ in their scientific or technical consciousness.

Since scientifically educated university students of the "white" and "rational" West have, by a political process, become attracted to the old but unscientific wisdom of the "brown" and "yellow" East, it is popular to suggest that these are two fundamental ways of consciousness. And it is also popular to consider that human nature is divided in two parts that correspond to the mentally different brain hemispheres.

Although, as I have said, I feel that much of this reasoning about societies and the brain is too facile, in one respect the evolution of all cultures and the differentiation of mental operations in the brain may have a real parallel. The majority of literate and numerate adults develop strong lateralization for speech writing and calculation in the left hemisphere. There are E.E.G data for Africans suggesting that illiterate people who do not depend on literacy skills, but belong to cultures that use highly cultivated powers of environmental perception and with language rich in myth and metaphor but unsuited to scientific argument, have relatively more activity in the right-hemisphere (Munday-Castle, 1975). If this is true, then cultural development may be fundamentally related to the ontogenetic process that separates analytical and symbolic communication and thought in the left side of the brain from syncretic awareness of relations and processes provided by the right hemisphere. This is not to say, of course, that relative development of the hemispheres is genetically fixed.

We have no reason to believe that in the most highly cultivated mental functions the special abilities of the right hemisphere are inferior to those of the left. It is even possible that the special abilities of the right hemisphere may become the more highly differentiated. However, the analytical, deductive mode of understanding, dependent on intense and precise communication between numbers of studious minds is more central in cultures with elaborate technology, elaborate education, and a social structure dependent on written language for all its functions. Apparently the innate modes of the human brain, as represented by the functions that differ in the cerebral hemispheres, may find expression in the highest ramifications of cultural evolution.

MODES OF THE INFANT MIND

Any theory of innate psychological processes must concern itself with the mental functions of infants. It is possible that at birth a human brain is so undeveloped that its inherent potentialities for conscious activity are not manifest. But if this is so one would expect the functions, when they do emerge, to reveal the form of innate constraints. This would be so even if development of the brain were strongly moulded by environmental stimuli. In Watson's (1914) behaviorism basic emotional drive functions and elementary motor reflexes were assumed to be active in an otherwise random chaos of infant behaviors and this view of man's mental heritage from nature is accepted by Skinner (1953). Psychologists reveal their theoretical biases by what they say an infant has built in. But even the most mechanistic learning theory assumes a foundation of structure that grows before experience performs miracles of psychological creation. Why should growth not continue to contribute? How does one define the contribution of experience?

For some years I have been studying infants in the first year of their lives, using descriptive methods in order to gain knowledge, not of reflex reactions, but of the ultimate spontaneous patterning in what they do (Trevarthen, 1977b). Films and television records reveal remarkable complex forms of action that prove the infant to possess outlines of a highly integrated primary intentionality. By primary intentionality I mean the capacity to originate coordinated acts that are directed to express a specific line of experience. The infant moves coherently in the direction of particular experiences, even before showing signs of assimilating those experiences and forming percepts of them. In this foundation the necessary conditions for development of consciousness, will, and cooperation with others are created. There are changes in the infant's behavior in the first year that are clear indicators of an intrinsic growth process. I therefore believe that a growing and self-regulated neural mechanism of intentional activity is essential to the growth of human intelligence.

Piaget and Modes of Intention

According to the now dominant theory of infant intelligence, the neonate is essentially a reflex being, lacking in organized intentions of any kind (Piaget,

1950, 1953). Both perceptual representation and coordinated actions (operations of purpose) are, in Piaget's view, undeveloped at this stage. In subsequent development the infant is said to create progressively more complex mental structures out of the chance adventures that lead to slightly dissimilar novel events. Goals arise *post hoc* and then, after several months, take a manifest role in directing the further course of experience. For example, the hands and the visual field discover the properties of objects and their various fates by chance and repetition in a space of other objects, screens, holes and so on. People are imitated and objects are played with by extension from the developing center of action which is the essence of the infant.

Piaget's theory is certainly one of an active, biologically generated psychological process. He asserts that a major contribution to growth of intelligence originates internally. Active principles in the mind interact and equilibrate between themselves to make more comprehensive principles that may govern transactions with the world more effectively. However, there is in the Piagetian system of psychological growth no preestablished pattern of growth and only one process of private or individual testing of relations to the world. The child is, in this view, intent at all stages of constructing mental rules by which to subject the objects and events of reality to actions. All different psychological states of motivation, of sociability, as well as of cognitive mastery are related to this unfolding and differentiating of propositions about knowing objects and doing things to them.

In theory, one could propose, on Piagetian grounds, certain fundamental modes of psychological function in early childhood. A child engaged in practising assimilation of the consequences of an operation and testing for effects produced when an act is repeated several times is in a self-directed, circular experience—a play (ludic) mode. A child imitating an effect—"trying to open" a match-box by opening its mouth, or acting like another person, or tracking an object—is in an identificatory, accommodatory and potentially communicative mode. A child systematically exploring a new synthesis of experience, constructing some creation, and overcoming obstacles and barriers to do so is in a performative, praxic mode.

But, Piaget does not give any indication that there are specialized innate neural mechanisms that, from the time of birth, define alternative modes as distinct adaptations. The modes of action would appear to arise out of the logic of circumstances. I find this very hard to comprehend. For example, it would seem to me that imitation, so central to the symbolic function of Piaget, would never arise or develop without a preestablished active and reactive sociability with others.

In fact, closer observation, using experimental methods that adjust to the infant's poorly developed actions, reveals that neonates move the parts of their body in coordination with external events in patterns that proves that there is far more intrinsic unity and variety of intention in the untutored brain than

Piaget assumes in his poineer study (1953). He appears to have mistaken a highly specific coordination of eye and hand ("hand regard")—a prerequisite of refined manual praxis that develops after four months—for a step in bringing together two movement systems which he assumes have no spatial integration at the start. Piaget is led to conclude that eye-hand coordination has no innate basis as such. There is a maturational coupling of two reflex systems and no inherent function. Another factor affecting his interpretations was his restricted interest in observing the adaptations of his infants to objects. This adaptation is poorly developed in the first three months. Adaptations to persons, described below, are much more precocious, but Piaget neglected these.

Both in timing and in form of action the infant is in possession of a unified yet differentiable motor apparatus, moving in a single space field from minutes after birth. Discrete reflex responses to stimuli are not the building blocks of this machinery of concerted action: they are peripheral and autonomous adjuncts that come into effect only when abnormal stimuli intervene to correct or protect more organized forms of movement.

The Start of Doing Things with Objects

Our observations of neonates give evidence of joint action of body parts and systematic orienting of them in combinations for apprehension of objects in space (Trevarthen, 1974e, 1975a, b). Conjugate, saccadic orienting of the eyes in pattern that in timing and in amplitude is remarkably close to that of an adult exploring a moderately extensive field may be observed minutes after birth. The eye orienting is coupled from the start to weakly and inadequately controlled head-turning movements. Newborns may orient to track auditory or visual stimuli from objects that are near them and that are displaced or changed slowly. The newborns do therefore possess the outline motor function for looking at things and bringing them to central vision.

When looking, neonates also make orienting movements of all limbs; hands and feet being pointed separately or in various combinations in the direction of the object. There is about the same accuracy with these orienting movements as there is in the direction of regard. Detailed measurements of the arm and hand movements that are aimed toward objects at this stage reveal that the reach and grasp pattern is already present, and that the wrist transport and hand rotation with opening and closing of the fingers, all aimed to the locus of the object of regard or hearing, have approximately the same temporal sequencing as the adult voluntary reach and grasp movement. We call this neonatal activity "prereaching." It is adapted in form to seizing objects, but it is ineffective. Usually the movement does not even extend far enough to reach the object, and the hand is extended then immediately withdrawn.

We have found that ocular orienting (which is saccadic and ballistic) and prereaching arm extensions (which surge and apparently have little visual or proprioceptive guidance), share a common 3 per second beat. This beat also appears in the action of neck muscles that rotate the head in pursuit of an object. When a 2- or 3-month-old tracks an object with head and eye, surges in the contractions of the neck muscles are tightly coupled to the saccades of the eyes; the two vary in frequency between 4 and 2 per second, depending on the overall rate of angular displacement. However, most of the variation of tracking rate is obtained by varying the length of saccadic jumps, not by varying their frequency.

Each of these highly coordinated, synergistic and periodic movement patterns is purposive in the sense that it has a clear shape adapted to the performance of an ultimate conscious operation (looking to see, reaching to grasp and manipulate), but all of them may be produced in elaborate and far from random form when there is no actual object present to serve as goal. All are (in outline) of the same form as adult movements which are clearly voluntary.

Recently, Bower (1974) has used head and eye orienting and prereaching movements to study the perceptual capacities of young infants. He has reported remarkable evidence, from appropriate shaping of reaching-out movements, that perception of the locus, form, and displacement of an object in motion is present in neonates. This leads him to present a theory which differs from that of Piaget in that it supposes a much more precocious capacity for perception of objects as goals for prehension. However, we find that each of the acts upon which the tests of neonatal perception depend, may be formulated by the immature brain without stimuli and presumably without perception of an object. The acts may be constituted in and of themselves as motor programs. This being so, achievement of the perception of a permanent object with identity, that persists through occlusions or transformations of stimuli on which its perception depends, must be related to the elaboration of intention which in the early months have only limited duration and limited receptivity to afferent guidance.

Twitchell (1965) has described the changes of reflex response to proprioceptive (arm stretch) and tactile (touching the hand) stimuli during the first weeks. His analysis gives the impression that the growth of voluntary reaching and grasping is dependent upon development in sensory command over motor patterns. I feel that the essential mechanism is an intentional one which, while specifically receptive to appropriate stimuli, is also organized in neuromotor processes that are developmentally related to body form. Both concerted and independent action of eye and hand develop by differentiation of their action together in a single pattern.

Observation of the growth of the visual and manual exploratory action of infants during the first year brings evidence that this differentiation of joint or several actions of parts, is a complex process. The mechanisms for guidance of proximal (upper arm and shoulder) and distal (forearm) muscles appear to mature at different times (Trevarthen, Hubley, & Sheeran, 1975).

From birth, the complete grasp and pull-in movement is stimulated by stretch of the arm extension muscles. Soon after, moving touch on the thumb side of the hand can cause the same response. At the same time (2-3 weeks) one may obtain clear reaching out towards a visual object with extended hand, this being usually followed immediately by the pull in or flexion movement. In the second and third month, when the muscles of arm and trunk are visibly filling out, the pattern elicited to a seen object gains in form, but it also becomes more vigorous and subject to disruption. When a slow, gentle response occurs, the whole cycle of aimed arm extension and retraction with oriented opening and closing of the hand may be beautifully apparent; but when the movement is more vigorous, the hand usually does not open and the arms flail in poorly aimed swipes. Towards the end of the fourth month the extension of the arm gains power to modulate and redirect itself in opposition to gravity and the inertial forces of the moving limb. At the same time, pulling-in reflexes to stretch extensor muscles diminish. We have shown that sight of the reaching arm is not required to guide it progressively towards the target. It is sufficient for the target to be located visually for the hand to be guided to it.

This heralds the begining of effective reaching to objects. From this point the infant is able, for the first time, to support the extended hand near an object, and to redirect the hand to bring it closer, or even to track a moving object in a chain of connections. Orienting and closing of the hand then becomes controlled by visual or touch information about the place of the object relative to the hand. This achievement starts the exploration of objects by hand to which all theorists attribute great significance for the further growth of intelligence.

But even the manipulation of objects under direct control of focal vision is not dependent entirely on stimuli. Film evidence shows that a separate mechanism for hand shaping in relation to the local form, rather than the general size and location of objects, is growing in parallel with the mechanism for aiming grasp.

Infants begin staring at their partly extended hand while rotating the wrist and opening and closing the fingers well before controlled reaching is achieved at about 16-18 weeks. This "hand regard" was seen by Piaget and considered by him to be hand locating. In fact, it is a form of convergent fovea-hand activity dependent on but separate from the orienting capacities of eye and arm. After 5 months infants who may reach and grasp efficiently, spend increasing amounts of time concentrating on small details (like crumbs on the food tray, string attached to toys, and so on), and on grasping these details carefully with the fingers. Preparatory to this, their visual fixation abilities undergo maturation. It is known that the accommodation of the lens and associated pupillary movements, which are outward signs of regulation of the foveal image on which high-acuity vision depends, mature at about four months. There is evidence that the central, foveal cone mechanisms attain maturity as receptors at this time. All this leads to the conclusion that out of a general orienting function, in which all partial orienting systems are innately coordinated, there are differentiated proximal and distal reafference devices for control of successive stages in the processes of partial orienting and focal attention to detail.

Developments of perceiving, tracking, handling, and remembering objects, which are rapid and extensive throughout the first year, therefore support the idea of different modes of subjective psychological operation related to orienting and attending. The brain mechanisms are related to the hierarchical organization of the body and its parts as the other work we have reviewed suggests. It is interesting that Twitchell (1965) reports a difference in the responses to touch of the two hands of very young infants. We note hand preferences in careful manipulation of objects in the second half of the first year. These preferences undoubtedly relate to innate cerebral lateralization of functions for which there is direct anatomical evidence (Levy, 1976).

Within the first two months infants show a highly elaborate form of activity that is specifically adapted to communication with persons. This is a much higher level or "mode" of operation than those already considered and one that clearly has very special significance for human intelligence. I do not conceive of intelligence as the achievement of an individual child. It is a social phenomenon.

Communicating with Persons

A two-month-old infant is capable of fixed attention to an object, with well-directed gaze, concentrated expression, slightly protruding upper lip giving a highly diagnostic "attentive" expression; and the attempts to reach and grasp as have been outlined. If this baby is then spoken to by the mother a total change in behavior occurs. The child looks closely at her face, principally focusing on her eyes, smiles in response to her speech, and then begins a complex expressive display of face movements, gestures and posturing, frequently looking away from her while most excited. Within 2 or 3 sec the infant looks back to the mother's face and watches her reply with interest. The activities directed to persons, and highly responsive to them, are different in form and in coordination from those directed to objects. The infants clearly have, at this age, different modes of psychological function that distinguish between persons as animate partners for communication, and objects that may simply be observed or reached towards.

Developments I have observed (Trevarthen, 1977b, Trevarthen, Hubley, & Sheeran, 1975) in the communication of infants suggest to me that the fundamental processes of perception and cognition, and also the deeper processes by which voluntary action grows, are in constant competitive interaction with mysterious but very powerful psychological mechanisms that ensure social cooperation in human intelligence. This last function, social cooperation, is of course the most special feature of human intelligence.

When I first began to observe the spontaneous activities of infants systematically, I quickly became impressed with the astonishing precocity of their sensitivity to persons and, above all, their powers of expression which influence attentive adults very strongly.

In the literature, there are many experiments showing that young infants prefer faces to other shapes, selectively attend to eyes, are extremely sensitive to human movement, are attracted to human voice sounds, particularly the female voice speaking softly. It has even been shown recently that two-month-olds perceptually categorize speech sounds in basic phonological forms (Eimas et al., 1971; Trehub, 1973; Eisenberg, 1975); they categorize along the same boundaries of hearing as we adults do when we distinguish physically similar sounds as sharply different. An example of this is the distinction between "ma" and "pa." Piaget (1953), Papousek (1961, 1969), Wolff (1969) and others have noted that one- or two-month-olds will express highly communicative signs of pleasure when they master tasks or engage in games with persons.

We have recently described elaborate communicative interactions between mothers and two- to three-month-olds (Trevarthen, 1974e, 1975b). Mother and infant engage in highly regular, conversationlike exchanges in which it is clear that the infant exercises the primary control of events. The mother, by attending carefully and responding in a friendly way, certainly provides an essential substrate for the baby to communicate, but she is in fact compelled to do so by the very detailed actions of the infant and by the organization into expressive episodes of these actions addressed to her.

Within these cycles of expression, to which the mother responds reciprocally, we find rudiments of the elaborate and culturally modified acts by which adults express their experiences, intentions, and interests to one another. Most astonishing are lip and tongue movements which we label *prespeech,* because they have the outline form of speaking, and because they occur in the appropriate place in the exchange for the function of utterances. Prespeech movements are frequently not voiced, although vocalization is associated with them from the start.

Coupled to prespeech are hand movements that are similar in form to stereotyped gesticulatory movements that adults make in communication. We have distinguished a "hand-wave" pattern and have found from our films that index finger pointing or "indicating" is a social communicative signal that is present in infants as early as the second month. There seem to be other stereotyped gestures of the infant which, though without meaning, are very close in form to gestures common to all races of men—gestures which were accurately described by Darwin (1872) more than a century ago.

The social response of infants takes place over a wide range of levels of animation. Sometimes expressive activity is restricted to the fingers and mouth, the eyes, the whole face, and so on. At other times the whole body is moving in larger bursts usually accompanied by excited shouts or calls that are less finely articulated. The mothers immediately and unconsciously interpret these changes in intensity of animation as expressing feelings and intentions of the infant.

Cutting across changes of excitement are changes of mood. In recent work (Trevarthen, 1977b), in which we systematically modify the mother's response with the aid of instructions to her, we have been able to show that the infant's expression of unhappiness or dejection on the one hand, and happiness or playfulness on the other, is tightly dependent on the "success" of communication. This leads to investigation of the structure of emotionality and its relation to the control of communicative action. I cannot develop this here, but we conclude, in general, that the concept of motivation is mistaken; that emotion regulates the complex mental mode of intersubjectivity, but that it does not drive or motivate it.

It is significant that a very rich period of embryonic communication takes place in the period 6–15 weeks when reaching is described as disappearing. We refer to this period as *primary intersubjectivity*. It establishes the first form of communicative interaction for its own sake. Primary intersubjectivity has become, for us, the prototype of diadic communicative interaction in humans. Adult and infant engage in mutually supportive and complementary acts that constitute a true phatic interaction.

When reaching appears at the end of the fourth month we note exceedingly important changes in the attentional predispositions and in the curiosities and spontaneous intentions of infants. Apparently a major organization of the whole mental system takes place at this time, leading to revolutions in cognitive ability, and also changing completely the rules of communication (Sylvester-Bradley & Trevarthen, 1977; Trevarthen, 1975b). This is the time when our subjects show, invariably, a "cooling" of their interest in chatting with the mother. In many instances babies at this time quite rudely refuse to indulge in friendly, smiling eye-to-eye contact and "protoconversational" exchange. A five-month-old may even actively avoid the mother's gaze, turning his/her head away as soon as she comes close to address the infant. This is done clearly to establish a different balance between attention to the mother and attention to surroundings and to objects nearby. The consequence is that the mother's interest in the infant changes as she is strongly led by the baby to change her tactics; and this leads her to become much more interested in joining in with what the baby is *doing* to objects. She also begins to communicate through objects offered to the baby or received from the baby, rather than by chatting.

After this period of transition we observe the development of a new form of communication, *secondary intersubjectivity*. This is triadic and cooperative play with and about things and experiences shared. No longer is communication merely between the two partners; it now has an outward direction as well, and functions to bring in topics. In the first part of this period of development the topics are established most often by the infant. Later the infant becomes delighted to receive hints about novel forms of activity from adults. In other words, towards the end of the first year the baby becomes a natural pupil to the teacher, that, in turn, the mother has become.

We wish to emphasize that our observations are quite inconsistent with the view that the child's learning ability is molded from without by the mother. Indeed, we think it more correct to say that the pupil role grows in the infant and this causes the mother to take on the teacher role. (The mother is no doubt also adapted to become a teacher in and of herself. She too is human, and it is the interaction of two humans which is developing through changes taking place in both of them.)

A special relationship grows between mother and infant or other primary caretaker and infant, and it is interesting to observe that the transformation of intersubjectivity around the age of six months is much more pronounced for this privileged person. When the baby shows a new refractoriness with the principal partner, other persons who may be described as "friends" are, we note, still treated in a highly sociable way. In other words it is the privileged relationship of the main "attachment" that undergoes most pronounced developmental changes.

For the present I accept a teleological explanation of the appearance of joint interest in tasks and objects. The change takes place as an essential step towards human cooperation. Ultimately the cause is a developmental change in the intersubjective mechanism of the infants brain correlated with changes in mechanisms that govern orientation and prehension directed to objects.

These observations show: (1) that cognitive development in the first year is integrated within social development; and (2) that the whole field of the developing infant intelligence brings together communicative competence and competence of the individual to perceive and operate upon the world of objects on his or her own. I think the dynamics of development, including periodic recessions in new components of performance, reflect mainly the developmental regulations in the social sphere (Trevarthen, 1977c).

Imitation

Maratos (1973) has carried out experiments which prove that very young infants are able to imitate specific acts of the mouth, voice, and hands, and also movements of the head. This imitation has a particular character, and like prereaching, it depends upon subtle state changes in the infant. Only brief intervals of optimal arousal or intentional readiness occur. These are characteristically periods of quiet alertness, that is, the baby is neither extremely active nor somnulent. Because the response is not preceded by well-formed overt orienting and vocalizing behavior, it gives the impression of simply popping out. I would call this type of imitation *magnetic* to emphasize that it is a fairly automatic expression of a complex recognitive and expressive machinery which is as yet not well controlled by reafferent—sensitive orienting systems.

The specificity of imitation (for example, tongue protrusion for tongue protrusion) proves that the neonate possesses the template for recognition without having benefit of learning by association of rudimentary reflexive sensory–motor schemata. It is interesting that such an innate capacity for imitation is firmly denied by behaviorists (e.g., Skinner, 1953, p. 119) with what seems to me to be an arrogant misapplication of the principle of scientific parsimony. Piaget (1962) also believes that the capacity for imitation of movements by parts of the body that the infant cannot see, must be developed with the aid of experience by progressive approximation. Magnetic imitation, we find, occurs first during primary intersubjectivity when the infant is very much involved in self-expression. As I have said, imitation during the second and third months is very different; in fact, reversed. During that time the baby is generally influenced by the support given from the mother and by the reinforcing effect of her sympathetic movements.

Another kind of imitation appears with increased frequency towards five months and develops considerably after that time. This involves the infant in a very marked orientation—an apparently puzzled or curious fixing of attention on the repeatedly presented model. In other words, the infant is led to imitate by an insistent demonstration action of the partner, and does so after much successive approximation through a series of tentative attempts. I would call this *discretionary imitation* because an element of deliberation or choice is evident in it. Piaget (1962) describes this behavior as "imitation through training," and then he calls it "pseudoimitation" and says that it does not last unless continually reinforced (like smiling). However, this type of imitation has benefit for the older infant in that new acts, already outlined in the repertoire of the infant, may be picked up in more elaborate form.

Around nine months the infants frequently becomes involved in imitative games in which some pickup by the mother from the infant is utilized by her, returned to the infant as a model, and then is reconstructed by the infant in some special form. This process leads to private languages of communication special to the mother/infant pair. This is not to say that some degree of deliberation is not evident even in the earliest magnetic imitation. It is clear from some of Maratos' (1973) records of sound production that the infant's imitative sound making is different from spontaneous sound making; it sounds more "strained" or "artificial."

Communication Evolves from Intending and Becomes its Tutor

The evidence for an innate mechanism for communication in infants is overwhelming. Clearly we have only begun to understand its complexity. From birth, infants detect persons and by six or eight weeks of age they begin elaborate acts that function only in the regulation of interpersonal transactions. Experiments to identify the cause of this selective response to persons have failed to show that it is caused only by a few basic innate release mechanisms that are triggered by sign stimuli. The infant is not just reacting to one or two features of face geometry, the pitch of the human voice, lively movement, the contrast in light reflections from the eyes, body contact, body odor. The list is already very large and is not yet complete. The versatile imitative capacities of one-month-old babies suggests that they have a built-in identifier of persons in close functional relation with the mechanism that causes their own acts of communication. For infants to imitate what adults do when they smile, nod their head and speak, wave their hands, or poke out their tongues must be reflected in a system of like design in the infant. Each form of model act must excite the mechanism that causes the same movement or its rudiment in the baby. Seeing the tongue protrude excited protrusion of the tongue.

How, physically, could the infant mind identify persons? What features of their behavior are diagnostic of them? Intentional behavior has a number of features that are not shared with inanimate things, and so an intentional agent may be equipped to respond to others like itself. To control complex movements the brain organizes patterns of motor output which detect themselves as well as their effects that are reflected back from the world as reafference. Given an unchanging, stable environment, the best way to move with control is in preprogramed, ballistic steps. All intentional movements have a saccadic (stepping) quality. Inanimate movement runs downhill, oscillates in simple ways, bounces, but it does not surge in self-generative impulses. Anything that tends to make unprovoked bursts of rhythm, like a spot of reflected sunlight, seems alive. This rhythmical vitality of movement is the first identifier of live company.

When the circumstances of intention are changing, complex, or uncertain, the brain must accurately distinguish self-made change in sensory signals from effects caused from outside. Awareness of the world is facilitated by a special sensitivity to one's own pattern of action. In a society of intentional agents each may detect the output of acts by others, as if they were produced by each agent itself. I believe that animal communication evolves by adaptation of the self-detecting, ego functions of the subject—agent, an adaptation that serves to pick up the effects of others with like subjectivity (Trevarthen, 1977b).

Infants do act with rudimentary intentionality. They can look to see the world; they outline attempts to move in the world and to seize hold of things near them in it. Therefore they possess the outline mechanisms necessary for conscious control of spontaneous acts. Recent experiments (e.g. Bornstein, 1975; Bower, 1974; Eimas et al, 1971; Fantz, 1963; Leehey et al, 1975; Lipsitt, 1969; McKenzie & Day, 1972; Papousek, 1961; Trehub, 1973) disprove the earlier theories that the infant was a confused, shapeless mind, incapable of orderly formulations of all except the absolutely necessary reflexive acts.

The relation between complex plans of action for a subject capable of an infinite variety of movements and perceptual scan with selective attending has been discussed. Attending to what is interesting, relevant, or exciting in surroundings has a natural design. It is progressive, periodic, and selective. Selection is obtained by aiming parts of the body that are specialized for information pickup in one direction and one modality at a time. The acts of orienting and attending may, in turn, give continuous data on the curiosity, recognition, or motivation, that the subject has for surroundings. Since young infants imitate eye, mouth, head, and hand movements appropriately, we know that they are able to separately identify body parts of people confronting them. They are thereby given the basis for observing attentions of others to surroundings. They are also sensitive to mood or feelings as this is transmitted in style of movement, sound of voice, and probably in many other ways.

It is, at first, astonishing to observe the similarity of form and timing between the rudimentary acts of infants and those of adults. This similarity becomes clearer as one makes more exact descriptions. The spontaneous design of a baby's behavior is essentially the same, in outline, as that of an alert aware adult. I believe this underlying generative structure is not merely a producer of acts of attention, but a detector of like behavior in others.

I think that, as the intentions of infants become more elaborate, gaining in discriminative power for objects and gaining in the range of time and space in which they represent conditions for acts, they also develop more complex perceptions and cooperations with other persons. The precocity of infant communications, relative to all the other cognitive things they can do, directed to objects and arrangements in space, suggests that the intersubjective process may become dominant and lead the process of attending and intending to the inanimate things. This explains why conspicuous revolutions in mental functions of infants and children appear to be accompanied by changes in their communication with persons. It is through changes in the way the acts of other persons are perceived that the infant develops new levels in knowledge and plans for action.

In humans the intersubjective mode dominates over the subjective one in the growth of the mind. The intentional infant grows by sharing intentions with others. It is the way we become capable, early in life, of having the kind of intentions about intentions, the kind of attention to experiences that is essential to play, language, and all cooperative work. This is the sense in which one may say culture is innate to man.

The role of shared intention and transmitted attention to experiences for the development of cultural intelligence is obvious. In 100,000 years the universe has been changed by this process. The intelligence of a child we test in IQ measures is more than just affected by the kind of social communication with persons to which each child has been exposed since birth. It is a summary of shared existence. Psychological function in humans is woven of individual experiences in combination with transmitted experience of others, and a special form of mind is required for this interweaving.

I think we are justified, on the basis of the clear functional distinctions observed in infancy, to consider individual or subjective cognitive enterprise to know the physical world as one innate mode of action. Intersubjectivity or psychological communication is another mode. Humans are innately social. They are "socialized" in the sense that plants are "photosynthesized."

To judge from a kind of behavior we have seen from time to time in our laboratory films, when the infant is engaged in some inner process to the exclusion of both persons and things, contemplation is a third primitive mode of activity in the human mind. It is one that regulates both the other outwardly directed and receptive modes.

There is evidence that these great modes of the mind compete for a balance of interaction in development. They are certainly capable of complimentary contributions to intelligence. I believe that differences in their relative strength and in their balance underly the principle kinds of individual difference in human intelligence. I think that recognizing them as real structures will help to understand abnormal minds and difficult periods in the growth of personality.

ACKNOWLEDGMENTS

Research on split-brain monkeys and with commissurotomy patients discussed here was supported by the Hixon Fund of the California Institute of Technology and by a United States Public Health Service grant to Professor Sperry. The infant research of Edinburgh has been supported by the Medical Research Council and Social Science Research Council of the United Kingdom.

The manuscript has been prepared at the Psychology Department of La Trobe University, Bundoora, Victoria, Australia, for whose generous assistance I am most grateful.

REFERENCES

Adrian, E. D. *The basis of sensation.* New York: Norton, 1928.

Bernstein, N. *The cordination and regulation of movement.* London: Pergamon, 1967.

Bogen, J. E. The other side of the brain. I Dysgraphia and dyscopic following cerebral commissurotomy. *Bulletin of the Los Angeles Neurological Society,* 1969, *34,* 73–105.

Bogen, J. E., & Vogel, P. J. Cerebral commissurotomy: A case report *Bulletin of the Los Angeles Neurological Society,* 1962, *27,* 169.

Bornstein, M. H. Qualities of color vision in infancy. *Journal of Experimental Child Psychology,* 1975, *19,* 416–419.

Bower, T. G. R. *Development in infancy.* San Francisco: Freeman, 1974.

Brinkman, J., & Kuypers, H. G. J. M. Split-brain monkey: Cerebral control of ipsilateral and contralateral arm, hand and finger movements. *Science,* 1972, *176,* 536–539.

Brinkman, J., & Kuypers, H. G. J. M. Cerebral control of contralateral and ipsilateral arm hand and finger movements in the split-brain rhesus monkey. *Brain,* 1973, *96,* 653–674.

Brunswik, E. *Perception and the representative design of psychological experiments.* Berkeley, Cal.: University of California Press, 1956.

Darwin, C. *The expression of emotions in man and animals.* Chicago: University of Chicago Press, 1965. (Originally published, 1872.)

Eimas, P., Sigueland, E., Jusczyr, P., & Vigorito, J., Speech perception in infants. *Science,* 1971, *171,* 303–306.

Eisenberg, R. B. *Auditory competence in early life: The roots of communicative behavior.* Balitmore: University Park Press, 1975.

Fantz, R. L. Pattern vision in newborn infants. *Science,* 1963, *140,* 296–297.

Fraenkel, G. S., & Gunn, D. L. *The orientation of animals.* Oxford, England: Clarendon Press, 1940.

Fritsch, G., & Hitzig, E. Über die elektrische Erregbarkeit des Grosshirns, Archiv fur Anatomie, Physiologie und Wissenschaftliche Medicin, *1870,* 37, 300–332.

Gaze, R. M. *The formation of nerve connections.* New York: Academic Press, 1970.

Gazzaniga, M. S. *The bisected brain.* New York: Appleton-Century-Crofts, 1970.

Gibson, J. J. *The senses considered as perceptual systems.* Boston: Houghton-Mifflin, 1966.

Gottlieb, G. (Ed) *Neural and behavioral specificity: Studies on the development of behavior and the nervous system, Vol. 3.* New York: Academic Press, 1976.

Greene, P. H. Problems of organisation of motor systems. In R. Rosen & F. M. Snell (Eds.) *Progress in theoretical biology (Vol. 2).* New York: Academic Press, 1972.

Jacobson, M. *Developmental neurobiology.* New York: Holt, Rinehart, & Winston, 1970.

Kinsbourne, M. Eye and head turning indicates cerebral lateralization. *Science,* 1972, *176,* 539–541.

Kinsbourne, M. Mechanisms of hemispheric interaction in man. In M. Kinsbourne & W. L. Smith (Eds.), *Hemispheric disconnection and cerebral function.* Springfield, Ill.: Charles C Thomas, 1974.

Kuypers, H. G. J. M. The anatomical organisation of the descending pathways and their contributions to motor control, especially in primates. In T. E. Desmedt (Ed.), *New developments in E.M.G and clinical neurophysiology, (Vol. 3).* Basel, Switzerland: Karger, 1973.

Lashley, K. S. The problems of serial order in behavior. In L. A. Jeffress (Ed.), *Cerebral mechanisms in behavior.* New York: Wiley, 1951.

Leehey, S. C., Moskowitz-Cook, A., Brill, S., & Held, R. Oreintational anisotropy in infant vision. *Science,* 1975, *190,* 900–902.

Levy, J. Possible basis for the evolution of lateral specialization of the human brain. *Nature,* 1969, *224,* 614–615.

Levy, J. Psychobiological implications of bilateral asymmetry. In S. Dimond & J. G. Beaumont (Eds.), *Hemisphere function in the human brain.* London: Paul Elek, 1974.

Levy, J. A review of evidence for a genetic component in the determination of handedness. *Behav. Genet.,* 1976, *6,* 429–453.

Levy, J., & Trevarthen, C. Metacontrol of hemispheric function in human split-brain patients. *Journal of Experimental Psychology: Human Perception and Performance,* 1976, *2,* 299–312.

Levy, J., & Trevarthen, C. Perceptual, semantic and phonetic aspects of elementary language processes in split-brain patients. *Brain,* 1977, *100,* 105–118.

Levy, J., Trevarthen, C., & Sperry, R. W. Perception of bilateral chimeric figures following hemispheric deconnection. *Brain,* 1972, *95,* 61–78.

Lipsitt, L. P. Learning capacities of the human infant. In R. J. Robinson (Ed.), *Brain and early behavior: Development in the fetus and infant.* New York: Academic Press, 1969.

Maratos, O. The origin and development of imitation in the first six months of life. Ph.D. thesis. University of Geneva, 1973.

Mark, R. F. *Memory and nerve cell connections.* Oxford England: Clarendon Press, 1974.

McKenzie, B. F., & Day, R. H. Object distance as a determinant of visual fixation in early infancy. *Science,* 1972, *178,* 1108–1110.

Meyer, R. L., & Sperry, R. W. Retinotectal specificity: chemospecificity theory. In G. Gottlieb (Ed.), *Neural and behavioral specificity: Studies on the development of behavior and the nervous system,* Vol. 3. New York: Academic Press, 1976.

Milner, B. Hemispheric specialization: Scope and limits. In F. O. Schmitt & F. G. Worden (Eds.), *The neurosciences: Third study program.* Cambridge, Mass.: M.I.T. Press, 1974.

Mundy-Castle, A. C. Cross-cultural electroencephalographic studies. In J. W. Prescott, M. S. Read, & D. B. Coursin (Eds.), *Brain Function and Malnutrition.* New York: Wiley, 1975.

Nebes, R. D. Dominance of the minor hemisphere in commissurotomized man for the perception of part-whole relationships. In M. Kinsbourne & W. L. Smith (Eds.), *Hemispheric disconnection and cerebral function.* Springfield, Ill.: Charles C Thomas, 1974.

Ornstein, R. F. *The psychology of consciousness.* San Francisco: Freeman, 1972.

Papousek, H. Conditioned head rotation reflexes in the first six months of life. *Acta Pediatrica,* 1961, *50,* 565–576.

Papousek, H. Individual variability in learned responses in human infants. In R. J. Robinson (Ed.), *Brain and Early Behavior: Development in Fetus and Infant.* New York: Academic Press, 1969.

Piaget, J. *The psychology of intellignece.* New York: Harcourt Brace, 1950.

Piaget, J. *The origins of intelligence in children.* London: Routledge & Kegan Paul, 1953.

Piaget, J. *Play, dreams and imitation in early childhood.* New York: Norton, 1962.

Pribram, K. H. *Languages of the brain.* Englewood Cliffs, N. J.: Prentice-Hall, 1971.

Skinner, B. F. *Science and Human Behavior.* New York: Macmillan, 1953.

Sperry, R. W. Neural basis of spontaneous optokinetic response produced by visual inversion. *Journal of Comparative Physiological Psychology,* 1950, *43,* 482–489.

Sperry, R. W. Mechanisms of neural maturation. In S. S. Stevens (Ed.), *Handbook of experimental psychology.* New York: Wiley, 1951.

Sperry, R. W. Neurology and the mind-brain problem. *American Scientist,* 1952, *40,* 291–312.

Sperry, R. W. Cerebral organization and behavior. *Science,* 1961, *133,* 1749–1757.

Sperry, R. W. Chemoaffinity in the orderly growth of nerve fiber patterns and connections. *Proceedings of the National Academy of Sciences of the United States of America,* 1963, *50,* 703–710.

Sperry, R. W. Embryogenesis of behavioral nerve nets. In R. L. DeHaan & H. Ursprung (Eds.), *Organogenesis.* New York: Holt. Rinehart & Winston, 1965.

Sperry, R. W. Mental unity following surgical disconnection of the cerebral hemispheres. *The Harvey Lecture Series,* 1968, *62,* 293–323.

Sperry, R. W. Perception in the absence of the neocortical commissures. *Research Publication Series: Association for Research in Nervous and Mental Diseases,* 1970, *48,* 123–138.

Sperry, R. W. Lateral specialization in the surgically separated hemispheres. In F. O. Schmitt & F. G. Worden (Eds.), *The neurosciences: Third study program.* Cambridge Mass.: M.I.T. Press, 1974.(a)

Sperry, R. W. Mental phenomena as causal determinants in brain function. In G. Globus, G. Maxwell & I Savodnik (Eds.), *Mind and brain: Philosophic and scientific approaches to the single "world knot."* New York: Plenum, 1974. (b)

Sperry, R. W., Gazzaniga, M. S., & Bogen, J. E. The neocortical commissures: Syndrome of hemisphere deconnection. In P. J. Vinken & G. W. Bruyn (Eds.), *Handbook of clinical neurology.* Amsterdam: North-Holland Publ., 1969.

Sylvester-Bradley, B., & Trevarthen, C. Baby talk as an adaptation to the infant's com munication. In N. Waterson & K. Snow (Eds.), *Development of communication: Social and pragmatic factors in language acquisition.* London: Wiley, 1977.

Trehub, S. E. Infants' sensitivity to vowel and tonal contrasts. *Developmental Psychology,* 1973, *9,* 91–96.

Trevarthen, C. Processur visuels interhémisphériques localisés dans le tronc cérébral. Leur mise en évidence sur des singes à cerveau dédoublé. *Comptes rendus des Séances de la Société de Biologie,* 1963, *157* (No. 11), 2019–2022.

Trevarthen, C. Functional interactions between the cerebral hemispheres of the split-brain monkey. In E. G. Ettlinger (Ed.), *Functions of the corpus callosum.* (Ciba Foundation Study Group, No. 20). London: Churchill, 1965.

Trevarthen, C. Two mechanisms of vision in primates. *Psychologische Forschung,* 1968, *31,* 299–337.

Trevarthen, C. Experimental evidence for a brain-stem contribution to visual perception in man. *Brain Behaviour and Evolution,* 1970, *3,* 338–352.

Trevarthen, C. Brain bisymmetry and the role of the corpus callosum in behaviour and conscious experience. In J. Cernacek & F. Podovinsky (Eds.), *Cerebral interhemispheric relations.* Bratislave: Slovak Academy of Sciences, 1972.

Trevarthen, C. Behavioral embryology. In E. C. Carterette & M. P. Friedman (Eds.), *Handbook of perception* (Vol. 3). New York: Academic Press, 1973.

Trevarthen, C. Analysis of cerebral activities that generate and regulate consciousness in commissurotomy patients. In S. J. Dimond & J. G. Beaumont (Eds.), *Hemisphere function in the human brain.* London, England: Paul Elek, 1974. (a)

Trevarthen, C. L'action dans l'espace et la perception de l'espace. Mechanismes cérébraux de base. In F. Bresson et al (Eds.), *De l'espace corporel a l'espace écologique.* Paris: Presses Universitaires de France, 1974. (b)

Trevarthen, C. Cerebral embryology and the split brain. In M. Kinsbourne & W. L. Smith (Eds.), *Hemispheric disconnection and cerebral function.* Springfield, Ill.: Charles C Thomas, 1974. (c)

Trevarthen, C. Functional relations of disconnected hemisphere with the brain stem and with each other: Monkey and man. In M. Kinsbourne & W. L. Smith (Eds.), *Hemispheric disconnection and cerebral function.* Springfield, Ill.: Charles C Thomas, 1974. (d)

Trevarthen, C. The psychobiology of speech development. In E. Lenneberg (Ed.), *Language and brain: Developmental aspects, Neurosciences Research Program Bulletin,* 1974, *12,* 570–585. (e)

Trevarthen, C. Growth of visumotor coordination in infants. *Journal of Human Movement Studies,* 1975, *1,* 57. (a)

Trevarthen, C. Early attempts at speech. In R. Lewin (Ed.), *Child alive.* London: Maurice Temple Smith, 1975. (b)

Trevarthen, C. Psychological activities after forebrain commissurotomy in man. Concepts and methodological hurdles in testing. In F. Michel & B. Schott (Eds.), *Les syndromes de disconnection calleuse chez l'homme.* Lyon: Höpital Neurologique, 1975. (c)

Trevarthen, C. Manipulative strategies of baboons and the origins of cerebral asymmetry. In M. Kinsbourne (Ed.), *The asymmetrical function of the brain.* Cambridge England: Cambridge University Press, 1977. (a)

Trevarthen, C. Descriptive studies of infant behaviour. In H. R. Schaffer (Ed.), *Studies in mother-infant interaction.* London: Academic Press, 1977. (b)

Trevarthen, C. Basic patterns of psychogenetic change in infancy. In H. Nathan (Ed.), *Dips in learning.* (Proceedings of the O.E.C.D Conference, St Paul de Vence, March, 1975), 1977. (c)

Trevarthen, C. Neuroembryology and the development of perception. In F. Falkner & J. M. Tanner (Eds.), *Human Growth: A Comprehensive Treatise.* New York: Plenum. 1977. (d)

Trevarthen, C., Hubley, P., & Sheeran, L. Les activités innées du nourrisson. *La Recherche,* 1975, *6,* 447–458.

Trevarthen, C., & Sperry, R. W. Perceptual unity of the ambient visual field in human commissurotomy patients. *Brain,* 1973, *96,* 547–570.

Twitchell, T. E. the automatic grasping responses of infants. *Neuropsychologia,* 1965, *3,* 247–259.

Von Holst, E., & Mittelstaedt, E. Das Reafferenzprinzip. *Naturwissenschaften,* 1950, *37,* 464–476.

Watson, J. B. *Behavior: An introduction to comparative psychology.* New York: Holt Rinehart, & Winston, 1914.

Whitteridge, D. Visual projections to the cortex. In R. Jung (Ed.), *Handbook of sensory physiology, Vol. VII/3/B.* Berlin: Springer, 1973.

Wolff, P. H. The natural history of crying and other vocalisations in early infancy. In B. M. Foss (Ed.), *Determinants of infant behaviour,* Vol. IV, 1969.

Yakovlev, P. I. Telencephalon 'impar', 'semipar' and 'totopar'. Morphogenetic, tectogenetic and architectonic definitions. *International Journal of Neurology,* 1968, *6,* 245–265.

Yakovlev, P. I., & Lecours, A. R. The myelogenetic cycles of regional maturation of the brain. In A. Minkowski (Ed.), *Regional development of the brain in early life.* Oxford and Edinburgh: Blackwell, 1967.

Zaidel, D., & Sperry, R. W. Memory impairment following commissurotomy in man. *Brain,* 1974, *97,* 263–272.

Zaidel, E. Auditory language comprehension in the right hemisphere following cerebral commissurotomy and hemispherectomy: A comparison with child language and aphasia. In E. Zurif and A. Caramazza (Eds.), *The acquisition and breakdown of language: Parallels and divergences.* Baltimore: Johns Hopkins University Press, 1976.

7
Attended and Unattended Processing Modes: The Role of Set for Spatial Location[1]

Michael I. Posner
Mary Jo Nissen[2]
William C. Ogden[3]

University of Oregon

EDITORS' INTRODUCTION

The distinction between ambient and focal perception emphasizes information about where *something is as opposed to* what *it is. The nature and identity of objects is more usually defined by their sensory qualities than by their position in space. Michael Posner, Mary Jo Nissen, and William Ogden apply chronometric techniques to ascertain whether position information is functionally processed in a different manner than sense modality information is processed. The functional processing difference on which their investigation is focused is that of attentional conscious perception as opposed to automatic unconscious perception. The authors find it useful in making this processing distinction to invoke "set"—one of the classical directive perceptual concepts. For them, set "involves the deliberate turning of attention toward the expected source of an item." In contrast to the relatively narrow meaning of set used in much of the history of psychology, this usage implicates set in a very broad sense, characteristic of processing mode.*

[1] Portions of this chapter were presented to the Psychonomics Society November 1973 and November 1975.

[2] Now at Department of Ophthalmology; University of Chicago Medical School.

[3] Now at Department of Psychology; New Mexico State University.

INTRODUCTION

One of the fundamental differences between processing modes is the distinction between exogenous, automatic, passive processes and centrally controlled, active, attended processes. While these processing modes usually appear as rivals in psychological theories, the persistence of the dichotomy undoubtedly arises in the fact that humans characteristically show both forms of processing. Without "habits," which allow automatic processing, life would place intolerable burdens on the highest integrative levels; but without endogenous plans, which change the significance of input, the human system would hardly be as flexible as both casual observation and experimentation reveal.

Automatic and Attended Processing

It is doubtful that psychological theories will soon be able to reduce either form of processing to the other. In our current state it appears necessary to develop frameworks broad enough to accommodate both modes of processing in the hope that experimentation conducted within such frameworks will produce a better empirical grasp of the two modes and their relations. Posner and Snyder (1975) attempted to define operational differences between automatic and attended processing modes. Three indicants exist that may be used to assess the automatic activation of psychological pathways: (1) activation may occur without intention by the subject; (2) without conscious awareness; and (3) in parallel with the activation of other pathways. In contrast, attended processes are intentional, give rise to conscious awareness, and tend to prevent the output of any other pathways from having access to attention.

Cost—Benefit Analysis

The differences between the parallel activation of automatic processes and the more serial character imposed by active attention provide a method for separating the two modes (Posner & Snyder, 1975). Automatic activation of a pathway by an input item produces facilitation (benefit) in the speed of processing subsequent items that share the same activated pathway. Attended processing also provides benefit to new items sharing the same pathways, but produces widespread inhibition (costs) in the processing of items that use different pathways. The costs arise from the need to shift attention from the pathway to which it has previously been committed to the new pathway. Thus attention to one pathway does not prevent automatic processes from operating on new input, but does reduce the availability of attention. Since attention is often needed to produce overt responses, costs in RT and related performance measures can be used to indicate the reduced availability of attention.

Posner and Snyder (1975) provide evidence that many complex aspects of processing simple letter and word stimuli may take place without attention as defined above. A priming stimulus may facilitate the processing of a subsequent array without producing any cost if an unexpected array should occur. However, if careful attention is paid to the prime it will produce costs along with benefits. When both benefits and costs are involved the former accrue more rapidly. This asymmetry in the time course of cost and benefit is taken as evidence that benefits in this situation arise from both automatic and attended processing, while costs accompany only the latter.

Although much internal processing of input items can proceed without active attention, it is possible to direct attention toward these same processes. In many situations attention is directed at the highest levels of coding, but this strategy will change with task demands. Fluent readers are frequently aware only of the word meanings, but increasing the difficulty of the material will often produce more careful analysis of orthographic and phonetic levels. The cost–benefit analysis outlined here can be used to study the ability of subjects to direct attention toward processes that may normally occur automatically.

The main theme of this investigation involves instructed shifts in the balance between attended and unattended processing, for which we use the term *set*.

Set

Set is one of the oldest and most widely used concepts in psychology (Gibson, 1941). While the term has been used in many ways, we use it in this investigation to signify processes involved in turning attention to a source of input signals that arise at some location in the environment. As we view it, set is an active process that arises from the subject's knowledge about the nature of the input to be received. The active nature of set is quite important. In previous work we have found that subjects have a general bias toward the visual modality (Posner, Nissen, & Klein, 1976) which they must actively overcome if nonvisual input codes are important. This bias, like the automatic activation that a letter or word will produce, does have important consequences for subsequent processing, but we will not use the term set for these effects. According to our usage, set involves the deliberate turning of attention toward the expected source of an item.

Within our general framework, studies of set should tell us something about the limits of attentional control over the processing of input items. It seems to us that one of the most fundamental questions to be asked about set is how one prepares to take in information from a particular place in the world. Each stimulus with which an organism interacts appears to occupy a particular position in space. Thus, we frequently attend to some source of signals, and this is usually accompanied by motor activity addressed toward the source. Yet little is known about the time course of such sets—the mechanisms required to effect them, or whether the sets are directed toward all stimuli arising from that position or only toward stimuli in a particular modality.

In this chapter we attempt to analyze sets induced by instructions to attend to a *source* of sensory signals. In the first experiments we trace the time course of this type of set without any effort to dissect the mechanisms through which it operates. In the second series of experiments we examine the role of peripheral sensory adjustments (eye movements) and motor preparation in mediating the set. In the third series of experiments we seek to separate attention toward a position in external space (object) from a pathway in the brain. In the final section we consider the implications of our results for an integration of theories of set.

EXPERIMENT 1: THE TIME COURSE OF SET

Method

In this experiment we asked the subjects to fixate on a central visual position. The position consists of a center line through a box occupying about $3°$ of visual angle. The stimulus was an X presented either to the left or the right of the center line. When the X occurred to the left of center, the subject was instructed to press the left key as quickly as possible, and when the X appeared to the right of center, to press the right key as quickly as possible.

Each subject participated in 6 blocks of 32 trials in each of 3 experimental sessions. The blocks differed only in the length of time between a warning signal and the imperative stimulus. These values were either 0 (no warning signal) or intervals of 50, 150, 300, 500, or 1000 msec. On half the trials the warning signal was a plus sign; on the other half it was an arrow pointing either left or right. In each block, 13 of the trials had the arrow pointing to the side on which the imperative stimulus would occur and 3 trials had it pointing in the opposite direction. Thus, the arrow was a valid cue to the position of the stimulus and response .8 of the time. The order of intervals was assigned randomly to each subject so that over 6 subjects, each interval appeared one time in each order on each day.

A trial began with exposure of the warning cue for the interval specified by the foreperiod. This was followed by the imperative stimulus which appeared $1°$ below the warning cue and either $.5°$ to the left or $.5°$ to the right of the center line. Following each response, feedback as to the correctness and speed of the response was presented for .5 sec, followed by a variable intertrial interval of .5 to 3 sec. After each block there was a rest period followed by the next block. Subjects participated over a 3-day period; the first day's data was not used.

Results

The response times for the second and third day were averaged and are shown in Figure 1, as are errors in Figure 2. The time course of benefit for the expected event is similar to that found by Sanders (1972) in a similar task. There are two important aspects to these data. Highly significant costs and benefits are found even when the cue leads the stimulus by only 50 msec. These effects, which are most striking in the errors, tend to increase over the first 150 msec following input and then decline. If an unexpected stimulus follows the arrow by as little as 150 msec, performance approaches chance. Of the 8 subjects, 6 show very strong peaks in error or reaction time at some intermediate value of foreperiod. These results suggest very strongly that the process of set is an active one. During the time that the subjects are developing a set, they are very susceptible to making errors if the wrong stimulus occurs. Once a set has been achieved, the error rate subsides somewhat, although very significant cost and benefits are still present.

It should be noted that the costs and benefits found in this task are nearly symmetric, particularly in the reaction-time data. Because this is a task of relatively low error rate, there is little room for a benefit in errors, and thus costs and benefits there are less symmetric.

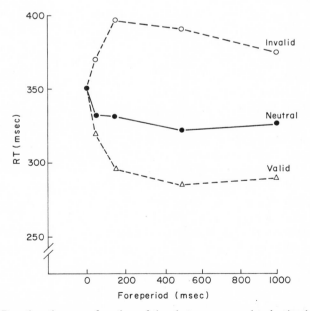

FIGURE 1   Reaction time as a function of time between cue and task stimulus for neutral, valid, and invalid position cues.

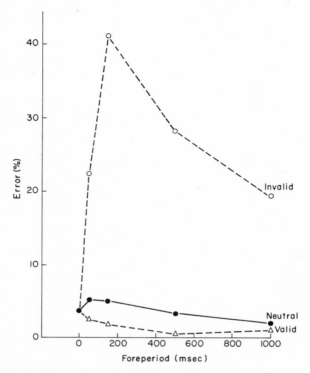

FIGURE 2   Errors as a function of time between cue and task stimulus for neutral, valid, and invalid position cues.

The neutral condition shows improvements in response time with foreperiod and increases in error at short foreperiods. This speed—accuracy tradeoff is the usual result of changes in phasic alertness that accompany noninformative warning signals (Posner, Klein, Summers, & Buggie, 1973; Klein & Kerr, 1974).

Discussion

Despite the experiment's very striking results, the mechanisms that mediate the result are unclear. A wide variety of "stimulus" and "response" mechanisms might be postulated. Four mechanisms that could produce this result are outlined:

1. One might expect a preparatory eye movement from the fixation stimulus toward the expected event. If such eye movements were effective one would expect better processing of the expected stimulus. In this experiment, we did not monitor the subject's eyes.

2. The subject may shift attention to a position corresponding to the likely input without actual changes in fixation. This would be a set mediated not by a direct change in the sense organ but by a change in the way in which the subject examines the input arising from the stimulus. Thus, any stimulus arising from the position in space to which the subject focused attention ought to be facilitated.

3. Note that such a mechanism could in principle be differentiated from a third mechanism which suggests that the set is mediated by a shift of attention to a position in the brain that would be contacted by the external event. The separation requires the use of multimodal stimulation which arises from a common position in the external world, but involves different input pathways.

4. The set might be carried by specific motor tendencies that have nothing to do with enhancement of the stimulus input. In our experiment, the subject could simply prime the muscles involved in the left or right index finger and obtain the set in this way.

In the remainder of the chapter we report experiments that are designed to help discriminate among these various accounts.

ATTENTIONAL CONTROL OF HAND AND EYE

There is little question that the position of eye fixation is related to attention. This fact has led to an enormous interest in the study of eye movements as a way of investigating attention (Kahneman, 1973). However, the fundamental questions of the relation of eye movement and eye position to "set" have not been settled. The question can be divided into two parts. The first deals with the degree of attention required to redirect the eyes. In many ways saccades seem to be forced upon us without the need for a conscious decision. On the other hand, we may choose to inhibit saccades or to make them voluntarily even without an external stimulus. In Experiment 2 we compare directly the control of hand and eye by attentional mechanisms. The second part of the question has to do with the relation of eye position to what is currently being attended. We frequently judge the attention of a person by eye position, but it seems possible for a subject to be looking in one place and to attend to another modality or even perhaps another position in visual space. In Experiment 3 we examine the relation between attention and the environmental location of stimuli.

In addition to anecdotal reports there are experimental reasons for believing that changes in eye position to visual stimuli are more automatic than other responses studied in the laboratory such as the key press discussed in the last section:

1. Eye movements are ballistic, or nearly so (Komoda, Festinger, Phillips, Duckman, & Young, 1973; Westheimer, 1954). Ballistic movements are more

difficult to control once initiated than are other types of movement. In addition the eye muscles give rise to poor proprioceptive feedback. For these reasons monitoring eye movements may require little attention.

2. The movement of the eyes is not much affected by the number of alternative stimuli to which one might move (Saslow, 1967). While it is not certain whether stimulus uncertainty affects eye movements at all, there is little question that the direct movement of the eyes toward positions in space is only slightly affected by stimulus uncertainty. This is symptomatic of a highly automated system.

3. The time between input and firing of collicular cells related to movement of the eyes is very short (Goldberg & Wurtz, 1972).

None of these three behavioral results is unique to eye movements. Other types of movement also may be ballistic, show little or no uncertainty effects, and involve rapid responses of motor cells. Thus, the eye-movement system may require minimal attention, but it can be brought under attentional control if so desired.

It is often assumed that the initiation of eye movements is quite separate from the systems that control other kinds of movement. This is undoubtedly true in a physiological sense, but it is less clear functionally. Megaw & Armstrong (1973) found some evidence for functional separation of the eye and hand systems. They showed that both hand and eye were affected by stimulus uncertainty, but that there was little change in reaction time when the two response systems were combined. They also reported that directional errors were far more frequent for the hand than the eye and thus a common error resulted in movement of the eye and hand in opposite directions. In this section we use methods similar to those of Megaw to determine the degree to which anticipatory eye movements are required for the set effects obtained in the last section and also to attempt to understand the degree of independence of the response systems that control hand and eye.

Experiment 2: Choice Reaction Time

Method. Subjects fixated a central cross on a cathode ray tube. The task stimulus was a .2° square of light that was presented 6.9° to the left or right of the fixation. The task was to move to the stimulus as quickly as possible. In Condition 1, subjects moved a lever toward the stimulus but were instructed to maintain fixation. In Condition 2 the subjects were instructed to move their eyes to the stimulus but not to move the lever. In Condition 3 subjects were asked to move both lever and eyes to the stimulus. Conditions were blocked in sequences of 96 trials. Subjects ran in 1 block of each condition on each of 3 days. Within each condition 1 of 3 cues, either a plus sign or a left or right arrow was displayed 1 sec before the task stimulus. If the plus sign was presented, the probability of the test stimulus appearing in either direction was equal; an arrow indicated a .8 probability of the event occurring in the indicated direction and a .2 probability of occurring in the opposite direction.

Two separate experiments were run that differed only in feedback conditions. In the no-feedback study subjects were given no information on their performance. In the feedback study subjects were given information on the RT for the hand, eye, or both, depending on condition. Eye movements were monitored by electrodes attached to the temporal aspect of each eye. A minicomputer controlled the stimulus sequence, located the onset of the saccade and lever movement for each trial, and displayed feedback information. All anticipatory movements were recorded and analyzed separately.

Results The results are reaction times for eye- and hand-movement systems for Days 2 and 3. All anticipation and directional errors have been removed from the analysis. Results for the eye-movement-only and hand-movement-only conditions are presented in Figure 3. The same results for the simultaneous hand and eye conditions are presented in Figure 4. The eye-system RTs are about 100 msec faster than the hand-movement RTs. It should be noted that our hand-movement measurement includes time required for the lever to reach the end position and thus overestimates RT. Megaw and Armstrong (1973) found that the hand-movement latencies measured by an accelerometer, were about 40 msec longer than the eye-movement latencies. However, both hand and eye

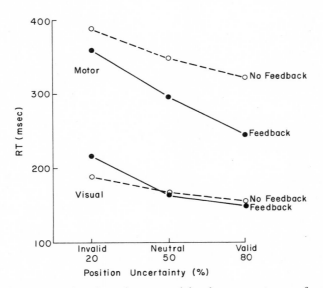

FIGURE 3 Correct reaction times for eye and hand movements as a function of cue condition (position uncertainty) for each feedback condition. All data are from eye alone and hand alone conditions of movement.

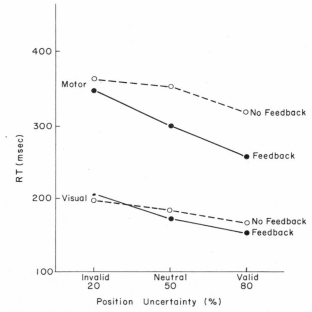

FIGURE 4 Correct reaction times for eye and hand movements as a function of cue condition (position uncertainty) for each feedback condition. All data from combined eye- and hand-movement blocks.

systems show significant effects of the expectancy manipulation: nearly symmetric costs and benefits due to expectancy in both systems.

Since the present data for the hand-movement system are free of artifacts due to anticipatory eye movements, it is clear that the set effects found in the first experiment cannot be dependent on overt eye activity. Even though the stimulus display, response, and method are quite different, the costs and benefits in this study are almost exactly the same size as those obtained in the first experiment with a 1000-msec cue interval.

The effect of the expectancy manipulation on the eye system is about half of that on the hand system (cost + benefit = 90 versus 45 msec). These differences are systematic across subjects and are of almost exactly the same size as those obtained by Megaw and Armstrong (1973). The smaller effects of directional uncertainty on the eye system can be interpreted in terms of the relative automaticity of the eye-movement system. Another interpretation might be that smaller effects are found with the eye system because of their overall faster RTs. However, this latter argument is weakened by the similarity of our results to those of Megaw and Armstrong who report motor RTs much more similar to eye-movement RTs than those in our study; and by a finding (subsequently

TABLE 1
Percentage of Visual Anticipation Errors

	Visual trials only			Visual and motor trials		
	20	50	80	20	50	80
No feedback	5.5	.9	4.5	3.6	.7	1.9
Feedback	9.1	2.1	6.8	7.0	3.7	6.3

reported in this chapter) showing that compatibility effects are much larger for the eye-movement system than for the hand-movement system.

There are a number of interesting differences between the way the eye-movement system and hand-movement system are affected by the imperative stimulus and the subjects' expectancies. Prior to the occurrence of the imperative stimulus, the eye-movement system is very much more affected by the expectancy manipulations than is the hand-movement system. Visual-anticipation errors occurred frequently as shown in Table 1. Their frequency is increased both by feedback and by reduced directional uncertainty from the cue, indicating that the errors are under the control of expectancy. Motor anticipations were essentially nonexistent in our experiment. This could be due to our less sensitive method of measuring the hand versus eye responses; however, Megaw and Armstrong (1973) also report that anticipatory errors were largely visual.

Once the stimulus occurs, the situation reverses and the eye is far less affected by expectancies than is the hand. This is most striking in the occurrence of directional errors (see Table 2). These occur much more frequently for the hand responses than for the eye. Under feedback conditions the hand moves in the direction of the expectancy and opposite to the direction of the stimulus five times as often as the eye does. The degree of independence of the two systems is highlighted by the relative frequency of these errors involving the movement of hand and eye in different directions. The tendency for the eye to be less influenced by attentional control than the hand in the presence of the task stimulus is also illustrated by the very weak effects of feedback conditions on

TABLE 2
Percentage of Directional Errors

	Trials								
	Visual alone			Motor alone			Both		
	20	50	80	20	50	80	20	50	80
No feedback	1.9	.4	.6	2.4	.8	.7	0	0	.5
Feedback	2.4	1.3	.7	12.0	2.5	.2	1.9	.2	0

the eye-movement latencies as compared to the hand movement-latencies (see Figures 3 and 4).

In summary, it appears that both hand and eye can be influenced by the subject's conscious attention, but that the visual stimulus exerts a much stronger control over the eye than over the hand. Thus, expectancies seem to dominate the eye-movement system only in the absence of a task stimulus, while they frequently dominate the hand even in the presence of the stimulus event.

Experiment 3: Simple Reaction Time

Both hand- and eye-movement systems show costs and benefits of about the same size regardless of whether the two systems are used alone or together. Clearly neither set effect depends on the other system. However, it is not clear whether the sets are mediated entirely by the control of the muscular output of each system or whether they also depend on the knowledge that the subject has about the source of the input. Neither our study nor that of Megaw and Armstrong (1973) considers the role of input location expectancies per se.

A number of years ago Mowrer, Rayman, and Bliss (1940) and Mowrer (1941) conducted a number of studies illustrating the effect of set independent of differential response priming. To do this they used a simple reaction time (RT) task but varied the modality or location of successive inputs. They found that successive stimuli in the same modality led to faster RTs to stimuli in that modality and delays when the modality was shifted. Since only one response was used, this result led them to suggest that the set obtained did not involve differential motoric processes. However, when they varied the spatial location of visual stimuli they found no effects of manipulating the subject's knowledge of stimulus location.

More recently, there has been a great deal of dispute about whether spatial uncertainty reduces stimulus discriminability when eye position is controlled. A number of investigators have argued that it does not, at least in an empty visual field (Grindley & Townsend, 1968; Mertens, 1956; Shiffrin & Gardner, 1972). Others have argued that knowledge of the signal location can improve performance even when eye position is held constant (Engel, 1974; Ericksen & Hoffman, 1973; Smith & Blaha, 1969). We studied two conditions to determine whether the set effects on RT would occur in the absence of differential responding.

Method.   In both conditions the same stimulus arrangement and cueing procedures were used as those described in the two previous experiments. In the first condition a total of 13 subjects were tested for 2 days. On 1 day they were instructed on each trial to move their eyes and hand in 1 direction (for example, to the left) and on the other day in the opposite direction in response to either stimulus. The second condition involved 8 additional subjects tested for 2 days each. On each day they received 300 trials, 1/3 with each cueing condition (see Experiment 2). They were provided a single key which they were to press with the right index finger whenever any test stimulus appeared. In both experiments stimulus uncertainty was the same as in the previous choice RT experiment; but since only a single response was possible, there was no way the subject's response could be differentially prepared based upon the cue validity.

Results. The results for the key-press condition are considered first since that experiment was simpler for the subjects and for the experimenters to interpret. Figure 5 shows reaction time as a function of cuing condition for the second day of the experiment. The costs and benefits are symmetrical and somewhat larger than those obtained for the eyes in the choice experiment, but somewhat smaller than those for the hand in the choice experiment. Figure 6 shows the effect of practice on the RTs as a function of cuing condition. It appears that the functions have reached a steady level by the second day, from which the times given in Figure 5 were taken.

Approximately 4% of all trials in this experiment involved an anticipatory eye movement. These trials were marked and the reaction times accumulated separately. The RT for trials with no anticipatory eye movement and for those with such a movement are given in Figure 7. The figure shows that RTs following an

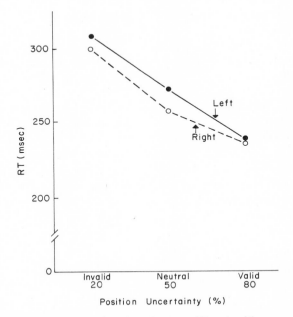

FIGURE 5 Simple motor RT as a function of cue condition (position uncertainty) for task stimuli presented to the left and right of fixation.

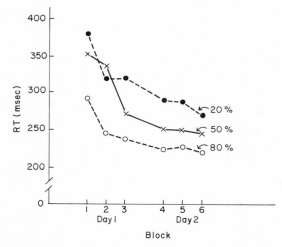

FIGURE 6   Practice functions for simple RT as a function of cue condition.

anticipatory eye movement are actually somewhat longer than are those for those trials in which the subject maintains fixation. Even if it were the case that some anticipatory eye activity was not picked up by our electrooculographic (EOG) technique, it is unlikely that this would have aided RT performance in our task.

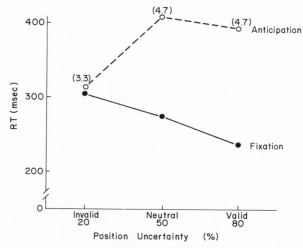

FIGURE 7   Reaction times in simple RT study for trials in which fixation was maintained and those for which anticipation movements occurred. Parentheses indicate percentage of anticipation errors.

The results of the simple RT study using combined eye and hand movements are somewhat more complex. On half the trials the stimulus event occurred on the same side as the instructed response (compatible) and on half the trials it occurred on the opposite side (incompatible).

As might be anticipated, the incompatible conditions are much more difficult for subjects to perform. Figure 8 shows the difference in RT for compatible and incompatible RTs for hand and eye. The most important point in this figure is that eye RTs are more affected by compatibility than are hand RTs. This is opposite the interaction found between response type and expectancy (see Figure 3), and thus it appears unlikely that expectancy has a smaller effect on the eye merely because the eye RTs are faster. It is consistent with the general point that the eye is more controlled by the visual stimulus input than is the hand.

Because this experiment is made very difficult by mixing compatible and incompatible movements, the costs and benefits obtained from expectancy are hard to interpret. Subjects tended to do better when the movement was in accord with their expectancy even if the stimulus was not. This result suggests an ability to set the responding eye muscles. Even clearer evidence for this proposition comes from an examination of the average times of subjects in the simple RT condition and in the corresponding choice RT conditions. The stimulus uncertainty is the same, but the compatible RTs are significantly faster in the

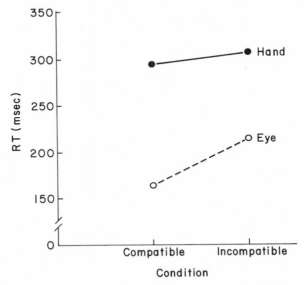

FIGURE 8 Simple RTs for eye and hand movements in combined blocks as a function of whether the test stimulus was presented in the direction of the movement (compatible) or in the opposite direction (incompatible).

simple condition, suggesting that subjects must be able to get ready to execute a particular muscular response with the eyes.

When we consider all the experiments outlined in this section it seems reasonable to conclude that set for spatial position may be mediated by a central system independent of overt eye movement or differential response priming. It is also established that the subjects can voluntarily prime the eye muscles to produce more efficient movement in the direction chosen by the subject. Finally, both hand and eye movements are under the general control of expectancies about where signals will occur and where responses are to be made. However, the eye movement system is so strongly influenced by the occurrence of visual input that expectancies and feedback appear to play a minor role once the visual input occurs.

Our demonstration that prior knowledge of stimulus position influences the speed of processing that stimulus event suggests that attentional mechanisms can be turned toward an input item prior to response selection. We explore the level of this effect in the next section.

INTERNAL VS. EXTERNAL LOCUS OF ATTENTION

Some of the benefits of set in our prototypical experiment must involve improvements in performance that are not due either to peripheral eye movements or to muscular tendencies. In these experiments, it is possible that the subjects attempt to turn their attention to locations in space even without moving external receptors or biasing responses. The way the subjects might do this seems to interact with the sort of model one has about how location is coded in the central nervous system. Phenomologically based models imply that position in space is essentially a multimodal concept based on the tendency of objects to exist at particular locations in the environmental field. On the other hand, physiologically based views imply that subjects may be turning their attention either to a particular hemisphere, or to some location in the nervous system which would be sensitive to the modality of the stimulation presented. Mowrer *et al.* (1940) showed that subject's expectancy about whether a stimulus would be auditory or visual could affect reaction time. Moreover, in our previous work (Posner *et al.,* 1976) costs and benefits were shown when subjects knew in advance whether to direct their attention to the auditory or visual modality. In those studies, the auditory information was presented over earphones, while the visual information was presented on a screen about .33 m in front of the subject. Thus, the locations in external space occupied by the signals were quite different. There is no way to tell whether the subject's attention is directed to different external positions in space marked by the input or whether it is directed to the pathway taken by that modality internally in the brain. In experiment 4 we decided to attack this question directly.

Experiment 4

Method. Subjects were provided with a pair of stimulus–response boards, each one of which consisted of a light and vibrator mounted together on a single board that also contained two keys. For each hand the vibrator rested under the subject's middle finger such that the little finger and thumb rested on keys and the light was adjacent to the subject's middle finger. In the center of the subject's field was an oscilloscope display. The subject's task was to determine whether the signal received was strong or weak. Two values of light and vibration were chosen such that subjects were easily able to discriminate the strong signal from the weak one.

Subjects worked for 5 consecutive days. On each trial they were shown 1 of 5 cues for 2000 msec, followed by the visual or tactile imperative stimulus. The cues could be an arrow pointing to the left or right, a plus sign, or the letters V or T. Each cue was valid 80% of the time and invalid 20% of the time. The plus sign was followed equally often by all possible signals. The subject was asked to press both thumbs if the stimulus was strong and to press the two little fingers if the stimulus was weak. Following each response the subjects received feedback as to the correctness of the response and the speed with which it was made. There was counterbalancing of the various conditions so that when the visual cue was presented, for example, the likelihood that the stimulus would occur left and right were equal and vice versa for the position cues.

Results. The basic data of the experiment consists of the costs and benefits obtained over the neutral (plus) condition when subjects were cued as to the location of the stimulus as opposed to the cuing based on the modality of the stimulus. Data for external position cues and for stimulus modality cues are shown in Figure 9.

A statistical analysis showed that effects due to both modality and spatial position cues were significant. However, as can be seen from Figure 9, the effects of modality were considerably larger.

Although knowledge of spatial position had a significant effect, it was almost entirely in terms of benefits when the stimulus occurred at the expected position. There were 0 costs for the tactile modality and only 4 msec of cost for the visual modality. Moreover, the benefits obtained (17 and 12 msec, respectively, for the two modalities) while significant, were accompanied by a small reverse effect on error. Even though it was possible for subjects to move their eyes in accordance with the cue or to change the position of their fingers with respect to tactile cues, knowledge of the position of the cue had little effect on the subject's performance.

A replication of this experiment subsequent to the writing of this chapter produced fairly strong costs following a direction cue when a stimulus occurred on the unexpected side. Benefits were about the same size as reported here and modality cues also gave results similar to the current ones. Moreover, crossing

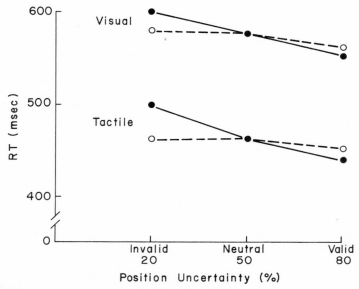

FIGURE 9 Reaction time for classification of stimulus input as strong or weak as a function of cue condition (position uncertainty) for visual and tactile modalities and for modality cues and position cues: filled circles, modality; open circles, position.

the hands, which makes the tactile and visual input of the same side go to opposite hemispheres, had no substantial effect on the results suggesting that location effects are not related to knowledge of the hemisphere stimulated. The reason for the increase in costs found in the replication over the results presented here is not apparent, but it does not change our general conclusion that benefits deriving from knowledge of where a stimulus is presented are less than those arising from knowledge of the modality of input.

Knowledge of the modality on which the cue was to be presented aided the subject much more than knowledge of spatial location. Both the visual- and the tactile-modality cues produced significant costs (25–40 msec) and benefits (20 msec) in RT which were both significant statistically. Errors were also reduced when the modality cue was correct. The costs and benefits were almost as large as those obtained in the previous experiments. There was no obvious difference in cost or benefits between the visual or tactile modality.

Discussion. Under the experimental conditions presented here, position in external space by itself does not seem to be a very helpful cue. If the subject knows that something will occur at a particular position in space, but does not know what will occur there, very little advantage is demonstrated. On the other hand, we have shown larger costs and benefits when the subject knows both what modality will occur and at which position it will occur. The latter condition allows the subject to focus attention on a particular position in internal space.

More experiments will be necessary to determine how general the dominance of modality over external position is. Our current experiments use relatively separate signals which have as their only relation their common position in space. It is possible that the results will differ markedly when stimuli that constitute a more natural object and simpler responses are studied.

CONCLUSIONS

This investigation has furthered our efforts to separate attended and unattended modes of processing. It has done so by showing that subjects can choose to attend to an expected pathway. This set can be established quite quickly and is an active process that is more labile during creation than it is once it is established (see Experiment 1). The set for spatial location can involve peripheral mechanisms such as priming of eye muscles and changes in fixation but it need not involve such mechanisms (see Experiments 2 and 3). It may be achieved by central processes alone without involvement of peripheral systems. The set for location seems to be best conceived as a bias toward the pathways activated by the expected input. Since input pathways are quite different depending on the modality of stimulation, subjects are better off if they know the modality than if they know only the external position of the input (see Experiment 4). If they know both modality and location (such as in Experiment 2 and 3) the set is probably more effective than when they know modality alone. From our previous work it can be suggested that exact knowledge of the nature of the input (like the identity of a letter) will yield even better set effects (Posner & Snyder, 1975). In general, the set seems more firmly established the more detailed the subject's knowledge of the pathway that a stimulus will use.

The finding of Experiment 4 that knowledge of modality is more important than knowledge of spatial position in achieving set is important. Our phenomenal experience is generally of objects rather than of separated sensory information. This view has been used by Gestalt psychologists to argue that the object should be thought of as the primary organization through which subjects perceive their environment. A similar view has been taken by Gibson (1966, p. 266). Modality information is thought of as a tool through which one perceives but not as a basis for perception itself. On the other hand, information-processing psychologists have argued that the channel (modality or position in space) is one basis for the selection of input. To our knowledge these two views have never before been brought into experimental opposition. The results of Experiment 4 suggest that the importance of modality of input as a basis for selection has been underemphasized by psychologists who base theories primarily on experiments using phenomenological report. Our chronometric evidence suggests that attention can be tuned to input prior to its being combined into evidence based on common location in the external world. While we feel this is a potentially important finding, we believe that further empirical demonstrations are necessary before a final judgment can be made.

The relation between attention and the performance of eye movements is a complex one. Attention can be dissociated from the fixation point to either a different position in the visual modality (see Experiment 2) or to a different modality (see Experiment 4). These complexities should caution us about too close identification of peripheral indicants such as eye position with the direction of attention. The notion that eye position is a direct measure of cognitive process or of internal observing responses cannot be taken completely seriously even though it proves a useful tool in many situations.

Gibson, in his (1941) influential paper on set, outlines the difficulty of operationally distinguishing between voluntary and involuntary processing modes. He argues that different operational definitions of set such as intention or awareness produce different classifications and that there is as yet no quantitative way to deal with the degree of volition involved in an activity. Gibson (1941) concludes that "controversies cannot be resolved until psychologists come to grips with the experimental analysis of phenomena like attitude, set, intention and expectation [p. 811]."

We agree that there is difficulty involved in developing sets of converging operations that are capable of dealing with the concept of automatic and attended modes in a quantitative way. Nonetheless the general framework outlined in our introductory remarks does provide a method for assessing not only whether an operation or activity requires mechanisms that subserve conscious report, but also the degree to which such mechanisms are involved in a given task. Our results suggesting smaller involvement of attention in the control of eye movements to visual stimuli than in the control of hand movements to the same input provide support for our general method. It seems likely that systematic chronometric investigations will produce a more detailed analysis of the characteristics of attended and unattended processing modes.

ACKNOWLEDGMENTS

These experiments were supported by the National Science Foundation under grant BMS73-00963 A02 to the University of Oregon.

REFERENCES

Engel, F. L. Visual conspicuity and selective background interference in eccentric vision. *Vision Research*, 1974, *14*, 459–471.

Eriksen, C. W., & Hoffman, J. E. The extent of processing of noise elements during selective encoding from visual displays. *Perception & Psychophysics*, 1973, *14*, 155–160.

Gibson, J. J. A critical review of the concept of set in contemporary experimental psychology. *Psychological Bulletin,* 1941, *38,* 781–815.

Gibson, J. J. The senses considered as perceptual systems. Houghton Mifflin Co. Boston, 1966.

Goldberg, M. E., & Wurtz, R. H. Activity of superior collicalus in behaving monkeys: Effect of attention on neuronal responses. *Journal of Neurophysiology,* 1972, *35,* 560–574.

Grindley, C. G., & Townsend, V. Voluntary attention in peripheral vision and its effects on acuity and differential thresholds. *Quarterly Journal of Experimental Psychology,* 1968, *20,* 11–19.

Kahneman, D. *Attention and effort.* Englewood Cliffs, N. J.: Prentice-Hall, 1973.

Klein, R., & Kerr, B. Visual signal detection and the locus of foreperiod effects. *Memory & Cognition,* 1974, *2,* 431–435.

Komoda, M., Festinger, L., Phillips, L., Duckman, R., & Young, R. Some observations concerning saccadic eye movements. *Vision Research,* 1973, *13,* 1009–1020.

Megaw, E. D., & Armstrong, W. Individual and simultaneous tracking of a step input by the horizontal saccadic eye movement and manual control systems. *Journal of Experimental Psychology,* 1973, *100,* 18–28.

Mertens, J. J. Influence of knowledge of target location upon the probability of obsecuation of peripherally observable test flashes. *Journal of the Optical Society of America,* 1956, *46,* 1069–1070.

Mowrer, O. H. Preparatory set (expectancy)–Further evidence of its 'central' locus. *Journal of Experimental Psychology,* 1941, *28,* 116–133.

Mowrer, O. H., Rayman, N., & Bliss, E. Preparatory set (expectancy)–An experimental demonstration of its 'central' locus. *Journal of Experimental Psychology,* 1940, *26,* 357–372.

Posner, M. I., Klein, R., Summers, J., & Buggie, S. On the selection of signals. *Memory & Cognition,* 1973, *1,* 2–12.

Posner, M. I., Nissen, M. I., & Klein, R. Visual dominance: An information processing account of its origins and significance. *Psychological Review,* 1976, *83,* 157–171.

Posner, M. I., & Snyder, C. R. Attention and cognitive control. In R. Solso (Ed.), *Information processing and cognition: The Loyola Symposium.* Hillsdale N. J.: Lawrence Erlbaum Associates, 1975.

Sanders, A. F. Foreperiod duration and the time course of preparation. *Acta Psychologica,* 1972, *36,* 60–71.

Saslow, M. G. Latency for saccadic eye movement. *Journal of the Optical Society of America,* 1967, *57,* 1030–1033.

Shiffrin, R. M., & Gardner, G. T. Visual processing capacity and attentional control. *Journal of Experimental Psychology,* 1972, *93,* 72–82.

Smith, S. W., & Blaha, J. Preliminary report summarizing the results of location Uncertainty Experiments I–VII. The Ohio State University, 1969.

Westheimer, G. Eye movement responses to a horizontally moving visual stimulus. *Archives of Ophthalmology,* 1954, *52,* 932–941.

8
The Functions of Vision

David N. Lee

University of Edinburgh

EDITORS' INTRODUCTION

Notwithstanding the traditional static displays used in psychological experiments, dynamic optical stimulation is the rule in everyday life. Such dynamic stimulation, typically generated by movements or transformations of objects in the world or by the movements of the observer, can be a particularly rich source of information. It has been argued that the changing optical stimulation accompanying the transformation of objects provides information both about the identity of the objects and about the nature of the transformation. Similarly, the changing pattern of stimulation due to observer motion provides information both about the spatial layout of the environment and about the progress of the observer moving with respect to it. In both these cases a single pattern of stimulation is the source of different kinds of information. This is one of the criteria for speaking of different modes of perceiving.

David Lee's chapter, as well as the following chapters by Mack and by Shaw and Pittenger, are all concerned in one way or another with the information available in dynamic patterns of optical stimulation. Lee focuses on the dynamic stimulation arising from movement of the observer, but he argues for a threefold distinction in the information provided by that stimulation. He argues that exteroceptive *information is provided about the layout of the environment; but he also suggests that the information provided about movement of the observer might usefully be broken down into: (1)* proprioceptive *information about motion of one body part with respect to another; and (2)* exproprioceptive *information about motion of the body with respect to the environment. Lee argues cogently that visual stimulation provides all these types of information.*

This chapter is about the functions performed by vision. The problem is of both theoretical and practical importance. An understanding of the functions normally performed by vision is clearly relevant to training skills; designing visual surrogates and training programs for the blind; diagnosing and correcting visual defects; and designing visual screening tests for drivers and pilots.

Let us start our enquiry by recognizing that the fundamental function of vision, as of any perceptual system, is the obtaining of information in the service of activity. Information is needed not only for planning acts but also for the ongoing control of them. As Bernstein (1967) has shown, there cannot exist an unequivocal relation between the efference directing the muscles and the form of an act. This is true since the effect of the efference will necessarily vary, for example, with the prevailing external forces on the limbs, which are not completely predictable. Therefore no act, however simple or stereotyped (like signing one's name), can be completely preprogrammed. Ongoing control, based on information about the course of the act, is necessary for its proper execution. In the absence of such information the act is ataxic.

What types of information are necessary for controlling activity? Gibson (1966) has proposed two basic types: (1) *exteroceptive* information about the layout of the environment and about external objects and events; and (2) *proprioceptive* information about the acts being performed. This is somewhat too broad a categorization in my view. It is important to distinguish two types of information about the course of an act, the one relative to the body, the other relative to the environment. Rather than invent two new terms, I propose to retain the term *proprioception,* but use it in a more restricted sense than Gibson (and in a sense closer to its classical meaning[1]), to mean the obtaining of information about the positions and movements of the parts of the body relative to the body. I further propose a new term, *exproprioception,* meaning the obtaining of information about the position, orientation or movement of the body as a whole, or part of the body, relative to the environment.

The three types of information, exteroceptive, proprioceptive, and exproprioceptive, are, I would argue, sufficient for performing any form of activity, and some, or all, are necessary for performing any particular activity. Exteroceptive information is used in planning an act relative to the environment; proprioceptive information is used in controlling the act; and exproprioceptive information is used in both planning and control.

Most of the perceptual systems are capable of obtaining more than one of the three basic types of information. They may be said to have different functional modes. The visual system is clearly trimodal as is the auditory system, though

---

[1] As Gibson (1966) has pointed out, the classical error, still current in textbooks, is to ascribe proprioceptive function solely to the receptors in the joints and muscles—the so-called proprioceptors.

auditory proprioception is confined to sound-producing acts such as vocalizing and playing a musical instrument. The articular system of receptors in the joints and muscles is solely proprioceptive. The combination of this system with the system of receptors in the skin is a trimodal haptic system. The vestibular system is solely exproprioceptive. The olfactory system is, in humans, primarily extero- ceptive, and only to a limited degree exproprioceptive. Taste is solely ex- teroceptive.

If we confine our attention to activity involving physical interaction with the environment or objects in it (that is, ignoring such activities as verbal com- munication), it is clear that vision is the most powerful exteroceptive sense. No one would, I suppose, dispute this. What I want to argue, however, is that vision is also the most powerful proprioceptive and exproprioceptive sense. Further, because of its trimodal power, vision normally functions as an overseer in the control of activity, developing patterns of action, and tuning up other perceptual systems and keeping them tuned. To support my argument I will consider different forms of activity, starting with the most fundamental.

BALANCE CONTROL

We take our ability to stay upright on our feet so much for granted that it is often not realized what a precisely controlled activity it is. It is, in fact, the most fundamental activity, for without it most other activities would not be possible.

How do we maintain our balance? Clearly we need exproprioceptive informa- tion about our orientation and movement relative to the environment in order that appropriate muscular corrections can be made. To obtain this information we need some form of sensory contact with the environment. There are three types: (1) inertial contact through the vestibular system; (2) physical contact through the feet; and (3) optical contact through the eye. Let us consider them in turn.

The receptors in the vestibular canals respond to angular accelerations of the head and to the resultant of linear accelerations and gravity. However, it seems clear from experimental and clinical evidence that the vestibular system is not sufficiently sensitive to account for the small angular accelerations that occur in fine balance (Birren, 1945; Lee & Lishman, 1975). Fine balance control ap- parently depends on other more sensitive exproprioceptive information.

The reliability of the exproprioceptive information from the feet and ankles is much dependent on the nature of the support surface. If the surface is broad and firm, the orientation and movement of the body relative to the environment is accurately reflected in the angle at the ankles and the pressures on the feet, which could be registered by the articular and skin receptors. However, if the support surface is narrow, compliant, or unsteady, so that the feet can move relative to the environment, the physical contact reference to the environment is uncertain and so the ankle—foot exproprioceptive information is unreliable. Also the efficiency of the information varies with the posture of the feet. In a novel stance, the pattern of feedback is unusual and practice is required to become attuned to it.

As Gibson (1950, 1958) has pointed out, whenever the head is moving relative to the environment there is an optic flow pattern at the eye, the spatiotemporal structure of which depends both on the form of the movement and on the structure of the environment. The optic flow pattern thus affords both exproprioceptive information about the movement of the head relative to the environment and exteroceptive information about the environment itself. The two types of information correspond to certain mathematical properties of the flow pattern (Lee, 1974). It is the visual exproprioceptive information that is used in controlling balance.

The power of vision in controlling balance has been demonstrated in human infants and adults by means of a "swinging room", a large bottomless box suspended just above the floor (Lee & Aronson, 1974; Lee & Lishman, 1975). Visual exproprioceptive information about body sway was manipulated by moving the swinging room around a subject standing on a stationary base. When the room is moved, the subject unconsciously and unavoidably "corrects" posture and either sways excessively or loses balance. That vision normally affords the most sensitive information for balance control is evidenced by the fact that, even for an adult standing normally, vision normally improves balance and body sway can be visually driven by 6-mm oscillations of the swinging room without the adult being aware of it. Balance control is finest when there is an object or wall close in front of the person, since this accentuates the optical change at the eye.

Vision is particularly important in learning a new stance. An infant learning to stand or an adult in an unpracticed stance is easily knocked off balance by moving the swinging room. It is often the case that balance is impossible without vision when first attempting a new stance. However, with practice in the stance, vision usually becomes noncritical. This indicates that vision, in affording the most sensitive information, can be used to tune up the other exproprioceptive systems. If vision were absent, therefore, the tuning up should not be as efficient. Observations on blind people support this. Edwards (1946) found that, when standing normally with eyes shut, blind and partially blind adults swayed about twice as much as normal adults with their eyes shut. It is also well known among teachers of the blind that congenitally blind children are normally retarded in learning to stand and walk.

It is most likely that vision plays just as important a role in dynamic balance control—walking, running, skiing, and so on. (One need only consider walking along a narrow beam.) However, little systematic work on this has yet been done.

ORIENTING

There are two basic types of orienting activity. There is *investigatory* orienting of the perceptual systems to part of the environment or the body, in order to obtain information, as in looking at or feeling something and turning to face a sound source. This normally precedes *performatory* orienting of the body, preparatory to performing an act such as pitching a baseball, kicking or catching a ball, executing a tennis stroke, and moving towards something.

What to orient to is based on exteroceptive information. *How* to orient is based on exproprioceptive and proprioceptive information. This distinction is somewhat different from the "what/where" distinction made by Trevarthen (1968) in his paper postulating two mechanisms of vision: focal and ambient. Whereas the concept of parallel focal and ambient mechanisms is made essentially on behavioral and anatomical grounds, the distinction I am making is in terms of information. Focal vision, served by the fovea, is intensive, and would seem to be mainly concerned with the pick-up of detailed exteroceptive and possibly proprioceptive information within a small region of behavioral space, for identifying objects, controlling fine praxic movements and so on. On the other hand, ambient vision, served by the whole retina, is extensive, and would seem to be mainly concerned with picking up proprioceptive and exproprioceptive information on a broad scale within the whole behavioral space, for controlling locomotion and orientation.

Let us consider first the simple case of investigatory orienting—moving the eyes to foveate a stationary or moving object. The control of the eye movement is clearly dependent on visual exproprioceptive information about the direction of the object relative to the eye, and presumably also on proprioceptive information about the orientation of the eye in the head, since the eye is moved relative to the head. Contact lenses deform the projection of the optic array onto the retina and so alter the exproprioceptive information. This disturbs eye movement control. For example, a lens that magnifies (as do those used in correcting for astigmatism) initially causes the eye to overshoot in making saccadic movements. This presumably accounts for some of the difficulty many people experience when first wearing contact lenses.

Moving down one stage, let us now consider investigatory orienting of the head to face a stationary or moving visible object. Control of the head movement depends again on visual exproprioceptive information about the direction of the object relative to the eye and on proprioceptive information about the orientation of the eye relative to the head. Lenses or prisms mounted in spectacle frames deform the optic array incident at the eye and so alter the visual exproprioceptive information. This disturbs head movement control (though not eye movement control, as do contact lenses), as anyone will know who has worn prisms or lenses of reasonable power or has tried to follow a fast moving object through binoculars.

How is proprioceptive information about the orientation of the eye in the head obtained? One possible source is vision itself, since most parts of the body are visible. The other possible source is the receptors in the extraocular muscles, and possibly also those in the tissues in contact with the eyeball. However, it seems clear that the nonvisual proprioceptive information is much poorer than the visual (see, e.g., Merton, 1964). One illustrative case is the autokinetic phenomenon, in which a stationary spot of light in a dark room appears, after a short while, to wander around. This indicates that the nonvisual proprioceptive system is subject to quite considerable drift. If it is used at all in registering the orientation of the eye, which seems not unlikely since vision has so many other tasks to perform, then it seems most probable that the system is kept tuned by vision.

Bower (1974) has argued that it is sight of the nose and eye orbit that affords the visual proprioceptive information about eye orientation. However, in view of the limited acuity at the retinal periphery, it would seem more likely to be sight of other parts of the body. Hay and Pick (1966) and Craske (1967) have both obtained evidence for a change in registered eye position after wearing wedge-prism spectacles, which alter visual proprioceptive information about the trunk and limbs but not about the nose and eye orbit.

While visual exproprioceptive information is with reference to the eye, auditory and olfactory exproprioceptive information is with reference to the head, since the ears and nose are immobile. Sounds are localized on the basis of the differential intensities and times of arrival of inputs to the two ears, and the form of the multiple input at each ear, which is produced by sound reflection in the pinna (Batteau, 1968). While auditory exproprioception might reasonably be thought to be independent of vision, this does not appear to be the case. It is well known that blind children are much less able in locating sounds than are sighted children with eyes closed. Even for normal adults, Warren (1970) found that auditory localization of invisible sound sources was better in the light than it was in the dark. It would seem, therefore, that vision can improve auditory exproprioception.

So far we have only considered investigatory orienting of the head, the home of most of the perceptual systems. Let us now consider performatory orienting of the body. Given that the head can be oriented towards a visual or auditory object, how is the body, or part of the body, oriented towards it? Clearly, in general, there needs to be proprioceptive information about the orientation of the head relative to the trunk and about the position and movement of the limbs relative to the trunk. How is this proprioceptive information obtained? Again there are two possible sources: (1) the articular system of receptors in the joints and muscles (which are classically referred to as *the* proprioceptors) and (2) vision. And again there is substantial evidence that visual proprioception is the more powerful, and indeed can dominate and recalibrate articular proprioception. One has only to try bringing the tips of one's index fingers quickly together with the eyes open or shut to demonstrate that vision can afford more sensitive proprioceptive information. Experiments on adaptation to wearing wedge prisms, which initially produce discordance between visual and articular proprioceptive information, so that one sees the parts of one's body somewhere other than where they are felt to be, provide strong evidence of visual recalibrating of articular proprioceptive information to bring it into agreement with the visual information (see Harris, 1965, for a review of the evidence).

Performatory orienting of the body to part of the environment can be achieved with great precision. Driving off in golf provides a clear example. It is noteworthy how much shuffling and looking at the hole, the ball and the body goes on in lining up the body, preparatory to executing the automatized, nonvisually controlled act of swinging the club.

As a final case of performatory orientation, let us consider a dynamic one: Walking straight towards something. Given that one is initially heading in the right direction, how does one maintain the correct course? Clearly one needs exproprioceptive information about one's motion path relative to the environment. There are three possible sources of this information: the vestibular system, the articular proprioceptive system (particularly the receptors in the feet), and vision. It is easy to demonstrate for oneself that the visual exproprioceptive information is by far the more sensitive. Simply start walking toward a distant point over an open stretch of ground and after a few paces either shut your eyes or keep them open for about 30 paces more. A similar experiment could be tried when driving along a straight stretch of road, but I would not recommend it.

BODY-CENTERED ACTIVITY

Thus far we have been concerned with the control of actions relative to the environment. Let us now turn to the control of actions relative to the body or a learned extension of the body, like a musical instrument. We may distinguish two types of body-centered actions: (1) environment-independent actions, like removing a splinter from the finger or playing a violin; and (2) acts that serve activity relative to the environment, like walking or executing a tennis stroke.

We have already touched on the control of body-centered acts in the preceding section. Control requires proprioceptive information, and the evidence is that vision affords the most sensitive information and can dominate and/or recalibrate the articular proprioceptive system, which is apparently subject to drift. This does not mean, of course, that the articular proprioceptive system is redundant. Clearly, acts frequently have to be performed without visual control. What it does suggest, however, is that vision is normally used to advantage as a sort of proprioceptive overseer to develop patterns of action and, at the same time, tune the articular proprioceptive system. Actions then can be performed later without visual control, albeit with intermittent checking by vision to correct for drift, thus freeing vision for exteroception and exproprioception.

Let me give some examples. A musical instrument, whether it be held in the hands, like a violin, or not, like a piano, becomes, for the player, an extension of the body. In developing technique on an instrument, the player normally uses vision both exteroceptively, in watching the teacher, and proprioceptively, in watching him- or herself. Once the skill has been sufficiently developed, the ongoing control is handed over to articular proprioception (and, of course, auditory proprioception and touch). This frees vision for its exteroceptive function of reading the music and planning the activity. But since, without vision, articular proprioception tends to drift, it has to be kept intermittently in tune by vision. Thus, practice on the piano is normally done under visual control. Also, when particularly precise control is required, vision is called into play. For executing large leaps over the piano keyboard the pianist's eyes flash from the music down to the hands. Better still, the pianist memorizes the music so that vision can be concentrated on its proprioceptive function.

Similar examples can be drawn from skills that serve activity relative to the environment. Again the action pattern is frequently developed and kept tuned with the aid of vision, either by using vision proprioceptively (as with the tennis player watching the racket and the ballet dancer watching him- or herself in the mirror), or by using vision exteroceptively, as in watching someone else demonstrate the action or watching a videotape of oneself. Once the necessary action patterns have been developed, the control of them can be handed over to articular proprioception, enabling vision to concentrate on the control of the movement of the body relative to the environment. The tennis player guides his or her body visually, but controls the tennis stroke nonvisually.

The motor deficiencies of the blind also illustrate the power of vision as a proprioceptive overseer. As Kooyman (1970) has pointed out from his experience as a physical education teacher of the blind, a person who has been sighted in his early life, even if for only a year or two, is normally much less handicapped than a congenitally blind person. The early vision apparently greatly facilitates the development of basic structures of movement and tuning of the articular proprioceptive system, providing a foundation for later development.

LOCOMOTING

No discussion of the functions of vision would be complete without mentioning the superordinate role of vision in controlling and guiding locomotion. An adequate coverage of such a vast topic is beyond the scope of this chapter, and so here I will just sketch out some basic points.

I have already mentioned, in the discussion of balance control, how the optic flow pattern at a moving eye affords both exteroceptive and exproprioceptive information. This information serves the two basic aspects of visual control of locomotion: steering the body through the environment and guiding individual locomotor acts. In the first category are such activities as running towards a place or a moving object, such as a ball or prey; running away from a predator; and steering oneself down a winding track, either in a vehicle or on foot. In the second category are such activities as guiding one's feet to step onto, down from, or around obstacles; jumping across gaps, over obstacles or down from a height; and stopping at insurmountable obstacles either when driving or on foot. Any such locomotor act has to be planned in advance and executed at the right time. Normal locomotor activity is a continual process of programming locomotor acts and controlling their execution. The programming of a locomotor act is probably based mainly on visual exteroceptive information (the width of the ditch, the layout of the stepping stones, and so on), and the timing of the act is probably based on visual exproprioceptive information about time to contact. This information is directly available in the optic flow pattern (Lee, 1974; Purdy, 1958).

There are countless everyday examples of the power of vision in controlling locomotion. Here are just a few to illustrate the points I have been making. As I am writing, the Winter Olympics are on television. The precision with which the skiiers adjust their posture that split second before launching off into space in the 90-m jump (to avoid performing uncontrollable aerobatics) is a beauty to behold. A more down-to-earth example is stepping off the sidewalk; one can get a nasty jolt if one did not notice the edge and so failed to adjust one's pace accordingly. In the same vein, running over smoothly undulating ground is no problem in the light, but in the dark or semidark it can be quite a bone shaker. Rough ground illustrates the point even more forcibly. The long jump, despite its apparently stereotyped form, relies on precise visual control. The jumper has to get his or her foot on the board, be in the right posture for the launch, and also be traveling as fast as possible. Though pacing out the run undoubtedly helps, it seems certain that the jumper must visually adjust the last few strides to the board.

As a final example, let us turn to driving. Stopping behind an obstacle is normally achieved in a remarkably smooth and controlled way. The locomotor act of depressing the brake pedal is obviously under precise visual control. It seems clear that the control must be based on visual exproprioceptive information about the adequacy or inadequacy of the current braking force. Such information is, in fact, directly available in the optic flow pattern at the driver's eye (Lee, 1976).

SOME PRACTICAL IMPLICATIONS

The thesis proposed here is that vision has three basic functional modes.

1. Vision is capable of obtaining the three fundamental types of information, exteroceptive, proprioceptive, and exproprioceptive, which are required for controlling activity.

2. Vision is more powerful than the other perceptual systems in each of these domains.

3. Because of its trimodal power, vision normally functions as an overseer in the control of activity, developing patterns of action and tuning up other perceptual systems and keeping them tuned.

Let us consider some practical implications of the thesis.

In training skills which ultimately have to be executed without visual control, as with many sports skills, vision should be used as fully as possible. The trend in coaching seems to be in this direction. Films and videotape are being used extensively. However, while valuable, these visual aids only afford second hand visual information. One needs also to structure the training program so that the trainee can exercise direct visual control over his or her actions. The visual information should be as fine as possible. For example, in training balance, there should be, if possible, surfaces or objects near the person to enhance the sensitivity of visual exproprioceptive information. The trainee should not, of course, become dependent on vision; during the training program steps need to be taken to reduce the dependence.

When one considers vision tests and the optical devices for correcting or enhancing vision, it seems clear that the designers had in mind only the exteroceptive function of vision. A classic example is the standard driving test of static visual acuity—a test which, for example, could be, and in fact is, passed by people with tunnel vision. What is needed are tests that measure the triple function of vision. The exteroceptively blinkered view of vision has led not only to inadequate tests but also to the design of optical devices that disturb the other functions of vision. Apart from restricting view of the body, which reduces visual proprioceptive information, most devices distort visual exproprioceptive information. They do so by deforming the optic array by lens systems, as do prescription glasses and telescopes; by optically changing the position and orientation of the eye relative to the head by mirror systems; or by both, as do binoculars. The adverse effects on visual functioning of such devices, not surprisingly, frequently give rise to a feeling of disorientation and tend to disrupt the control of balance and movement. Opticians are, of course, aware of these effects, but do not seem to consider it part of their job to do anything about them.

As a medical example, let us consider someone suffering from dizziness and/or inability to balance. This is usually due to some form of exproprioceptive deficiency or dysfunction. The disorder may lie in the patient's visual, vestibular, or articular system. What the patient needs is help in improving exproprioceptive efficiency. If the disorder is a result of visual malfunction, it may be possible to alleviate it by suitable spectacles or contact lenses (if the understanding and techniques were available). If, on the other hand, the vestibular system is damaged, as in Ménière's disease, then the patient needs to be taught how to make more efficient use of other exproprioceptive information. For example, by keeping near to walls or large objects the patient can enhance visual exproprio-ceptive information. By avoiding compliant, uneven or unsteady surfaces, and wearing firm-soled shoes, the patient can enhance the exproprioceptive informa-tion from the feet. And by using, for example, a walking stick with a tripod foot, the patient can obtain additional exproprioceptive information through the hand.

A common type of dizziness is that experienced at heights. This is probably due, in part at least, to a conflict between visual and nonvisual exproprioceptive information. When the surroundings are a long way off, small movements of the head produce no detectable optical change. Therefore, as far as the visual system can tell, the body is stationary. Too much reliance on vision would lead, therefore, to increased body sway and a feeling of instability. The solution would be to look at something close by, as a rock climber looks at the rock face, removing the exproprioceptive conflict and, at the same time, gaining very sensitive visual information for controlling rather precarious balance.

Motion sickness is another common complaint that is also likely to be a result, in part, of a visual–nonvisual exproprioceptive conflict. For example, when reading in a car and thus confining one's visual field to the interior of the vehicle, the way one feels onself to be moving is different from the way one sees oneself to be moving. Looking outside, particularly forward through the wind-shield, removes the conflict. A person rarely feels motion sick while driving. This probably results not only from the absence of exproprioceptive conflict but also from the driver being able, with the aid of vision, to adjust his or her posture to the motion of the vehicle and so avoid harsh accelerations of the head.

To conclude, let us turn to blindness. A blind person needs help in compensat-ing for loss of visual proprioception and exproprioception as well as for loss of visual exteroception. This need is recognized in modern programs of physical education for the blind (see, e.g., Kooyman, 1970), which aid the development of articular proprioception through dance, gymnastics and so on. However, in designing aids for the blind, such as ultrasonic devices, the principal aim seems to have been to provide an exteroceptive aid. As much effort should be directed toward providing both proprioceptive and exproprioceptive aids for the blind.

REFERENCES

Batteau, D. W. Listening with the naked ear. In S. J. Freedman (Ed.), *The neuropsychology of spatially oriented behavior.* Homewood, Illinois: Dorsey Press, 1968.

Bernstein, N. *The co-ordination and regulation of movements.* Oxford: Pergamon Press, 1967.

Birren, J. E. Static equilibrium and vestibular function. *Journal of Experimental Psychology,* 1945, *35,* 127–133.

Bower, T. G. R. *Development in infancy.* San Francisco: Freeman, 1974.

Craske, B. Adaptation to prisms: Change in internally registered eye-position. *British Journal of Psychology,* 1967, *58,* 329–335.

Edwards, A. S. Body sway and vision. *Journal of Experimental Psychology,* 1946, *36,* 526–535.

Gibson, J. J. *The perception of the visual world.* Boston: Houghton Mifflin, 1950.

Gibson, J. J. Visually controlled locomotion and visual orientation in animals. *British Journal of Psychology,* 1958, *49,* 182–194.

Gibson, J. J. *The senses considered as perceptual systems.* Boston: Houghton Mifflin, 1966.

Harris, C. S. Perceptual adaptation to inverted, reversed, and displaced vision. *Psychological Review,* 1965, *72,* 419–444.

Hay, J. C., & Pick, H. L., Jr. Visual and proprioceptive adaptation to optical displacement of the visual stimulus. *Journal of Experimental Psychology,* 1966, *71,* 150–158.

Kooyman, W. J. J. Physical education of pupils with defective vision, and problems of orientation. *The Teacher of the Blind,* 1970, *58,* 99–105.

Lee, D. N. Visual information during locomotion. In R. B. MacLeod & H. L. Pick (Eds.), *Perception: Essays in honor of James J. Gibson.* Ithaca & London: Cornell University Press, 1974.

Lee, D. N. A theory of visual control of braking based on information about time-to-collision. *Perception,* 1976, *5,* 437–459.

Lee, D. N., & Aronson, E. Visual proprioceptive control of standing in human infants. *Perception & Psychophysics,* 1974, *15,* 529–532.

Lee, D. N., & Lishman, J. R. Visual proprioceptive control of stance. *Journal of Human Movement Studies,* 1975, *1,* 87–95.

Merton, P. A. Absence of conscious position sense in the human eyes. In M. R. Bender (Ed.) *The oculomotor system.* New York: Harper & Row, 1964.

Purdy, W. C. The hypothesis of psychophysical correspondence in space perception. (Doctoral dissertation, Cornell University, 1958.) University Microfilms No. 58-5594.

Trevarthen, C. B. Two mechanisms of vision in primates. *Psychologische Forschung,* 1968, *31,* 299–337.

Warren, D. H. Intermodality interactions in spatial localization. *Cognitive Psychology,* 1970, *1,* 114–133.

9
Three Modes
of Visual Perception

Arien Mack

New School for Social Research

EDITORS' INTRODUCTION

Arien Mack, like Lee, is also concerned with perception during observer motion. The empirical basis of her paper is a set of ingenious experiments on perception during pursuit eye movements. The underlying question is how the observer responds to stimulation that potentially provides information about local events on the retina (proximal-oriented perception) and distal events in the world (constancy-oriented perception). Mack notes the parallel between this distinction and the classical distinction of visual fields and visual world or sensation and perception. All of these distinctions imply alternative perceptual experiences arising from the same retinal stimulation. Like Lee, Mack proposes a finer threefold distinction. The constancy mode of perception is divided into one specified by object–object relations and one specified by subject–object relations. The proximal mode of perception is perception mediated exclusively by retinal properties of the pattern of stimulation.

It is difficult to discuss my own research in terms appropriate to the theme of this volume. The problem is not an unfamiliar one. It occurs whenever an attempt is made to go beyond the specific and restricted questions addressed in the laboratory to the question of how what is learned there is relevant to a more general, theoretical account of the perceptual process. It is one thing to look for the answer to a specific question (for example, how to account for certain visual illusions associated with a particular kind of eye movement), and quite another

171

and more difficulty thing to try to state what the relevance of that question is to perceptual processes generally. In this chapter I attempt to determine that sort of relevance. The results of an investigation of the perception of motion and stability during pursuit eye movements (PEMs) are considered and applied to the concept of perceptual modes.

As a working definition, the term *perceptual mode* is used here to refer to a kind of perception made possible or elicited by a set of more or less specifiable stimulus conditions. In order to qualify as a mode of perception, these conditions must be sufficiently general to include all or most of the dimensions of visual perception such as size, shape, position, motion, and color. Thus, this definition excludes depth or size perception as a mode of perception. A mode is considered to be a superordinate category embracing all dimensions of perception.

Given this admittedly vague definition, there seems to be a clear modal distinction between perception in the proximal and perception in the constancy mode. This distinction in many ways parallels the traditional distinction between sensation and perception; between perception of the visual field; and perception of the visual world (Gibson, 1950). With the appropriate stimulus conditions either mode is possible for any perceptual dimension although some stimulus conditions may make one mode mandatory and the other impossible.

Proximal perception is perception that is fairly strictly determined by the retinal stimulus and by that alone. *Constancy perception* is perception that tends to be faithful to some aspect of the distal stimulus despite changes in the proximal stimulus produced by changes in the imaged object's, the observer's orientation, position, and so on. Thus in the case of size or shape perception, it is possible to distinguish between size or shape constancy perception where the retinal shape or size of the stimulus is only one of the factors that determine the percept, and the proximal perception of size or shape where the percept is solely determined by the size or shape of the image.

There seem to be at least two situations in which proximal perception is likely to occur spontaneously. The first is an impoverished or reduced cue condition where there is no information or only minimal information available that would make constancy perception possible. Using size or shape perception again, as an example, proximal percepts are likely to occur where there is no information or little information about distance or slant. If an observer in a dark room views a luminous rectangle tilted with respect to the frontal plane from a distance of 2 m, the perception will most likely be of a trapezoid in the frontal plane, that is, the perceived shape will be determined by the trapezoidal shape of the image in the absence of information about the slant of the surface. Under genuinely reduced stimulus conditions, constancy perception would seem by definition not possible.[1]

---

[1] There are those who would not accept this formulation. Gogel (1969), for example, maintains with respect to size perception, that there is no such thing as a proximal

The second condition that appears to foster proximal perception is one in which constancy perception is also possible. It is what is referred to as a *full cue condition*. It is a condition in which perception takes on a bimodal character. Both proximal and constancy perception may occur in rapid succession. The conditions that elicit this kind of bimodal perception are not infrequent. If, for example, railroad tracks or street lights lining both sides of a street are viewed from a position in which they recede directly in the median plane, the two modes of perception seem to be almost simultaneously present. There is the proximal perception of the perspective convergence of the tracks or lights involving an awareness of retinal size relations and the constancy perception that the tracks or lights remain parallel and of equal size.

Stimulus conditions that allow both constancy and proximal perception are characterized both by providing sufficient subject–relative information to facilitate constancy percepts (in the example cited there is information about distance derived from both oculomotor and visual sources), and by certain specifiable attributes of the retinal array. These retinal attributes are ones that make salient some absolute and local quality of the image or images. They are conditions that facilitate internal proximal comparisons. Thus in the case of the receding railroad tracks or street lights the visual-angle differences between successively receding ties or pairs of lights is accentuated by the contiguity and adjacency of their images. Retinal extents are more readily perceived when the imaged extents are both parallel and aligned and are less readily perceived when they are in different positions relative to each other. Thus, proximal perception of size occurs, for example, when extensity differences within the image are emphasized or made salient by the alignment of increasingly smaller projected extents. Stimulus conditions that facilitate proximal perception under full cue condition are therefore those in which the alignment of images within the retinal array maximize proximal comparisons, allowing some absolute attribute of the proximal stimulus to intrude into or determine perception. However, while under full cue conditions, the vividness of retinal relations may foster proximal perception, it must be stressed that it is some absolute characteristic of the proximal stimulus that determines the percept. Proximal perceptions are not relational, although they are facilitated by certain image relations.

The reason for insisting on the absolute character of proximal perception is derived from the contention that all truly relationally determined percepts are in the constancy mode. This brings us to a second modal distinction, a distinction between two modes of constancy perception: a subject-relative mode and an object-relative mode. Constancy percepts in the subject-relative mode are conjointly determined by: (1) sensory information concerning some absolute characteristic of the proximal stimulus, for example, visual angle; and (2) sensory information concerning some characterisitic of the imaged object's relation to

---

perception of size. In the absence of distance information, Gogel argues some specific distance, a function of what he calls the "specific distance tendency" is used by the perceptual system in arriving at a perception of linear size.

the self, for example, its distance. The sources of this latter kind of information are frequently, although not necessarily, extra-retinal. It may be generated from efferent, proprioceptive, or vestibular signals, that is, it may be body-generated information. For example, when the perception of size is in the subject-relative constancy mode, proximal information concerning image size is used in conjunction with sensory information about the object's distance. This latter information may be derived from: (1) extra-retinal oculomotor information about distance (for example, from convergence); and/or (2) visual pictorial information about distance (from pictorial cues to distance such as linear perspective). As a second example, when the perception of motion, stability, position, or orientation is in the subject-relative constancy mode, the subject-relative sensory information is exclusively nonvisual and body-generated. The relevant information is derived from information about head and/or eye position and head and/or eye movement. Thus when the perception of object motion or stability is in the subject-relative constancy mode, it is a conjoint function of image displacement information and information about head and/or eye motion.

Subject-relative constancy percepts are constancy as opposed to proximal percepts even when the sensory information about subject-object relations is inaccurate. For example, the perception of size, which is a function of image size and distance information, is still a constancy percept where distance information is faulty as is the perception of object motion when there is inaccurate eye or head motion information. This is so because in both instances it is not some local characteristic of the retinal stimulus which is the sole determinant of the percept, and this is the distinguishing feature of proximal perception.

Constancy percepts in the object-relative mode are determined by strictly visual relations. They are distinguished from: (1) subject-relative percepts by the fact that subject-relative information is never a determinant of these perceptions; and (2) proximal percepts by the fact that they are not determined by local and absolute image characteristics. Examples of object-relative constancy perceptions are plentiful.

Brown (1931) has shown that perceived velocity may be determined by the rate of displacement of an object relative to its surroundings. Thus, a subject may perceive the velocity of an object moving within a large frame of reference as equal to the velocity of an object moving through a small frame when their rates of displacement relative to their frames of reference are equal. This, of course, means that velocities which are objectively very unequal are perceived as equal. The object in the large frame must move much faster for its velocity to appear equal to that of the object moving within the small frame. Rock and Ebenholtz (1959) have shown a similar kind of transposition for size perception. Lines enclosed in unequal sized frames appear equal in length when, within certain limits, the lines bear the same relations to their frames of reference. This, of course, also means that lines of very different physical lengths are perceived as equal. These are perceptions determined by visual (retinal) relations and are in no sense proximal. In both of these instances proximal percepts would be percepts determined by local image characteristics—in one case by the retinal velocities of the moving objects and in the other by the retinal extensities of the enclosed lines. Perceptual matches based on retinal velocity or extent would result, in these instances, in what would appear to be far more veridical percepts. Unequal retinal velocities or extents would not appear equal. A distinctive feature of these relationally determined percepts then is that the absolute characteristics of the images seem to be lost or masked.

There are other examples: Witkin and Asch's (1948; Asch & Witkin, 1948) work on perceived orientation of a rod within a frame; Duncker's (1929) work on induced movement; and the fact that a rectangular frame placed asymmetrically with respect to an observer's median plane will lead the observer to mislocate the straight ahead direction and displace it toward the center of the visual frame (Roelofs, 1935) are all instance of object-relative constancy perception.

Another distinguishing feature of object-relative constancy perceptions is that they generally seem to override or swamp subject-relative perceptions which are, in terms of available sensory information, possible in these situations and would occur if nonvisual, body-generated information were taken into account. In the case in which a spatially vertical rod enclosed by a spatially tilted frame is perceived as spatially tilted, the percept determined by taking into account head- or body-position information—the percept that the rod is vertical and the frame is tilted—is lost. In fact object-relative determined percepts not only generally dominate those based on conjoint visual and body-generated information, but also often lead to the misperception of body position or orientation; such percepts seem to swamp or mask this source of information. If one perceives the vertical rod as tilted, one also will probably misperceive and misdescribe the direction of the eye movements needed to scan the rod. If one misperceives the straight ahead direction by virtue of the fact that an asymmetrical frame is present in the field, one will also misperceive eye position. A turned position of the eyes will be reported as eyes straight ahead in the head. If one removed the frames of reference which are operating here to determine the percepts, the perception of orientation or egocentric direction will be based on the taking into account of subject-relative body- and/or eye-position information. These are all instances of what has been called *visual capture,* a phenomenon characterized by the fact that visual information concerning body, limb or eye position, dominates or suppresses nonvisual body-generated position information. Object-relative determined percepts thus not only mask the local absolute image characteristics of a stimulus, but also tend to produce visual capture, to mask body-generated position information, as well.

There is a final distinction to be made between subject- and object-relative modes of constancy perception. Only when constancy perception is in the subject-relative mode is proximal perception possible. That is, only then can perception take on a bimodal (proximal-constancy) character. Only then will proximal perception occur either spontaneously, by virtue of the nature of the retinal array, or by adopting the proper analytic attitude. This follows from the fact that when perception is object-relative, the absolute and local attributes of the image are lost to awareness and thus cannot intrude or be brought into perception. When perception is subject relative, local and absolute image attributes participate in the perception and may, under the appropriate conditions enter awareness.

This feature of object-relative constancy percepts may explain a number of optical illusions of size (like the Ponzo & Müller-Lyer illusions). If these illusions are object-relatively determined percepts and are not, as has been argued by Gregory (1962), instances of misapplied constancy in the subject-relative mode, it would explain why it is so difficult, if not impossible, to perceive the equal-sized line segments in the Ponzo and Müller-Lyer configurations as being of equal size. The perception that these line segments are of equal length would involve an awareness of their equal retinal extensities which is made impossible when perception is in the object-relative mode.

Having distinguished between a proximal and a constancy mode and between constancy percepts that are object relational and those that are subject relational (distinctions which have no particular claim to originality), the task is now one of explicating the relevance of these distinctions to our work on the perception of motion and stability during PEMs. We have been concerned with a possibly less familiar form of constancy, the constancy of position. We have attempted to understand a set of phenomena that appear to reveal a clear and sometimes gross loss of position constancy during PEMs.

Position constancy may be defined as the perception that objects maintain their positions in space, despite the movement of the images of stationary objects on the retina occasioned by every movement of an observer's head or eyes. It is generally believed that when position constancy occurs, the perception is a conjoint function of information about image displacement and sensory information about observer movement. A comparator or matching mechanism, is postulated which compares retinal- and observer-movement information. When the information "matches," image motion is attributed to the self. A "mismatch" leads to the perception of object movement. Thus, if the eyes turn $10°$ to the right and the retinal stimulus displaces $20°$ to the right in the same time interval, the object will be perceived to move by $10°$. This, of course, assumes accurate eye movement information. This account of position constancy clearly places it in the subject-relative mode. (A point to be made in what follows is that position-constancy perception may also be in the object-relative mode.)

While position constancy seems to characterize most of our perceptions, (our eyes are constantly moving, causing images to displace, yet the world appears stationary), there have been questions raised about the presence of position constancy during PEMs. Stoper (1967, 1973) has argued that the perception of motion and the position of the nontracked stimuli during pursuit are determined solely by retinal position and retinal motion, and thus are proximal percepts.

Recent work in our laboratory has involved a reexamination of some of the illusory movement phenomena that occur during intervals of pursuit and that suggest that there may be no position constancy. One of the phenomena, and the only one discussed here, is referred to as the Filehne illusion. Filehne (1922), reported that the stationary objects lying in a plane parallel to the path of a moving object (his finger), which he followed with his eyes while his head was held stationary, appeared to move in the direction opposite to that of the tracked object (and by the same amount). As described by Filehne, this illusion seems to represent a complete loss of position constancy, and the complete dominance of the proximal perceptual mode. The retinal displacements of the images of the stationary background objects caused by the pursuit movements exactly match the displacements of the eye; therefore, the background should appear stationary unless, of course, pursuit movements are characterized by proximal perception. But why should this be so? This question is particularly germane since the perception that the tracked target is moving cannot be explained in these terms. The tracked target is more or less retinally stable, depending on the quality of the tracking, yet it is clearly seen to move; this should only be the case if the system uses information about the eye movement.

In terms of the previous analysis, proximal perception is likely to occur either under impoverished stimulus conditions or when internal retinal comparisons are compelling. Stoper has argued that the absence of position constancy during pursuit (as evidenced by such phenomena as the Filehne illusion) is due to the fact that no information concerning the eye movement is available to the perceptual system. This seems to be an explanation which should be included in the category of impoverished conditions. Were this the case, it would account for the proximal perception of apparent background movement, but not for the perceived movement of the retinally stable, tracked target. If there is no information about the eye movement available to the perceptual system, then the eye should be assumed to be motionless; this assumption is matched by the absence of retinal displacement of the tracked target and so it should appear stationary. Stoper (1967) recognized this difficulty and therefore was forced to create a rather complex theory to account for the perceived movement of the tracked target. I have not considered this theory here, since our own work suggests that that analysis is not correct.

The work we designed to reexamine the Filehne illusion led us to a quite different account of the illusion, one that is consistent with the proposed modal analysis of proximal and constancy perception. To briefly summarize our findings: in our initial investigation (Mack & Herman, 1973) there was only a very partial loss of position constancy for the background during target tracking.

Subjects were required to track a small, luminous target as it moved from left to right in front of a background array which consisted of black vertical stripes and randomly interlaced rectangles and which completely filled the subject's visual field. The tracking target traveled at a constant velocity (either 3.5° or 10.5° per sec). Subjects were required to report whether the background appeared to be stationary or moving, and if moving, to give the direction of movement. We used a version of the nulling technique to measure the illusion. Over a series of trials the background was either stationary or moving at some fraction of the tracking target speed in the same or opposite direction (1/4, 1/8, 1/2, 3/4, and 1° per sec, respectively). If the retinal displacement of background stimuli are not evaluated in terms of PEM information, then on no trial should a subject have reported that the background was stationary, since on every trial the background pattern displaced over the retina. When the background was physically stationary, it actually displaced at the same rate as the eye that was pursuing the moving target. When it moved in the same direction as the target, it displaced at a slower rate, and the faster it moved in that direction, the slower its rate of displacement. When it moved in the opposite direction, the background displaced at a faster rate; and the faster it moved in this opposite direction, the faster its rate of retinal displacement.

Data from this study indicates that the stationary background appeared to move on only about 20% of the trials in which it was stationary. At the slowest speeds of background movement in the direction of target movement, the background tended to be perceived as stationary significantly more often than at the slowest speeds of background movement in the opposite direction. This difference diminished as background speeds increased.

From the fact that as the rate of background movement in the direction of the target increased, the perception of its movement becomes increasingly veridical, we were able to infer with some confidence that it is not simply the retinal displacement of the background during intervals of PEM that causes the background to appear to move. Because as the background speed in this direction increases, the rate and, therefore, the amount of its retinal displacement decreases, but the probability of perceiving background movement increases.

The results of this investigation seem most adequately described as an instance of perceptual underconstancy, that is, as an instance of a partial loss of position constancy for background objects during PEMs rather than as an instance of a complete failure to account for retinal displacement in terms of eye-movement information. This description of the data assumes that retinal changes are evaluated in terms of eye-movement information and attributes the departure from complete or perfect constancy to some error in the evaluation process. For reasons subsequently discussed we have come to believe that the error in the evaluation process is the result of the nature of the information about the rate of the PEM with which the evaluator mechanism must operate. We have come to believe that this information indicates that the eye-movement rate is consistently less than it actually is.

The hypothesis that there is an underregistration of the rate of PEMs becomes quite plausible in light of the fact that the perceived speed of a moving object is significantly less when that object is tracked than when it is observed while fixating a stationary point in the object's path (Fleischl, 1882; Aubert, 1887). This phenomenon is frequently referred to as the Aubert–Fleischl paradox. That it occurs when the moving object is the only object visible in the field (Brown, 1931; Mack & Herman, 1972, 1973) would seem to reflect the postulated underregistration of PEM rate. For in this situation it is difficult to imagine what the source of the speed percept is (other than the registered information about the rate at which the eyes are traveling), assuming of course, that the eyes are tracking accurately. If this reasoning is correct, the Aubert–Fleischl paradox is rather direct evidence of the underregistration of PEM rate. (For a more complete statement of this reasoning, see Mack, 1975; Mack & Herman, 1973).

Following this initial set of studies indicating a small position-constancy loss, further work was done by Herman (1975) as his doctoral research. He attempted to resolve the apparent contradiction between the results we obtained and those reported by Stoper (1967), which showed much larger losses of constancy during PEMs. While we found at most about a 20% loss of constancy for the stationary background, Stoper (1967) reported that under some conditions the constancy loss was as great as 76%.

Briefly, Stoper's task was to have an observer track a point moving from left to right across a blackened oscilloscope screen. When the tracked point reached the midline of the screen, a small Y-shaped stimulus was flashed slightly above it and to its right. At some set time interval ranging from 0 to 1734 msec later, a second small vertical line stimulus was flashed in one of a number of positions slightly below the path of the tracked point. The observer reported whether the second flashed stimulus appeared to the right or left of the first flashed stimulus. Using the method of constant stimuli, Stoper derived the point of subjective alignment of the flashed stimuli. The largest (76%) position-constancy losses occurred at the shortest time intervals—up to 306 msec—and became increasingly smaller as the time between flashes increased. At the longest interval (1734 msec), Stoper found only a 36.2% loss of constancy. These differences were essentially ignored and Stoper concluded that the perceptual system has no access to PEM information so that perceived location during pursuit is strictly a function of retinal location and is proximally determined.

In thinking about Stoper's data and about the discrepancy between his results and ours, it occurred to me that, rather than perception being either in the proximal or constancy mode during pursuit, this might be a case when perception was consistently in the constancy mode but either: (a) subject-relatively determined by the taking into account of eye movement information which our initial work indicated was certainly available; or (2) object-relatively determined, that is, determined by the relative displacement of the pursued to the background stimulus.

We reasoned that in the short interval conditions, the locations of the flashed stimuli relative to the tracking target may have been so compelling as to override the perception of location based on taking eye position into account. This may have occurred, we thought, because of the proximity of the flashed stimuli to the tracked target in these conditions. It seems that the experiment was designed so that in the short interval conditions during which the eye could only have traveled a short distance beyond the position of the first flashed stimulus, the physical position of the second stimulus tended to be close to that of the first, which also meant that it was fairly close to the tracking target. If, as a result of the proximity of the flashed stimuli to the tracking target, their position was perceived in relation to the tracking stimulus, the results would indeed look like those based on a failure to take eye position into account. Perception of location based on the location relative to the tracking target would be indistinguishable from proximal perception based on the absolute retinal locations of the stimuli and the failure to take eye position into account. As the time interval between flashes increased, the physical distance between the tracked stimulus and the second flash was always greater, thus possibly lessening the salience of perceived position relative to the tracked target and allowing for perception of position based on taking eye position into account. Were this the case, the increase in position constancy at the longer intervals would become explicable. An alternative view is that in short interval conditions both factors contribute to the position-constancy loss, the underregistration of PEMs and relative location; while in the longer interval conditions relative location of the stimuli to the tracking target plays a diminishing role in the perception.

This argument involves at least two assumptions both of which seem well grounded. One of them is already familiar: object-relative percepts override those conjointly determined by retinal image displacements and body-generated head and eye position information. The second is that relational determination of perception is most salient when stimuli are near each other. All of Gogel's (1974) work on what he has called the adjacency principle supports this second assumption.

To test our explanation Herman (1975) carried out the following experiments. The first was essentially a repetition of our earlier work on the Filehne illusion with two major modifications: (1) the character of the background stimulus; and (2) the length of time during which the background was visible. Rather than use a large background array which filled the visual field, the background stimulus in these more recent experiments consisted of a single point of light. This modification was prompted by our speculation that the large background in our earlier work may have acted as a stable frame of reference, thus spuriously decreasing the magnitude of the Filehne illusion. (Duncker's, 1929, work on induced movement demonstrated a tendency to perceive a large and surrounding framework as staionary.) By using a single point as the background stimulus and a short vertical line (.5°) as the tracking target, we were able to eliminate this possible confounding factor. By varying the duration of background exposure, we were able to begin to address the question of whether the perceived apparent motion of the background had a relationally determined component.

In both conditions of the first experiment in this series the subjects tracked the vertical line as it moved from left to right over a 15° path at a constant velocity of 5° per second. Eye movements were recorded with Cornsweet's Double-Purkinje Image-Eye Tracker. Both the tracking and background stimuli were generated on a fast-phosphor oscilloscope and were viewed through a smoked plexiglass filter so that the display appeared in an otherwise black field. When the tracking stimulus reached the center of its path (had traveled 7.5°), the background stimulus appeared and was aligned with and bisected the target. The background stimulus moved at a velocity that was varied on each trial in .25° steps from stationary to 5° per second in either the same or opposite direction as the target.

In the first condition the background stimulus remained visible for 1.2 sec during which time the tracking target traveled 6°. In the second condition the background point remained visible for only .2 sec during which time the target traveled only 1°.

Our prediction was that there would be a greater loss of position constancy for the background in the short (.2-sec) background exposure condition than in the longer (1.2-sec) exposure condition.

In the short interval condition we believed that the relative displacement between background and tracking target would be more salient because of the close proximity between background and target. Background and target were never separated by more than 2° and on most trials by less, and thus were always foveal. In the long interval condition the maximum separation between background and target was 12° by the time the background stimulus disappeared. We reasoned that at the longer time intervals, the increased distance between background and target might make the object-relative displacement less salient so that the perception of background movement might now be primarily or entirely determined by an accounting for image displacement in terms of PEM information.

Subjects who had been pretrained to smooth track the target reported at the end of each trial whether the background point appeared to move with or against the target or appeared stationary.

In the long interval condition the mean background velocity which appeared stationary was .96° per second in the direction (with) of the tracking target which represents a 19.2% loss of position constancy. In the short-interval condition the mean background velocity which appeared stationary was 3.35° per second in the direction of the target which represents a much greater, (67%), loss of constancy. The difference between these results is highly significant and is in line with our prediction. The results support the hypothesis that object-relative displacement is a more salient determinant of perceived motion when background and target are contiguous; and when salient it results in a greater apparent loss of position constancy.

The correspondence between the results of the long interval condition where the mean constancy loss was only about 19% and those from our initial investigation of the Filehne illusion involving a large background, in which we obtained a comparable mean constancy loss of about 20%, clearly demonstrates that the much greater position-constancy loss reported by Stoper (1967) cannot be attributed to the stabilizing effect of a large background array.

In the next experiment we were able to create conditions in which object-relative displacement between background and target was completely eliminated. Thus we were able to address the question of whether or not the loss of constancy in the long interval condition is less because: (1) of the weakening of object-relative displacement as a determinant of perceived motion of the background that occurs as a function of the increased separation between tracking target and background; or (2) as relative displacement becomes less salient, the perception of background motion is determined primarily by eye-movement information in conjunction with simple background-image-displacement information. If the decrease in position constancy in the long-interval condition is simply due to a weakening of the object-relative displacement as a source of movement information and is not evidence that another mode of perception remains or becomes operative, then eliminating relative displacement between background and target should eliminate all loss of constancy. If, on the other hand, this other mode of perception is operative in the long interval condition, namely that based on image displacement and degraded or underregistered PEM information, then we should expect a small but significant loss of position constancy when relative displacement is eliminated.

By eliminating relative displacement we can also ask whether it is, as Stoper (1967) and others have argued, the simple retinal painting of the background image uncompensated for by PEM information which causes the loss of constancy. If this argument were correct, we should expect as large a loss of position constancy when object-relative displacement is eliminated as when it is present. Were such results obtained, there would be evidence supporting the proximal account of the position-constancy loss during PEMs and we would be at a loss to explain the differences between the results of our short and long interval conditions and the differences Stoper (1967), himself, found.

We were able to eliminate object-relative displacement by trading on the fact that subjects can be trained to continue to make PEMs for an interval following the disappearance of a moving target. Experiment 2 was a modification of the short-interval (.2 sec) condition of the first experiment—the condition which produced the strong illusion. The modification involved the blanking of the tracking target immediately preceding, during, and immediately following the .2-sec interval in which the background point was visible. Specifically the tracking target appeared, as in the first experiment, and moved at 5° per sec for 1.3 sec covering a 6.5° path. The screen became completely black for .2 sec. The background point then appeared 1° to the right of where the tracking target disappeared. This is the position the tracking target would have been in at that moment had it been continuously visible and thus the background stimulus appeared in the same position it had appeared in, in the experiment just described. The background remained visible for .2 sec and either stationary or moving left or right. It then disappeared and the screen remained black for an additional .1 sec, following which the tracking target reappeared at the point it would have reached had it been continuously visible. During this time it traveled an additional 6° before disappearing. Only subjects who were able to continue to smooth track during this .5 sec interval in which the tracking target was absent were tested. The 6 subjects tested again reported whether the background appeared stationary or; if moving, they gave the direction of movement.

The mean velocity of the background that appeared stationary was .79° per second with the target. Because the eye-movement records showed that the eye has a tendency to slow from about 5° per second to about 3° per second during the blank interval, we computed the percentage of constancy loss in terms of a 3° per second PEM and also repeated the short-interval condition of the first experiment using a continuously visible tracking target traveling at 3° per second. The results of the blanked target condition represent a 26% loss of constancy. The results of the replication of the short-interval condition, using a continuously visible 3° per second tracking target, yielded a 74% loss of constancy.

The 26% loss of constancy obtained when relative displacement was eliminated clearly represents a significant loss of constancy and one which seems entirely due to the underregistration of PEM information which is used in evaluating the simple image displacement of the background. The fact that this loss of constancy is very significantly weaker than it is in the comparable condition in which the tracking target is continuously present (26 versus 74%, respectively) strongly supports the view that there are two modes of perception that may operate to produce the Filehne illusion. When object-relative displacement is made salient by the contiguity of background and target, it has a strongly determining influence on perception. When relative displacement is entirely eliminated, the perception of background motion and stability is determined by the relation between eye- and image-displacement information; and there is a much smaller loss of position constancy.

In addition to validating our explanation of the loss of position constancy during PEMs, the results of these experiments argue strongly against the view that the perception of location, motion, and stability during pursuit is proximal, a function of simple retinal location or movement. As previously noted, if the perception of background location or movement was determined simply by retinal position or movement, the position-constancy loss obtained in the experiment where object-relative displacement was completely eliminated should have been as great as in the comparable condition in which the tracked target was continuously visible. It was not. The fact that we obtained between a 67 and 74% loss of constancy in the short-interval conditions in which the tracking stimulus was continuously visible (which is comparable with the largest position constancy loss reported by Stoper, 76%, in his shortest interval conditions), further supports the view that Stoper's (1967) short interval results were a function of object-relative location—of perceiving the location of the background stimuli relative to the tracking stimulus.

Thus the distinction between subject and object relational perceptions seems to account well for the discrepant results concerning the magnitude of the position-constancy loss during PEMs, whereas it seems inappropriate and mistaken to account for these differences in terms of a proximal—constancy distinction.

It seems worth noting that this distinction between percepts that are determined by object-relative relations and those that are subject relative not only clarifies our data, the differences within Stoper's (1967) data, and the differences between his data and our own, but it also has an additional asset. It places this phenomenon, the Filehne illusion, squarely within the context of more general characteristics of motion perception. We know, as the result of many other peoples' work, that there are at least two sources of motion perception. One is the subject-relative displacement of objects in the field, the displacement of an object relative to the observer; and the other is object-relative displacement, the displacement of objects with respect to each other. We know from the work of Shaffer and Wallach (1966) that the threshold for the detection of object-relative motion is appreciably lower than that for subject-relative motion; and we know from the work of Duncker and others on induced motion that the perception of object-relative displacement dominates the subject-relative percept of motion. Lee's work (Chapter 8, this volume) on induced motion of the self makes this point excessively clear. When an observer fixates a stationary point surrounded by a frame that is moving below the subject-relative-motion detection threshold, the frame is perceived as stationary and the enclosed point is perceived as moving. This perception occurs despite the fact that the image of the stationary point is stationary on the retina and it is likely that the perceptual system has access to the information that the eyes are stationary, are fixating. These two pieces of information should lead to the subject-relative based percept of a stationary point. They don't. The object-relative displacement that occurs between frame and point is attributed to the point despite image displacement and eye-movement information to the contrary.

The fact that the position-constancy loss for the background objects during intervals in which a moving object is tracked is much greater when object-relative displacement governs perception than it is when the perception of background movement is based on subject-relative displacement (on eye- and image-movement information) is, thus, completely congruent with what we know about the differences between subject-relative and object-relative motion perception. When object-relative displacement operates as a source of perceived background movement during PEM, it is clearly dominant. The stationary background stimulus is perceived to move by quite a considerable amount despite the fact that the perceptual system has fairly good eye-movement information, which if used would result in a far more veridical perception of background behavior. When object-relative displacement is eliminated or made less salient by increasing the distance between background and tracking target, then the subject-relative perception of background activity takes over. This results in a much smaller constancy loss.

I might add that many of the phenomena described by Johansson (1950) also seem interpretable in terms of this distinction, a point first made by Wallach (1968). Let me cite one example. When an observer views two points of light moving in phase along paths at right angles to each other so that they describe a ∟, the observer perceives the two points moving obliquely towards and away from each other. In other words the object-relative displacement of the two points with respect to each other, strongly dominates the perception of movement path overriding the subject-relative perception of movement path—the perception that the points are moving along paths that are at right angles to each other and vertical and horizontal with respect to the observer. Johansson noted that if one of the two points is tracked by the eyes (say the horizontally moving one), a different percept occurs. The path of movement of the tracked point is perceived veridically whereas the path of the other point is perceived obliquely. The untracked vertically moving point is perceived to move obliquely toward and away from the tracked horizontally moving one.

It can be argued that the perception of the untracked point is determined entirely by its retinal path and is therefore a proximal percept. If one tracks the horizontally moving point, the vertically moving point in fact does trace an oblique on the retina; but based on what we know about object- and subject-relative motion perception and on our work on the Filehne illusion, I am convinced that this is not the basis of this perception. In fact, the situation just described is identical to the one we used to study the Filehne illusion, the only difference being that the untracked point moves at right angles instead of along a plane parallel to the plane of the tracked one. For this reason it seems to me that one must account for the perception that the untracked, vertically moving point is traveling obliquely in terms of object-relative displacement, the displacement of the untracked with respect to the tracked point. The extent and direction of movement of the tracked point is perceived more or less veridically as it is, I believe, in our work on the Filehne illusion; whereas the path of motion of the untracked point is perceived only in relation to the tracked one—is object-relatively determined. It is displacing obliquely relative to the tracked point.

We intend to try and verify our account of this phenomenon by using Herman's (1975) technique for eliminating object-relative displacement. We will blank the tracked point while moving the untracked point vertically, and, if this is correct, we should find that our subjects perceive the path of the vertically moving point as far less oblique than when the tracked point is visible. Some oblique motion should occur even here, however, due to the underregistration of the PEM information.

In conclusion then, visual perception may be in a proximal or constancy mode and if in a constancy mode, it may be determined either by object relations or by the relation of an object to a subject. It would seem that human beings are such visually dependent creatures that visual relations—object-relative based percepts—may not only lead us to misperceive the external world but may also lead us to misperceive what we ourselves are doing.

REFERENCES

Asch, S. E., & Witkin, H. A. Studies in Space Perception I and II. *Journal of Experimental Psychology*, 1948, *38*, 325–337.

Aubert, H. Die Bewegungs empfindungen. *Pflugers Arch.*, 1887, *40*, 459–480.

Brown, J. F. [The visual perception of velocity.] *Psychologische Forschung*, 1931, *14*, 199–232.

Duncker, K. Über induzierte Bewegung. *Psychologische Forschung*, 1929, *12*, 180–259.

Filehne, W. Über das Optische Wahrnehmen von Bewegung. *Zeitschrift für Sinnesphysiologie*, 1922, *53*, 134–135.

Fleischl, E. Physiologisch-optische Notizen. *Sitzungsberichte der Akademic der Wissenschaften*, 1882, *86*, 17–25.

Gibson, J. J. *The perception of the visual world.* Boston: Houghton Mifflin, 1950.

Gogel, W. The sensing of retinal size. *Vision Research*, 1969, *9*, 1079–1094.

Gogel, W. C. Relative motion and the adjacency principle. *Quarterly Journal of Experimental Psychology*, 1974, *26*, 425–437.

Gregory, R. L. Distortions of visual space as inappropriate constancy scaling. *Nature*, 1962, *199*, 678–680.

Herman, E. The role of pursuit eye movements in the perception of motion: An investigation of the Filehne illusion and other related phenomena. Unpublished Ph.D. thesis, New School for Social Research, 1975.

Johansson, G. *Configurations in event perception.* Uppsala, Sweden: Almkvist & Wiksell, 1950.

Lee, D. N. On the functions of vision. This volume.

Mack, A. Perception during pursuit eye movements. *Psychologia*, 1975, *18*, 31–62.

Mack, A., & Herman, E. A new illusion: The underestimation of distance during pursuit eye movements. *Perception & Psychophysics*, 1972, *12*, 471–473.

Mack, A., & Herman, E. Position constancy during pursuit eye movements: An investigation of the Filehne illusion. *Quarterly Journal of Experimental Psychology*, 1973, *25*, 71–84.

Rock, I., & Ebenholtz, S. The relational determination of perceived size. *Psychological Review*, 1959, *66*, 387–401.

Roelofs, C. O. Optische Lokalisation. *Archiv für Augenheilkunde*, 1935, 395–415.

Shaffer, O., & Wallach, H. Extent of motion thresholds under subject-relative and object-relative conditions. *Perception & Psychophysics*, 1966, *1*, 447–451.

Stoper, A. Vision during pursuit eye movement: The role of oculomotor information. Unpublished doctoral dissertation, Brandeis University, 1967.

Stoper, A. Apparent motion of stimuli presented stroboscopically during pursuit movement of the eye. *Perception & Psychophysics*, 1973, *23*, 201–211.

Wallach, H. Informational discrepancy as a basis of perceptual adaptation. In S. J. Freedman (Ed.), *The neurophysiology of spatially oriented behavior.* Homewood, Ill.: Dorsey Press, 1968.

Witkin, H. A., & Asch, S. E. Studies in Space Orientation IV. *Journal of Experimental Psychology*, 1948, *38*, 762–782.

10
Perceiving Change

Robert Shaw

University of Connecticut

John Pittenger

University of Arkansas, Little Rock

> The gradualness of the change is the criterion
> by which I am led to regard the percepts as
> all belonging to one "thing."
> BERTRAND RUSSELL (1927, p. 245)

EDITORS' INTRODUCTION

Robert Shaw and John Pittenger examine perception of dynamic optical stimulation produced by transformations of objects. They are concerned with the information in such stimulation that specifies the transformation or event. They ask whether the perception of a slow event, for example, movement of the hour hand of a clock, is qualitatively different from the perception of fast events, for example, movement of the second hand of a clock. A traditional view of the perception of slow events is that such perception depends on comparison of static percepts at successive instants of time. In other words, perception of change depends on focal identity perception. Shaw and Pittenger present a logical argument that this cannot be so. They suggest that perception of slow and fast events occurs in the same mode.

There are two major problems to be addressed by perceptual theory: how do animals and how do humans perceive change and nonchange in the world around them. But under which of these two topics do we place the perception of extremely slow changes, such as the growth of animals and plants or the erosion of rocks and earth due to wind and torrents? Should we consider the detection of information specifying such extremely slow events under one mode[1] of perception while considering fast events (like balls bouncing or horses running) under another mode of perception? Or, perhaps, the perception of both slow and fast events takes place in a common mode of processing because the information specifying each is essentially the same.

The hypothesis we wish to investigate is whether or not the perception of all changes can be treated in a unified way by making events (rather than static objects or patterns) the primary focus of perceptual analysis. This event-perception approach seems to avoid the fallacies that occur in the more traditional accounts of the perception of change. Subsequently in this chapter, we review some of the evidence in favor of the event perception hypothesis. Our main goal in the chapter is to argue that the perception of change, even extremely slow change, is immediately experienced; there is no necessary intervention of mediating cognitive constructs such as specific memory for static objects or intellectual inferences, for it is surely a philosophical conundrum to assume that the experience of change can somehow arise from the experience of static things.

Another issue, not to be confused with the above conundrum, arises from a misunderstanding of Gibson's (1966) well-known claim that perception is the pickup of invariant information over time. It is sometimes argued, quite erroneously, that if perception is the pickup of invariant information, then all such information must be static in nature; hence, either change must be illusory or beyond the ken of a theory based on invariant information. This conclusion not only is unwarranted but shows a gross misunderstanding of the concept of invariance. For, to the extent that change proceeds according to some style, then to that extent change can be specified by invariant perceptual information. A motor can run invariantly, a couple can waltz invariantly, or a flower can grow according to a natural rhythm—an invariant policy of growth. None of these are static phenomena, rather they are distinct *events* precisely because they do exhibit different patterns of change.

Moreover, since much of psychology is directed toward the study of adaptive responses to change (like cognitive development, learning, reorganization of memory, and problem solving), it behooves us to develop, if we can, an adequate theory of event perception. To achieve such a goal we must ultimately provide precise definitions for those naturally occurring, invariant transformations which underly the varieties of change experienced by both animals and people.

---

[1] The term "mode" should be reserved for those psychological processes that are functionally disjoint and perhaps, even complimentary in the strong sense that (1) they depend in no essential way on the functioning of the other, although (2) they may be subsumed under a more generic concept. Traditional examples of distinct but related modes of psychological processing traditionally recognized are *focal* versus *ambient* vision, *parallel* versus *serial* information processing, and *voluntary* versus *involuntary* acts.

THE EVENT PERCEPTION HYPOTHESIS

An *event* can be defined as a *minimal change* of some specified type (including its continuants) wrought over an object or object complex within some determinate region of the space–time continuum. The type of minimal change involved and, hence, the nature of the event class, is relative to scale of the space–time region selected. In quantum physics the minimal region of change is apt to be measured in microns and microseconds, while in relativity physics light years or parsecs are more appropriate measures. Obviously, neither of these two scales is appropriate for describing ecologically significant events for animals and humans, that is, activities involving objects that play a significant role in the attempts of animals and humans to cope with change at the scale of the terrestrial environment.

Assuming for the moment that we are intuitively clear about the nature of objects that may be involved in terrestrial events, such things as trees, rocks, cars, houses, highways, cities, thimbles, baseballs, animals, apples, people, and so on, the main concept to be clarified in the above definition of an event is that of minimal change. By "minimal change" we mean the least transformation of a property of an object (like its color, size, texture, orientation, distance from other objects, and so on) needed to specify unambiguously the exact nature of that change. Such a minimal change can be said to constitute the *symmetry period* of the event (Shaw, McIntyre, & Mace, 1974). Generally speaking, the symmetry period of an event is that perceivable or measurable region of space–time over which the unique qualitative aspects of an event are defined.

Thus for every event the symmetry period entails a type of change that can be specified in terms of variations in extensive magnitude (such as color, texture, distance, size, and so on) and intensive magnitude (such as duration, frequency, phase, and so on). In other words, answers to questions such as *what changed?* or *what type of change was it?* are precisely specified in the observables made available by the event for an observer who has been properly tuned by evolution and experience. Typically then, except in cases of nonspatial change, such as in color or weight, an event has both a spatial period and a temporal period.

It is important to note, however, that the scale of the spatial or temporal periods of an event is relative, being dependent upon the nature of the event per se rather than upon an a priori determined, absolute unit of measure for change in general. Thus, we should expect no general solution to the so-called perceptual "quantum" hypothesis for events asserting the existence of a minimum visible or its analogue for other sensory modalities.

The temporal period of terrestrial events may vary extensively, ranging from milliseconds and seconds to minutes, hours, days, or even years. For instance, a flash of lightning lasts only a few milliseconds, while the evaporation of a puddle after a rain may take hours; the growth and blossoming of a flowering plant takes a whole season, while the period of growth of a human from infancy to adulthood may take nearly 30 years. Similarly, some change may take place over very small distances, say a few millimeters as when a blade of grass bends in the wind, or over many square miles, as when the weather changes from bright and sunny to dark and stormy.

Clearly, there can be no single value for the spatial–temporal period of all events, yet a successful perceptual theory must account for cases as different as:

1. I *saw* the lightning strike the tree.
2. I *watched* the puddle evaporate during the afternoon.
3. I've *observed* the roses blossoming each spring for several years.
4. I *noticed* that my nephew had grown into a man during my years of absence.

Consequently, we try to show that the perceptual predicates in the above cases are literally and not just metaphorically true.

Few people balk at calling very fast events of short duration *perceptual*. In this case by "perceptual" we mean an event that is seen rather than inferred somehow from memory or logically deduced from the observed effects of change. On the other hand, to claim that very slow events, that is, those that may take hours, days, or even years to develop, are also perceptual is understandably met with considerable incredulity. But this is indeed the claim we wish to make. Not only do we believe this claim to be theoretically necessary if we are to have a unified theory of event perception, but that it can also be justified on empirical grounds. We do indeed *see* events that may take years to transpire in accord with the same laws of event perception that allow us to see anything, even something traditionally presumed to be so static as the shape of an object (Shaw *et al.*, 1974). To understand why this is so requires a careful consideration of how we perceive change in general.

THE TRADITIONAL ACCOUNT OF HOW WE PERCEIVE CHANGE

In this section we examine the nature of the perceptual information specifying change in general. As pointed out above, change can be either kinetic or qualitative in nature, as when an object moves or a leaf changes color. However, for an exemplary case of change, and one that we all understand at least at the intuitive level, consider the perception of change due to the motion of an object.

It is accurate to say that we perceive the motion of the second hand of our watch while we do not perceive the motion of its hour hand. The standard explanation for this is that we do not see the motion of the hour hand because it moves too slowly. Yet we *do* see that the hour hand has moved from place to place, since on one sighting it is seen to occupy a position near one numeral on the face of the watch and on a later sighting, to occupy a new position near another numeral.

To account for the differing in the perceptual experience of motion of the second hand, as compared to the perceived change of position of the hour hand, an important distinction must be made between the perception of *motion* and the perception of *displacement.* The former experience necessarily entails the latter but not vice versa. However, before analyzing this difference, let us consider still another example.

On a clear night one can often see meteorites flash across the sky (a case of perceived motion) but cannot see the relative motion of the stars due to the rotation of the earth on its axis. However, after watching the sky for several hours one is able to detect that some constellations have disappeared over the eastern horizon while others have appeared over the western horizon (a case of perceived displacement, but not of perceived motion).

Several important questions must be answered if we are to understand the relation existing between perceived motion and perceived displacement:

1. What perceptual information is available in the light to the eye when something is seen to move versus simply being seen to have changed positions?

2. What role, if any, does memory play in "seeing" that an object has undergone a displacement from one location in the environment to another?

3. Is any kind of inference involved in concluding that such a displacement has taken place when in fact no motion of the object over the intervening space was perceived?

A full accounting of each of these questions is required if we are to validate our claim that the perception of "slow" events and "fast" events is governed by the same laws because the perceptual information made available in each case is essentially the same.

There is a danger, however, that how one states a problem may preclude its solution. For instance, the problem of how we recognize that very slow changes have occurred is often described as follows: we perceive that the hour hand of a watch has moved because we *remember* where it was and then compare that stored image with the percept of where we now see it. It is inferred that the difference between the first and second images results from a rotary motion of the hour hand from one place on the face of the watch to another place. It is assumed that the motion must be inferred because presumably it was too slow to be actually seen.

This analysis, what we will call the *image-comparison model,* surely deserves to be called the classical statement of the problem. But notice that it necessarily assumes that three distinct psychological processes—perception, memory, and inference—are involved in making a perceptual judgment that a slow event has occurred. If this were the case, then calling the phenomenon "the perception of change" would be a misnomer. However, as we shall see, not only is there something nonintuitive and logically cumbersome about this model, but also some very strong and quite unrealistic assumptions are made about the nature of the information that must be perceptually processed, stored, and compared.

In essence this approach is nothing less than a bald denial that change as such cannot be perceived but rather must be inferred from a comparison of two static patterns. This view therefore assumes that perception is nothing but the passive registration of a static characterization of stimuli rather than a direct apprehension of change itself. As such it is at loggerheads with the event perception hypothesis. We believe the image-comparison model, in spite of its traditional popularity, to be a fruitless endeavor, since it is based on a complete misunderstanding of the nature of the perception of change.

First, in this model it is assumed that in perceiving change we must obtain a specific memory for each pattern (like the scene, object, or event) about which we might later experience a change. For how else, so the argument goes, might we detect the difference between earlier and later versions of the same pattern?

This first requirement (that there be specific memory for the patterns to be compared) poses what seems to be an insurmountable obstacle to any perceptual theory or pattern recognition model that attempts to explain the capacity for optimization that all such systems naturally exhibit. Is it possible for the system to recognize readily variant forms of the same pattern in spite of changes in orientation, illumination, intervening media, or context? Since there is no way for the system to know in advance what feature dimensions might assume different values due to such salient environmental effects, then it is necessary that as complete a characterization as possible be stored. Such a complete and specific representation of a pattern is usually called an "image." This approach also assumes that in order to perceive the end state of a pattern-changing process as a transformation that arises continuously out of earlier states (such as seeing a flower grow over a long period of time or a person's face age), then we must somehow store specific images of all the earlier states and "integrate" over them. This assumption seems patently false.

Just as the perceived displacement of an object does not require that we see all of its intermediate positions, as in the case of apparent motion phenomena, such as phi, neither is it necessary that we see all intermediate growth states of a plant or face as they mature. Thus, such a requirement is wholly unrealistic, since if satisfied memory would consist of an unlimited store of specific images accumulated since birth. Perhaps, it is wiser to assume that nature strives for information-processing procedures more optimal than this. If so then the requirement that specific images of the world and its furnishings are somehow stored might be given up.

The second major assumption of the image-comparison model is that somehow the so-called Höffding step is accomplished (Neisser, 1967). This requirement assumes that the specific image of a pattern seen earlier can somehow be retrieved from among the astronomical crowd of other stored images and placed in a buffer to be compared with the specific image of the pattern the system is currently attempting to recognize. But notice that in order to accomplish this feat either all of the myriad stored images must be randomly retrieved and compared or there must be a procedure by which the identity relation can be established between the current image of the transformed pattern and the image of its progenitor pattern stored earlier. In other words, in order to recognize that a change in a given pattern has occurred, the perceptual system must first discover the identity of the pattern being processed by correctly associating its image with the image or images initially derived from the source pattern. Unfortunately, to solve the pattern-identification problem requires that the system be able to get the current input together with its stored counterpart, for how else might the comparison needed to determine their mutual identity (or difference) be accomplished?

Thus the second requirement of the image-comparison model lands the theorist smack in the middle of the chicken-or-egg dilemma. To make the Höffding step requires that the system solve the pattern identification problem, but to solve this problem requires that the system first make the Höffding step. As a result we not only must give up the specific image requirement but we must also give up the requirement that the Höffding step be accomplished before the image-comparison step can itself be successfully dispatched.

Although there have been many earnest attempts by computer scientists working on pattern-recognition models to circumvent this dilemma, no real success has been achieved when the patterns to be recognized are those that occur in nature. Unfortunately, little recognition of how seriously debilitating this dilemma is for the image-comparison model seems to have leached over into psychology. Indeed, some version of this model perennially recurs with all its attendant difficulties still intact.

This dilemma cannot be simply ignored by the serious theorist as being only some verbal sleight of hand, for the image-comparison model is indeed founded upon a vicious circle, that is, logically speaking, the theory chases its own tail. The chief mistake obviously arises from the assumption that the perception of change is founded upon the comparison of specific images of patterns that can somehow be retrieved at will. But this is a very mysterious somehow, for the criterion needed to retrieve the appropriate image from the plenum of stored images is nothing less than knowledge that such an image is potentially related to the new image by some specified transformation—a transformation that can be nothing other than the change to be perceived.

Hence, to perceive a change the system must already somehow know the change. But to assume that the model knows the change is to assume exactly that which the model is supposed to explain!

For these reasons the image-comparison model encounters a logical impasse at its very inception, even before the heart of the model, the image-comparison step, is reached. Too often the impasse is ignored rather than resolved. By focusing the theory primarily on the comparison step, the Hoffding step is considered to be merely a "coding" problem, a domain of problems in which the seriousness of the retrieval problem is too easily overlooked.

For instance, many a theorist has been lulled by the belief that if only the images of the pattern before and after its change are appropriately encoded, then their shared identity will be obvious to the system and the retrieval problem will disappear. This belief seems to be fostered most by approaches that depend too much on techniques of internal simulation, that is, techniques by which pattern recognition models are developed and tested solely within the innards of the computer.

Possessing no roving eye or active organ by which to explore its perceptual environment, the self-contained system must be fed upon data predigested by the programmer, who, of course, does indeed possess a knowledge of the environment born of continous, active perceptual exploration. Armed with this perceptual knowledge the theorist, often with only intuitive awareness, encodes the pattern data in such a way as to delimit arbitrarily the number of semantic variables so that retrieval decisions required of the system may be kept within manageable limits. However, even when such boot-strapping engineering solutions attain some degree of success, they fail to provide a general theory for the semantics of coding variables; hence, they fail to provide an explanation of their own success or a means for succeeding in other pattern contexts, especially natural ones.

Such glib attempts to wave away the dilemma inherent in image-comparison models ultimately run aground on the so-called "normalization" problem, a problem that arises whenver constraints on the selection of coding variables are arbitrarily relaxed or relaxed in favor of more natural pattern processing. Here patterns cannot be appropriately encoded in their original form of presentation but must first be preprocessed or "normalized" by reorienting, magnifying, minifying, or completing, or in some other way cleaned up so as to fit the coding variables, preselected for the system by the naturally biased programmer. Of course, the variables selected are those that are consonant with the comparison tests to be executed later, a bias which thereby restricts the nature of the pattern changes that can be recognized.

Again we come full circle in our analysis to what seems to be the culprit of the piece—the assumption that specific static patterns must be encoded in the first place in order to be stored and compared. Perhaps, if the comparison step could be avoided, then the need for detailed pattern codes (specific images) could also be avoided and ultimately the problem of the Höffding step could be avoided.

The goal of the image-comparison model is to detect differences existing among patterns. If this pickup of pattern differences could be accomplished without the need of a comparison step, then no specific pattern images would be necessary and in this way the pattern-identity problem would be circumvented.

One strategy might be to restate the problem of perceiving change in such a way as to avoid the problems inherent in the classical formulation. For instance, what if we assume that difference relations among patterns need not be computed by a comparison procedure but may be directly *perceived*?

In the next section, we attempt to show that abstract difference relations may themselves be perceived, thereby obviating the requirement for the comparison step and the need for encoding specific images of patterns to be compared. If such a tactic succeeds, then no mediation by nonperceptual processes such as memory and inference would be necessary and no longer would the phrase "perception of change" be a misnomer.

THE DIRECT PERCEPTION OF CHANGE

There are subtle nuances to the identity problem discussed in the previous section that need to be discussed before attempting to explain how change as the creation of an abstract-difference relation among variant forms of the same object might be directly perceived. The image-comparison model not only fails because it ensnares the theorist in a vicious circle, but it also fails because no comparison tests—even in principle—are capable of proving that a given object is or is not a variant form of an object experienced earlier.

Indeed, all that any comparison procedure can show is whether or not two objects are structurally similar, evidence which, even if true, has no logical bearing on the issue of their existential identity. Consequently, a principled solution to the existential identity problem, unlike what is often called "the pattern-identification problem," must do more than merely assign similar patterns to the same equivalence class in accordance with certain formal criteria (shape, color, size, texture, and so on). Rather, it must also provide means for deciding if two distinct things exist, or if only one exists. Such a decision must ultimately be rendered independently of the objects' formal similarity. No test of similarity due to shared features, however, exhaustive, is either logically necessary or logically sufficient to prove existential identity, for existence (and hence existential identity) is not an attribute but a predicate—the predication of a shared ontological state. This view is in keeping with the existentialists' claim that *existence precedes essence,* that issues regarding existence must in all cases be resolved before those regarding essences (attributes) can even be addressed. The truth of this is illustrated in the fact that identical objects may appear dissimilar while similar appearing ones may be actually distinct.

To see why formal similarity is logically irrelevant to the issue of the existential identity of objects consider the following pair of hypothetical cases:

1. Assume that sometime in the near future the process of complete cloning is perfected so that a perfect duplicate of any given person might be grown in a super test tube when tissue containing that person's DNA code is combined with appropriately synthesized enzymes. Furthermore, assume that the resulting android is a perfect physical facsimile of the person, right down to fingerprints, scars, number of hair follicles, skin blemishes, dental work, and so on. Assume also that by techniques of intensive psychoprogramming the android is given all of the memories, personality traits, tastes and desires of the person being simulated. Question: *Would there now be two such people or only one?* Given

that neither that person nor his android Doppelgänger had an acceptable alibi, how would a jury rationally decide which to convict for an alleged crime committed in front of several acute witnesses? Clearly, in such a case similarity is an irrelevant issue.

2. Now consider a case in which a master criminal succeeds in obtaining a completely different body through a brain transplant. In addition, the master criminal also undergoes psychosurgery and shock treatments that totally erase the memory, alter personality, and reprogram the individual with new memories and sufficient learning to allow the "criminal" to assume the life of a successful, law-abiding citizen. Question: *Would there now be a new person in every sense of the word or just the same old person in a new guise*? Again similarity or difference in formal aspects seems of little value in determining the issue of existential identity.

The following conclusions can be drawn from a careful study of these two cases: in the first case of the android Doppelgänger, to determine that it is not the person, requires a method by which each being might be traced back to its origins. However, if the thread of lineage of either is broken, then no definitive results are logically possible. On the other hand, if no gap exists in the recounting of their respective biographical histories, then ultimately the negative case can be decided, since it will be discovered that each being derives from a unique source.

Regarding the positive case, however, a bizarre possibility exists, namely, that their lineages, what the mathematician Minkowski (1908) called their "world lines," ultimately converge on the same source point. In such a case the only reasonable conclusion one might draw is that they were in fact the same person who, quite mysteriously, possessed a true double reality. Given the recent "many-world" hypothesis entertained by some quantum theorists (DeWitt & Graham, 1973), the possibility of such an outcome is not as ridiculous as may first be thought. We, however, ignore this possibility for now, since it would be quite rash to accept a theory that has such bizarre ontological consequences unless forced by overwhelming evidence to do so.

Turning now to the second case, there is only one way of determining if the criminal has been only cosmetically transformed by science or whether a second distinct person has actually been created who is entirely innocent under the law of any wrongdoings committed by a malevolent alter ego; it must be shown beyond the shadow of a doubt that the transformation was not really continuous but involved an abrupt change or identity gap—that one person had been creatively substituted in the place of another.

Thus, the two above cases suggest an important conclusion regarding the nature of perceptual information sufficient to specify that only a benign change in an object, person, or pattern has occurred: *The perception of the persistent identity of an object that undergoes a change over space—time logically presup-*

poses that there is perceptual information available which specifies the continuity of the transformation underlying the change.

At first this conclusion may not seem particularly dramatic, especially given the lengthy line of argument that we have taken to get here; but what is important is that this conclusion is the exact opposite of the principle assumed by the classical interpretation of the problem of how change might be perceived: We do not perceive change by comparing specific descriptions of patterns but by determining that one can be continuously transformed over space–time into the other. Where at first it seemed natural to assume that the perceived nature of change depends upon the available information specifying the identity of the objects involved, it now must be concluded that the reverse is true, namely, that the perceived identity of the objects depends upon the availability of perceptual information that they afford being related by some continuous transformation. Thus, it is the perceptual information for the continuity of the transformation that is of paramount importance in accounting for the perception of events rather than the perceived identity of the structures involved in the event transformation.

A possible objection to this argument might be raised. Is perceptual information specifying the transformational continuity that exists between variant forms of an object truly sufficient to guarantee their existential identity? Perhaps, one might argue, it is possible that two noncontemporaneous objects may be related by a continuous transformation, and yet still be existentially distinct. The proper reply to this question is that if so, then we would not be able to tell (excluding the possibility, of course, that the two objects could be arranged side by side), that is, that we allow them somehow to become contemporaneous. But even this test of twoness versus oneness is not logically foolproof since such contemporaneous arrangement of the objects might in principle (if not in fact) be achieved hypothetically by the use of a time machine or by the "many-worlds" hypothesis of quantum mechanics. However, as argued earlier, the wiser course is simply to suspend judgment regarding speculative hypotheses that entail bizarre ontological consequences, since they presently lack any significant scientific support.

In our opinion the wisest course is to accept the hypothesis that people do in fact settle issues of existential identity of noncontemporaneous objects by picking up perceptual information specifying their continuous transformability into one another over space–time. Indeed, to require more than this is to fall into an ontological sink hole of scientific perplexity. According to Russell (1927), Alfred North Whitehead stubbornly claimed that observable evidence alone is never sufficient to settle issues of existential identity, rather they can only be resolved by knowledge that one's percepts of the objects in question derive from the same underlying "substance." To this Russell (1927) replied:

> We have already seen that the physical object, as inferred from perception, is a group of events arranged about a center. There may be a substance in the center, but there can be

no reason to think so, since the group of events will produce exactly the same percepts; therefore the substance at the center, if there is one, is irrelevant to science, and belongs to the realm of mere abstract possibility [p. 244].

This reply still seems to us to be a cogent rebuttal to the recalcitrant critic of the continuity-of-change hypothesis previously offered, who feels justified in demanding greater certitude than that two noncontemporaneous things are the same simply because their mutual transformability is perceptually specified.

THE PERCEPTION OF MOTION
VERSUS THE PERCEPTION OF DISPLACEMENT, REVISITED

At last we return to the question originally posed regarding the difference between the perception of motion and the perception of displacement. If we can understand how we perceive displacements (for example, that the hour hand on our watch has moved), then we may be in a position to understand how we perceive other very slow events, such as the drying up of puddles, the growth of plants, or the aging of human faces. Given the above argument against the image-comparison model, we now know that however such events are perceived it must be in some other way than by inferring the change from a comparison of the static dregs of their invisible dynamism. Several lines of empirical evidence support the contention that the "difference" information picked up by the perceptual systems is abstract and general rather than concrete and specific. We now review some of the evidence.

A simple demonstration that you can perceive motion without the need to perceive the static contours of the object undergoing the motion is easily made. If, under a light bulb, you hold a pencil between your fingers over a sheet of white paper, the distance of the pencil from the paper can be adjusted so that no shadow of the pencil on the paper can be seen. However, if you wiggle the pencil back and forth, then the motion of its shadow cast onto the paper will become immediately apparent. Similarly, if some object moves into your peripheral vision, you will detect its presence as an event long before its shape, size, color, or texture is accurately appreciated by foveal vision.

Under both of the above circumstances what is specified in the changing light pattern at the eye is a definite motion of an indefinite object. Clearly, then, perceptual information for change does not depend on the recognition of static contour, but on the pickup of abstract information for change. If so, then no dependence upon the comparison of static images need be assumed, and one might conclude that change can indeed by directly perceived.[2]

---

[2] Evidence for the distinction between focal vision required to perceive shape and ambient vision required to perceive change has accrued over the past two decades. See for instance Lettvin, Maturana, McCulloch, and Pitts (1959) and Trevarthen (1968).

The word "abstract" literally means "conceived apart from concrete realities, specific objects, or actual instance." Thus, the claim that perceptual information for change (motion, growth, and so on) is abstract in nature is to claim that such information is general rather than specific, being manifested in some manner other than as a difference among static copies of the structure undergoing the change.

Additional evidence for this claim is provided by the so-called *phi* phenomenon, a type of apparent or optical motion in which a definite displacement is perceived in spite of the fact that nothing definite is seen to move (Kolers, 1972). It is interesting to note the boundary conditions under which apparent motion will be seen. In the typical phi-motion situation, two forms some distance apart are briefly illuminated. When the temporal interval separating the onset of the flashing of each stimulus is sufficiently short, the two stimuli are seen as being simultaneously flashed. On the other hand, when the flash interval is sufficiently lengthened, then the two stimuli appear to flash successively. However, when the temporal interval ranges over values longer than the former condition but shorter than the latter one, then an apparent movement is seen to occur between the two stimuli. In other words, apparent motion is specified only for a restricted range of temporal values of the flash interval. Furthermore, it can be shown that the effective range of values for the temporal interval varies directly with the spatial interval separating the two stimuli.

The relevant point of the optical motion phenomenon, for our purposes, is that motion between two places is perceived even when no such motion actually occurs. In the cited case, one wonders why discrete flashes specify a motion when such information is more nearly the analogue of a displacement than of a continuous motion. Yet observers invariably report seeing something translate across the intervening space between the two positions. Sometimes this "something" seems to be an object, while at other times it seems to be a motion of no definite thing. It must be that perceptual information specifying discrete displacement is, under some circumstances, identical to that specifying continuous motion. We return to this interesting point subsequently.

The apparent-motion phenomenon also illustrates how the condition of existential identity is intrinsically necessary to the perception of displacement, (and thereby to the perception of motion as well) for when the temporal interval is either too long or too short, then two successively present objects or two simultaneously present ones are seen, respectively. Thus, a quantitative change in a variable—the temporal period of the apparent event—yields qualitatively distinct percepts, that is, the perception of two things is transformable into the perception of one thing or vice versa.

Consequently, it seems that the information conveyed by the appropriate spatio–temporal interval is nothing other than abstract information for existential identity per se. The two percepts, continuity and identity, are inextricably intertwined so that one cannot be present without the other. Following Gibson

(1966), we suggest that the nature of the continuity information specifying identity is always some form of invariance under transformation.

If this is true then might not the information specifying displacement and motion be essentially identical? If so, then perhaps perceived motion and perceived displacement are phenomena of the same type in that both depend on the pickup of information specifying the persistent identity or invariance of successive objects or events undergoing a spatial change. As argued previously, this is tantamount to the pickup of information for a continuous transformation underlying the change; in this case the transformation specified is a translation. Could it be, therefore, that the perceived difference between displacements and motions—that the former is slow and discrete while the latter is faster and continuous—is not an essential difference?

Perhaps, displacements and motions lie on the same continuum of perceptual information so that one is readily transformable into the other by a simple operation, for example, by a scale change which shortens or lengthens their respective spatial or temporal periods. Or to put the hypothesis more generally: could it be that slow and fast events, at least so far as perception is concerned, are phenomena of the same type, and are thereby governed by the same explanatory principles? But what would constitute convincing evidence that this is so?

In the next section we attempt to provide evidence that the above hypothesis is indeed true by showing that information for slow events can be transformed into information for fast events, and vice versa. The transformation that accomplishes this is known as the Principle of Similitude, a principle that may ultimately help unify the field of event perception.

THE PRINCIPLE OF SIMILITUDE AND EVENT PERCEPTION

Poincaré (1905/1952) once posed the puzzle of whether there would be any detectable consequences if during our sleep the world and all its furnishings were suddenly increased in size by some scale factor, say a thousand times. A study of what Lord Rayleigh (cited in Bridgman, 1922) called the "Principle of Similitude" or what Bridgman (1922) later called *dimensional analysis* now allows us to provide a definitive answer to Poincaré's question. Assuming that mass increases proportionally, then simple changes in the magnitude of things are not always benign, that is, they sometimes move the phenomenon from a stable to an unstable state. For instance, a miniature building, a small animal, or plant may not be able to support its own weight if increased radically in size. This follows from the fact that not all dimensions of the supporting structure change proportionally when the object is scaled up in size. The cross section of a supporting member will change only linearly while the surface area of the object is squared and its volume is cubed. Consequently, since the strength of a supporting member is directly related to its cross section, whereas its weight is a function of its volume, then an enlarged version of the object will be disproportionately heavier than its supporting members are strong.

Hence, an object that is continuously enlarged will finally collapse under its own weight. This point of collapse where the phenomenon becomes grossly unstable is called a *critical point*. The Principle of Similitude, or *dynamical symmetry* as Thompson (1942) called it, is exemplified in the spindly legs of certain insects as compared to the more massive legs of larger creatures, such as elephants or dinosaurs, which must be disproportionately larger in cross section in order to counter the disproportionate effect of gravity on their great bulk. (So much the worse for science-fiction stories founded upon the premise of marauding giant insects.)

There is another sense in which scale changes may not be benign and yet bring about no gross instability in the phenomenon as a physical system. Instead of changes that affect the substantive variables of an object, event, or system (weight, size, velocity, and so on), changes can be brought to bear which affect only the variables of perceptual information associated with the phenomenon. Here gradual changes in quantitative measures may under some circumstances bring about radical qualitative changes in what is perceived.

Threshold effects and other nonlinearities, so avidly investigated by psychophysicists in their study of sensory and perceptual systems, are instances in which critical points have been found to exist in parameters of perceptual information. Such nonlinear effects occur, not because physical parameters of phenomena have been modified, but because the conditions under which they are measured or observed have been.

For instance an object may move so slowly that its motion is not seen, although after a long while its relative displacement can be detected. However, if the velocity of the object is increased, a critical point is eventually surpassed so that its motion becomes apparent. As its velocity is increased still further, due to perceptual persistence presumably arising from hysteresis of neural processing, another critical point is surpassed so that only an optical "smear" is seen. Imagine, for instance, an airplane propeller as it begins rotating faster and faster, or the blur of the road surface as seen from a window of an automobile as it moves from rest to top speed.

The difference between the perception of motion and the perception of displacement is that, in the former case, both the spatial and temporal periods of the event are visible, while in the latter case only the spatial period is. Could it be that this is the essential difference between fast and slow events of all kinds? If so, then a fast event would be specified whenever the observer is able to pick up information for both the spatial and temporal periods of an event while a slow event would be specified whenever only information for the spatial period is directly apprehended. Thus, if the temporal period of a slow event can be perceptually specified, say through the application of a benign scale transformation that alters the time scale of the event, while leaving the substantive variables unchanged, then it should be seen as a fast event rather than a slow one. This effect can be created in two ways: (1) by magnification of the light emanating from an event; or (2) by optical compression of the normal rate at which the event is perceptually sampled.

To see how magnification of perceptual information from slow events may transform them into fast events by making their temporal periods apparent, consider what happens when the hour hand of a watch is scrutinized through a microscope or when a star is observed through a telescope. In both of these cases our perceptual experience that something *has moved* is transformed into one of seeing that something *is moving*.

When viewed through a magnifying instrument, the visual angle of the observer (defined as the angle the apex of which is at the nodal point of the eye and the sides of which extend to the edges of the visual field provided by the optical instrument) is increased over that of the unaided eye. This makes the moving object (the hour hand or star) appear to traverse a wider spatial interval in the same time it originally required to cross a smaller one. This scale transformation of the spatial period of the event has the obvious effect of increasing the apparent velocity of the object (where apparent velocity is a function of the rate of change as measured in degrees of visual angle per unit of time).

In this case, the transformation of similitude applied is benign since it accomplishes an apparent shortening of the temporal period of the event beyond a critical point without changing to any extent the real velocity of the object in question. Therefore, by selecting an appropriate magnification of the information from a slow event, it can be effectively transformed into a fast event. (Mathematically, this can be shown to be a result of applying a transformation of similitude to a central projective transformation.)

As a magnification accomplishes a scale transformation of the temporal period of an event in an indirect fashion by lengthening the relative spatial period, so can a change in perceptual sampling rate determine a direct scale transformation of the temporal period of any event. By using the method of "lapsed-time" photography the apparent temporal period of a very slow event, such as the growth of a flower, can be transformed into that of a fast event. This method of photography allows a movie to be made in such a way that scenes separated far apart in time become temporally adjacent, thereby shortening the temporal period beyond the critical point where it can be seen.

An appropriate rendering of the Principle of Similitude for event perception would provide a beginning on the problem of explaining the significant effects of scale transfomrations on perceptual information conveyed by various kinds of events.

SUMMARY:
EVENT PERCEPTION AS THE PICKUP OF
ABSTRACT INFORMATION

In the foregoing it has been argued that the information for the perception of change does not—indeed cannot—arise from tests comparing the degree of similarity of detailed "images;" on the contrary, such information has been shown to be abstract and general rather than concrete and specific. Moreover, a necessary condition for the perception of change is the pickup of information specifying the continuous transformation underlying the change; for it is this information that is needed to specify the existential identity shared by variant forms of the objects involved in the event.

It was also shown that some scale transformations can be benign in that they effect a change in only the apparent temporal period of an event without requiring substantive changes in its physical parameters. Scale transformations such as magnification (expanding the apparent spatial period over which an event is seen), in contrast, achieve an indirect transformation of the apparent temporal period of slow events. Other scale informations, such as lapsed-time photography (varying the rate of perceptual sampling), achieve a direct transformation of the apparent temporal period of slow events.

The Principle of Similitude potentially provides a means for predicting the occurrence of critical points on the continua of perceptual information arising from gradual changes in scale factors, such as the lengthening of spatial periods or the shortening of temporal ones. The concept of critical points lying on information continua explains why perceptually distinct experiences sometimes arise in spite of the fact that only continuous variations in event variables have occurred.

Taken together the above arguments provide strong prima facie evidence in favor of the unified-event hypothesis that slow events and fast events are phenomena of the same sort, processed in the same mode, and, therefore, governed by the same perceptual principles.

ACKNOWLEDGMENTS

Preparation of this paper was supported in part by a Career Development Award to Robert E. Shaw from the National Institute of Child Health and Human Development (1 KO4-HD24010), and by grants to the University of Minnesota, Center for Research in Human Learning, from the National Science Foundation (GB-35703X), the National Institute of Child Health and Human Development (HD-01136 and HD-00098), and the Graduate School of the University of Minnesota. Thanks are also due the Center for Advanced Study in the Behavioral Sciences and Haskins Laboratories for the support given Robert Shaw during the writing of this chapter.

REFERENCES

Bridgman, P. W. *Dimensional analysis.* New Haven: Yale University Press, 1922.

DeWitt, B. S., & Graham, N. (Eds.). *The many-worlds interpretation of quantum mechanics.* Princeton, N. J.: Princeton University Press, 1973.

Gibson, J. J. *The senses considered as perceptual systems.* Boston: Houghton-Mifflin, 1966.

Kolers, P. A. *Aspects of motion perception.* New York: Pergamon Press, 1972.

Lettvin, J. Y., Maturana, H. R., McCulloch, W. S., & Pitts, W. H. What the frog's eye tells the frog's brain. *Proceedings of the Institute of Radio Engineers, 47,* 1959, 1940–51.

Minkowski, H. Space and time. Translation of an address delivered at the 80th Assembly of German natural scientists and physicians at Cologne, September 21, 1908. Reprinted in Lorentz, H. A., Einstein, A., Minkowski, H., & Weyl, H. *The principles of relativity,* London: Methuen & Co., 1923, pp. 75–91.

Neisser, U. *Cognitive psychology.* New York: Appleton-Century-Crofts, 1967.

Poincaré, H. *Science and method.* London: Dover, 1952. (Originally published 1905.)

Russell, B. *The analysis of matter.* London: Allen & Unwin, 1927.

Shaw, R., McIntyre, M., & Mace, W. The role of symmetry in event perception. In R. MacLeod & H. Pick, Jr. (Eds.), *Studies in perception: Essays in honor of J. J. Gibson.* Ithaca, N. Y.: Cornell University Press, 1974.

Thompson, P. W. *On growth and form.* Cambridge, England: Cambridge University Press, 1942 (2nd ed.).

Trevarthen, C. B. Two mechanisms of vision in primates. *Psychologia Forschung 31,* 1968, 299–337.

11
Modes of Perceiving: Abstracts, Comments, and Notes

M. T. Turvey

Sandra Sears Prindle

University of Connecticut and Haskins Laboratories

Intuitively, deliberations on modes of perceiving are intended to flesh out something of the special manner in which man apprehends his world. In principle, the importance of the enterprise lies in the fact that even an elementary cataloguing of modes would significantly fetter the construction of theories of perception and cognition. It goes without saying that in evolving the perceptual styles of man and animals, nature did not build "general-purpose machines," rather she built "special-purpose machines"; and whatever plasticity man and animals manifest is a "special-purpose plasticity." Nevertheless, one has the impression that oftentimes theory-making proceeds untrammeled by a serious consideration of natural constraints and seems to be oriented toward a general-purpose, context-free perceiver.

Unfortunately, while it is the case that deliberating on modes of perceiving is well motivated it is not immediately obvious what it is that one is deliberating. The concept of "mode" is an intuitive object: tacitly we can appreciate the catalytic value of the concept in thinking about matters of perceiving and knowing but we cannot say what a "mode" is, precisely and unequivocally. Partly in response to this equivocality our approach to summarizing the volume takes the following form. First, we précis the various papers conveying, ideally, the larger point made by each. Second, and in conjunction, we seek fundamental themes that weave these larger points together in the hope that these themes will identify major constraints on the theory of perception. Third and separately, we gather together some elementary and rough thoughts of ours on the abstract notion of "style." These we present as notes toward a tenable characterization of the concept of mode in psychology and in this respect our remarks in this final chapter may be regarded as complementing those of Pick and Saltzman in the initial chapter.

ABSTRACTS AND COMMENTS

A contrast that comes rapidly to mind when one thinks of modes of perceptual processing is that between unconscious and conscious, or as Posner and his colleagues described it, (Chapter 7) the contrast of automatic and attentive. Processing of the former kind, we are told by Posner et al., is very much a parallel affair, while that of the latter is considerably more serial. The significant consequence of attentive processing is that it consumes a portion of the limited resource capacity, thereby curtailing the processing of other concurrent signals, and further, that it induces inertia in the processing apparatus. When there is the intentional selection (attentive) of a particular psychological channel or pathway, it takes effort and time to shift attention to another channel when needed. The costs, therefore, of attentive processing are manifestly plain; among its benefits, we may suppose, is a finer grain of analysis.

Inasmuch as the mode of attentive processing can be set by instruction we may ask: To what, precisely, is my processing directed when I am instructed to attend to a given location? It is this question which guides the series of ingenious experiments reported by Posner, Niessen and Ogden (Chapter 7). The conclusion is curious and provocative. Apparently there is little benefit to be gained by knowing ahead of time the external location at which a signal will occur if I do not know the modality which will convey the signal. By inference, attentive processing cannot be directed to a location with the same efficacy that it can be directed to a modality; preference is for knowing the messenger rather than knowing from where the message is coming.

With respect to the inertia induced by the mode of attentive processing, Posner and colleagues (Posner, Niessen, & Klein, 1976) have recently interpreted the peculiar phenomenon of visual capture as being indicative of an inertial asymmetry between switching from vision to another modality and switching from another modality to vision. One is reminded that visual capture refers to the dominating role that vision has in the human conscious experience. When the information for vision and another modality are in conflict, vision is the likely victor. Thus, I will experience my hand as tracing out a curved line when in fact it traces a straight line that has been prismatically distorted for visual consumption (Gibson & Radner, 1937). The relation between visual dominance and the inertial aspects of attentive processing is thus expressed: experiment suggests that vision is not an especially efficient alerting system because the time to switch into vision from another modality significantly exceeds the time to switch between two nonvisual modalities. If the human animal was not in the visual modality at the time of occurrence of an ecologically significant optical signal, it would be, on this account, at a distinct disadvantage. Consequently, one hypothesizes that, in response to evolutionary expediency, human conscious experience has come to be biased toward the visual pickup of information. That the bias is software rather than hardware is suggested by the following observation made when prismatic distortion of vision accompanies haptic exploration: if vision is attended to, the haptic system undergoes an adaptive shift, but if the haptic system is attended to, it is vision that is recalibrated (Kelso, Cook, Olsen, & Epstein, 1976). With other things being equal, it is vision that is attended to by choice.

Herein lies a rationalization of the "primacy of vision," which dovetails with Lee's deliberations, for these also sought to express the supremacy of visual perception. We shall see that, while the account of visual primacy derived from Posner's (see Posner, Nissen, & Ogden, Chapter 7) work emphasizes the costs of vision, that of Lee (Chapter 8) emphasizes the benefits of vision.

The term "modality" enjoys considerable usage. It is a term befitting the convention of classifying senses according to the qualitatively different conscious experiences. Following this convention, the special sense of vision is a source of visual sensation and the special sense of proprioception is a source of sensation of one's own movements. But is has been remarked upon by Gibson (1966), and echoed enthusiastically by Lee (Chapter 8), that it is far more sensible to classify the senses in terms of such activities as looking and listening than in terms of passive conduits transporting qualitatively different sense data. When approached from this perspective, the term "perceptual system" is substituted for the term "senses." And whereas the fundamental role assigned to the senses is that of providing raw materials for the creation of conscious experience, the fundamental role assigned to perceptual systems is that of obtaining information in the service of activity, as Lee so elegantly puts it.

A promissory note of Gibson's (1966) approach is that different perceptual systems can be sensitive to the same information. Here information is defined as information about the environment in a sense of specificity to it; and it is in this sense of the term that is intended by Pick and Saltzman (Chapter 1). The claim is that the pickup of information of a given type is not necessarily the prerogative of any one perceptual system. It is a claim that is easily glossed over but its ramifications are considerable (see White, Saunders, Scadden, Bach-Y-Rita & Collins, 1970); for those who think in terms of special senses—or special modalities—it is anathema.

Lee (Chapter 8) reminds us that in the regulation and control of activity three kinds of information are needed: information about surface layout and events; information about relations and changing relations among the limbs; and information about the motion of the body relative to the environment. His argument is that vision supplies all three—it is trimodal—and does so better than the other perceptual systems. Hence, we have the "primacy of vision." Essentially, the relation of vision to the other perceptual systems is that of overseer: vision tunes and calibrates those systems, which would otherwise be imprecise sources of information relative to the guidance of activity. A dramatic demonstration of vision's role with respect to body-related (proprioceptive) information is provided by Gross, Webb, and Melzack (1974). When asked to plot the position of an arm that rested without moving out of view (it was hidden by an opaque shield), participants could do so quite accurately if the delay from last seeing the arm was relatively short. However, with the passage of time, the position of the resting arm was felt to migrate to one of two positions: flection—adduction or extension—abduction.

It is but a small leap from Lee's work to that of Mack (Chapter 9 of this volume). For the contentions between traditional and Gibsonian perspectives—between indirect and direct realism—that were merely interlineal in Lee's chapter are brought to focus in Mack's. A departure point is that thorny issue on which Boring and Gibson collided: Can the visual world be apprehended independently of the visual field? Its cognate is perhaps better known: Can perception be indifferent to sensation? This issue takes many forms that are by no means identical. The gist, however, is unmistakable. It is a matter of whether or not the world can be perceived first hand—directly, or only second hand (by virtue of some surrogate)—indirectly.

Mack distinguished between proximal and constancy perception. Put bluntly, proximal perception is determined solely by the absolute properties of the retinal image; in contrast, constancy perception is determined by these image properties only partially, or not at all. Obviously the central concept is that of the retinal image and we may, after Gibson (1950), identify two versions of the concept for they are of significance to Mack's remarks. In the one, the image is defined as the anatomical pattern of cells that are excited: this we call the anatomical image. In the other version, the image is defined as the ordinal pattern of excitations indifferent to the location of cells excited: this we call the ordinal image. It was Gibson's (1950) intuition that seeing in terms of the anatomical image and seeing in terms of the ordinal image were two different ways of seeing, two different modes, if you wish.

Generally, when one talks about the retinal image it is the anatomical image one has in mind. And related to this conception is a tendency to talk about the light at an eye in terms of Euclidean geometry and thus to emphasize absolute metrical values. Euclidean geometry was all that was known to the ancients and to the intellectual ancestry that established the conventions, the fundamental assumptions, of contemporary visual theory. In contrast, the conception of the ordinal image encourages the adoption of projective geometry and its emphasis on abstract relations preserved over projective transformations.

When one describes the retinal image or proximal stimulus in Euclidean terms, there is an apparent lack of correspondence between the image and its distal referent. Consequently, insofar as perception tends to be veridical, it follows that the light at an eye underdetermines perceptual experience. The appropriate perception arises by virtue of processes that supplement the retinal image. Most generally these processes are thought of as memorial or problem solving in nature. The observer in this, the traditional viewpoint, is much like Sherlock Holmes who must attempt to determine what actually transpired from the limited data or clues available to him. We refer to this point of view as constructivism, in order to emphasize the central hypothesis that visual perception is built out of a number of ingredients—some of which are provided by the retinal image and some of which are provided by other, extra-visual sources (Turvey, 1974, 1975).

Let us now return to Mack's three modes of perception. By all accounts the proximal mode is evident only when the conditions of observation are highly constrained, for example, a two-dimensional nonchanging display exposed briefly against a homogeneous background and viewed from a stationary point of observation. In a phrase, the mode of proximal perception is precipitated by impoverished stimulation.

The subject-relative constancy mode is most obviously an example of constructivism, for the ingredients in the perception recipe include absolute and local anatomical image properties and nonvisual information about eye, head, and body orientation. In subject-relative constancy one must go beyond the light to an eye in order to determine perceptual experience. By our interpretation subject-relative perception uses the anatomical image. And what we would like to believe is that only in rare and artificial circumstances does the anatomical image play a determining role in experience. In short, operating in the proximal and in the subject-relative constancy mode are unnatural recourses for the visual perceptual system.

We are led therefore to the viewpoint that object-relative constancy perception is representative of the style in which the visual perceptual system maintains contact with the environment. In the object-relative mode abstract relations in the structured light at an eye provide the optical support for visual perception and they do not need supplementing by nonvisual data. Mack informs us that visual perception in the laboratory may sometimes be in error because of the curious bias of the visual system to operate in the object-relative mode when the subject-relative mode is more felicitious for the conditions of observation. But we should not be surprised by this fact. If it is the case that the optical flow pattern at a moving point of observation is structured adjacently and successively in ways that are specific to the observer's movement and to the properties of the environment, as Gibson (1966) and Lee (Chapter 8) argue, then we should suppose that evolution optimized the visual perceptual system of man and beast to be sensitive to this structure. It is the abstract relational information in the ordinal image understood, more precisely, as the ambient optic array and not the metrical character of the anatomical image which has constrained the evolution of visual systems. And if that invariant information is specific to the environment, then as the optical support for visual perception, it "merely" has to be detected; it would not have to be supplemented by other sources of knowledge.

Let us summarize to this point. Our quest for the natural style in which man perceives has realized two dividends. One is that—*ceteris paribus*—vision pre-empts conscious experience because it is the most abundant supplier of information about the environment and about one's self and because, as far as perceptual systems go, it is potentially more costly not to be visually attentive and considerably more laborious to become so. The other dividend is that, although visual perception may operate in a subject-relative or constructive-like mode, this is not its more natural and preferred style. We pursue the latter proposition in Shaw and Pittenger's chapter 10 of this volume.

As remarked earlier, theorizing on matters of visual perception has tended to begin with the retinal image understood as an anatomical arrangement. But we can comment, further, that theorizing has tended to take as its departure point the understanding of the retinal image as a static bidimensional form. The consequence of this attitude is twofold: the analysis of pattern or form perception is taken as propaedeutic to the theory of visual perception; and change, defined as the transformation of an object over time, is said to be inferred from a succession of static retinal images.

The conceptualization of the optical support for visual perception as static and bidimensional has a long tradition. We owe to the tenth century Arab scholar Al Hasan the first comprehensive exegesis of the relation between the image on the retina and visual perception. Through Berkeley and Von Helmholtz the tradition has been popularly maintained, and it is the source of the fundamental, though rarely commented on, suppositions of contemporary visual information processing theory and research (see Haber, 1971; Neisser, 1967). Obviously, if we assume that a two-dimensional static description of the world is the starting point, the given, of visual experience, then we have identified the task of perceptual theory: to explain the means by which we arrive at static three-dimensional descriptions (depth perception, object perception) and dynamic three-dimensional descriptions (events). As we have already anticipated, the traditional explanation is that such perceptual experiences are constructed via the assistance of memory.

Suppose, however, that our intuitions about perception are guided not by history and the retinal image, but by the concepts of evolution and ecology. Such being the case, we would recognize that locomotion and the continuous orienting of the perceptual apparatus to the environment are the sine qua non of successful adaptation. We would recognize, in short, that dynamically transforming optic arrays would be the norm and static, frozen optic arrays would be the exception. Further, we would appreciate that an animal would wish to know not simply what kind of object it was looking at but what kind of change the object was undergoing. Perception of the *forms* of change is of paramount importance to adaptation. In sum, from an evolutionary–ecological perspective we might be led to conjecture that the proper departure point for a theory of visual perception is kinetic events and not two-dimensional static forms (Gibson, 1966; Johannson, 1974). This conclusion, of course, is cognate with that which we reached above in our discussion of Mack's chapter.

An event, Shaw and Pittenger inform us elsewhere (Pittenger & Shaw, 1975), is composed of two things: the object or complex of objects undergoing the change, and the change itself. The optical support for the perception of the former (the object) is referred to as the structural invariant, and that for the perception of the latter (the change) is referred to as the transformational invariant. This construal of the structure of events follows from Gibson's (1966) working hypothesis of ecological optics, namely, that for any isolable environmental property there is a corresponding isolable property in the transforming optic array, *however complex*. By arguing that there are higher-order invariants specific to the styles of change, Shaw and Pittinger express the unorthodox view that the perception of change is direct. They argue, in paraphrase of Gibson's (1966) notorious aphorism, that the perception of change is not based on the perception of static forms but, rather, on the detection of formless invariants over time.

Recent examinations of comparatively simple events, such as an object moving at constant velocity or accelerating from one position to another, reveal that the perceptions of velocity and acceleration are not based on the prior discriminations of spatial and temporal extent (see Lappin, Bell, Harm, & Kottas, 1975; Rosenbaum, 1975). Explanations of perceived velocity and acceleration in the constructivist mode would necessitate epistemic mediation, for example, having discriminated at least two spatial positions, that is, taking two retinal snapshots, and having monitored the time elapsed between the two positions, then velocity could be computed by means of a simple formula. The evidence, however, favors the view that velocity and acceleration are not constructed percepts, but directly perceivable attributes of stimulation. This conclusion reflects the larger point that Shaw and Pittenger wish to make, namely, that the nominalistic attitude toward accounts of perceptual experience is fundamentally in error. We can phrase this differently and positively: what Shaw and Pittenger wish to emphasize is the primacy of the abstract.

If this thesis is not already foreign enough for most students of perception to appreciate, it is made all the more so when one considers that in our lifetimes events range from the order of milliseconds to the order of scores of years. How is it possible, we ask, to apprehend slow events without the mediation of "memories"? What can it possibly mean to *detect* the transformational invariant of a slow event such as, say, aging? Shaw and Pittenger point a finger in the direction we might go in search of an answer. More tangibly, however, they lay bare the absurdity of the conventional story of memory mediation. For if my apprehension of a slow event is by virtue of inferences from memory, then I must have some way of collecting the relevant memories, and this implies that I have knowledge of the transformation that relates them to each other. But the transformation that relates them one to another is what I have to infer; it cannot be presupposed. Even if we permit a fortuitious gathering of the relevant memories the memory-mediation story fails to work; for now we must attribute to the inferential processes a priori knowledge of transformations in order that we might infer from the nominal data which event transpired.

In the preceding we have developed the intuitive notion that visual perceptual theory should be anchored in event perception, that is, in the perception of the transforming optic array. Obviously, within such a framework a static two-dimensional arrangement must be regarded as a type of "frozen" event in which the structured light at an eye has been reduced in its efficiency as a specifier of environmental facts. Belaboring the point somewhat, we may claim that truly static perception is artifactual arising at a relatively late phase in evolution. The perception of paintings, photographs, and the like exemplify the limiting case— and it is just this kind of perception that is examined by Hagen (Chapter 2 of this volume). Her questions are straightforward and they follow naturally from the preceding remarks: Is perceiving pictures much the same as perceiving the ordinary environment, or is there something special going on with pictures? Is there either something special about the information pictures contain or something special that we do with that information? As we might anticipate, Gibson's (Gibson, 1971) intuitions on these matters are essentially that the perception of pictures and the perception of the scenes they depict do not differ qualitatively, for the essence of pictures is that the information they convey is structurally equivalent to that of the scenes they depict. In a phrase, picture perception, like event perception, is not epistemically mediated.

Experimentation over a wide range of conditions reveals that when pictures (slides, photographic prints, line drawings) are viewed from the right station point and are apparently equated for static monocular surface-layout information, the perception of the real scene is alwasy superior to that of the facsimile. This could be because of the perceptual advantages that accrue from moving the eye over a real scene versus moving it over a picture. Alternatively, as Hagen suggests, it could be because when faced with the task of appreciating the three-dimensional structure specified by the pictorial information one must suppress the concurrent information specifying that the "frozen" event is actually two dimensional. In either case, the Gibsonian (Gibson, 1971) thesis that picture perception can be direct like ordinary perception (that is, not epistemically mediated) is not appreciably harmed.

A different conclusion, however, is implied by the "Pirenne paradox." An observer's appreciation of the three-dimensional scene depicted by a two-dimensional picture is significantly enhanced when he or she adopts the wrong station point. This is paradoxical inasmuch as the perspective information provided by a picture is only equivalent to that provided by a real scene at the center of projection for the picture. Pirenne's interpretation (Hagen, Chapter 2) of this paradox is clearly in the constructivist mode: Looking at a picture off center enhances one's awareness of flatness and induces one to bring to bear knowledge about the internal components of the picture; by so doing one not only *compensates* for the perspectival asynchrony, but in addition and more importantly, facilitates the perception of the internal components. The problem with this interpretation as we see it, is that it is not obvious why viewing a picture from an incorrect station point should trigger a compensatory attitude any more than the actual knowledge that one is in the context of picture viewing. We venture that a more useful approach to the Pirenne paradox lies in noting in what ways a perspective from the wrong station point could be more informative about the internal components than a perspective from the correct station point. Is it that the perspective accompanying an off-center station point specifies the perspective at the on-center station point; in short, that at the wrong station point one has, in some curious fashion, *two* perspectives on the static object?

All this concern with perception from particular points of view and with the perception of pictures as a possibly particular kind of seeing leads us, without too much difficulty, to perceiving—more precisely to visualizing—from *no* particular point of view. Exemplary of such visualizing is imaging and it has been Paivio's contribution (Chapter 3 of this volume) to restore imaging to respectability in academic psychology.

The mechanisms of imaging are part and parcel of a "nonverbal" system which is said by Paivio to mediate both our experience of the environment and our nonverbal actions. This imagery system operates independently of the "verbal" system which supports our linguistic endeavors whether they be performed by ear, eye, or hand. It is the case as Paivio argues, that the verbal system is dependent on the nonverbal, for while the former communicates what we know about the environment the latter is the primary source of that knowledge. Nevertheless, the two systems are distinguished by the kinds of objects which comprise their respective memory components. For the imagery system the objects are said to be perceptual analogs while for the verbal system they are discrete linguistic entities (for example, words).

But how should we characterize the perceptual knowledge that Paivio refers to? On the assumption that the relevant entities are discrete and static images we might be drawn to symbolic logic, formal grammars, machine theory and the like to characterize them. On this assumption an image could be treated as a symbol and perceptual knowledge viewed as a symbol-manipulating system. Since language can be similarly characterized, the possibility opens up that Paivio's imagery and verbal nodes are fed by one and the same symbol-manipulating system. This approach is favored by Anderson and Bower (1973), among others, but regarded with skepticism by Paivio.

We have remarked several times in this summary that the informational support for perceiving and acting consists of abstract invariants defined over time and, further, that the kernel units for perceptual theory are kinetic events. If Paivio wishes to maintain that the perceptual knowledge which feeds his imagery system is continuous with perception then we might wish to propose that perceptual knowledge is most appropriately characterized in terms of events, rather than static images, and, cognately, in terms of dynamic abstract invariants.

Our facility with metaphor provides a case in point. If I am requested to remember the sentence "Rabbits are like children skipping rope down the sidewalk," then an effective prompt at a later date is "Kangaroos move like a basketball being dribbled" (Verbrugge, 1975). Why should this be so? It stretches the imagination to believe that the equivalence between the two sentences lies in semantic features common to rabbits, children, skipping ropes, kangaroos, and basketballs, or that it could be realized by compounding static images. We may conjecture that the two sentences share a common abstract invariant: periodic up and down motion relative to the ground plane, and it is the detection of this invariant that determines their equivalence.

We alluded above to imaging as perceiving from no particular station point. In a delightful mix of words Verbrugge (1975) remarks that "language is more like a piano score—an invitation to create meaning [p. 2]." In his perspective, the listener seeks structure among the virtual objects suggested by a sentence much like seeking structure in the optic array—except in the linguistic case doing so from no particular station point. The suggestion is that the style in which we perceive language is not *qualitatively* different from the style in which we perceive or visualize the environment. Our guess is that if Paivio's nonverbal and verbal systems conflate at all, it is not because they use a common propositional format, but because they are both oriented to the abstract invariants which specify events.

Let us pursue the verbal mode a little further. With respect to language perception by ear there are three aspects of that perception that we might distinguish: (1) we can identify a semantic mode in which we experience the meaning of what we hear; (2) a phonological mode in which we experience what we said distinct from what it means; (3) and an acoustic mode in which we experience certain nonlinguistic aspects of speech (see Halwes & Wyre, 1974). Paivio's remarks and our comments in the preceding paragraphs were directed at the semantic mode; MacNeilage (Chapter 4 of this volume) focused on the phonological and the acoustic.

MacNeilage's bone of contention is the thesis that perceiving in the phonological mode is qualitatively different from perceiving in the acoustic mode.

More precisely, MacNeilage takes issue with the claim that what underlies the experience of language at the phonological level are processes which are fundamentally articulatory in nature. We may recognize strong and weak versions of this claim. In the strong version the processes responsible for phonological experience are identical to the neuromotor processes of articulatory coordination involved in speaking but with the motor commands inhibited at some level prior to inducing mechanical muscular events. In the weak version, phonological experience is constructed from the acoustic data by virtue of knowledge about what human vocal tracts can and cannot do.

The data often cited in support of the motor or articulatory theory of speech perception are no longer as compelling as they might once have been. Thus, one of the cornerstones of the theory, categorical perception, is now known to be indigenous to neither speech nor humans. Nevertheless, there are some curious observations which point to an intimacy between perceiving and producing speech that cannot be dismissed lightheartedly. Among these we might include the tight coupling between hearing and speaking vowels witnessed by the exceptionally rapid shadowing of Chistovich's (1961) subjects and a recent and provocative discovery, compatible with the weaker version of the theory, that has been made by Liberman and Dorman (see Liberman, 1975). If two syllables such as /bɛb/ and /dɛ/ are arranged very closely together in time, one of the stop consonants is "masked" so that the listener hears /bɛ/ instead of /bɛb/. However, this perceptual impairment can be readily eliminated by having the two syllables spoken by two different vocal tracts: no matter how temporally proximate is the presentation of the two syllables, as long as they are produced by different vocal tracts they can be heard as separate phonological events. In the perspective of the weaker version of the articulatory theory, this result is interpretable in terms of the listener's tacit knowledge of vocal tracts which specifies that although the rapid transition from one stop consonant to the other is impossible for a single speaker, it can be achieved easily by two speakers.

However, the thrust of MacNeilage's survey is not to be denied: there is relatively little to recommend a motor theory. The hypothesis that speech is perceived by reference to how it is produced is countered by the hypothesis that speech is produced by reference to how it is perceived, that is, the motor theory of perception is nullified by an acoustic theory of production. In view of the latter, we might not wish to regard either phonological perception or production as parasitic on the other but, rather, that perceiving speech and producing speech are related through an abstract structure that is common to both but indigenous to neither (Turvey, 1977). At least for the lowly cricket there is a suggestion that perception and production are manifestations of the same structure: a common gene might mediate the male's song and the female's perception of it (Hoy & Paul, 1973).

Perhaps the larger point to be made with respect to a comparison of perception in the phonological and acoustic modes is that nonphonological auditory perception has not been treated fairly in theory and research. In studying the auditory perceptual system, insufficient weight has been given to its primary role of detecting environmental sources of mechanical disturbance. Ecologically, the role of audition is to identify the source of sound and the behavior of the identified source (see Schubert, 1975). The auditory perceptual system, like its visual counterpart, is oriented to events; but our understanding of auditory perception outside of speech, is based on the perception of sounds that are more nearly abstract than event related.

Consider the common use of artificial sounds in the laboratory; examples are steady-state pure tones or steady-state short bursts of random noise. The most notable feature of the perception of sounds such as these is that they resist reliable identification (Pfafflin & Matthews, 1966; Webster, Woodhouse, & Carpenter, 1970). In part, this seems to be owing to the fact that sounds relating to ecological events—the class of sounds to which the auditory perceptual system has been attuned by evolution—involve rapid transients in intensity. These transients are concomitants of the onsets and offsets of the mechanical disturbances to which the sounds correspond. In the absence of these transients, specification of the identity of the source of the sound is far from ideal (see Luce & Clark, 1965, 1967; Saldanha & Corso, 1964).

Speech perception is the perception of sound as modulated by articulatory events. But the nonspeech perception with which it is often compared is the perception of sounds that have been stripped of ecological validity. A pure steady-state tone specifies no event whatsoever. The contrast between speech and nonspeech perception or linguistic and nonlinguistic perception is, in our opinion, more often a contrast between event perception and nonevent perception. Such being the case, speculation on how the perception of speech differs from that of nonspeech is premature. Imagine hearing a can or a dish fall to the ground. We can ask with Schubert (1975) "Was the can large or small; of heavy or light construction; was it in contact with a hard surface like concrete or an absorbant one like earth or grass? Did the dish shatter or bounce [p. 102]?" Conjecturally, we answer these questions on the basis of the fact that the objects and substances involved, and their interactions, modulate the acoustic array in specific and invariant ways. But what do we know of such invariants and their detection? The answer, unfortunately, is very little. Nevertheless, it is the character of this kind of auditory perception to which the character of speech perception should be compared. There is one modest difference between the two kinds of perception which comes to mind immediately. Differentiating nonspeech environmental events probably takes full advantage of the exteroceptive expertise of vision; in contrast, it is roughly apparent that vision's role in the differentiating of speech events is minimal.

At this juncture let us anthologize our review and comments thus far. To the primacy of vision we have now added the primacy of abstract relational information defined over time. The latter is meant to contrast with the more common attitude which asserts the primacy of nominal, punctate, and momentary entities in perception. Furthermore, we have promoted kinetic events as opposed to static retinal images or steady-state sounds as the ecological entities to which evolution has attuned perceptual systems and thus the proper departure point for theorizing. Admittedly this promotion does not reflect the bias of all of the authors of this volume but, ideally, our remarks have been sufficient to support our intuition that the event concept provides a unifying theme.

We come now to the remaining two chapters, those of Halliday (Chapter 5) and Trevarthen (Chapter 6). If the chapters discussed thus far can be categorized as being directed to the what and the how of perception, that is, to the issues of what there is to be perceived and how it is perceived, then those of Trevarthen and Halliday may be categorized as being directed to the who of perception—the epistemic agent or algorist (Shaw & MacIntyre, 1974). As Shaw and MacIntyre (1974) remark, the questions of the "what," the "how" and the "who" of perception form a closed set of questions with answers to any one coimplicating answers to the other two. It is fitting, therefore, that the authors of the final chapters in this volume emphasize the member of the above triad thus far omitted.

Briefly, Trevarthen's major points are these: (1) psychologists are insufficiently sensitive to the implications of anatomy—particularly the somatotopic principal—for perception and action theory; (2) perceptual systems should be considered in the light of mechanisms for action; and (3) contrary to time-honored claims, infant behavior is intentional. This last point is also the larger point of Halliday's chapter.

The organization of the vertebrate midbrain provides an instructive example of both Trevarthen's first and second points. If a map is drawn of the projection from the eyes to the midbrain tectum in the coordinates of the eye, then, for animals with frontal-oriented eyes and animals with lateral-oriented eyes, the two maps are quite dissimilar. However, if the maps are drawn in the coordinates of the behavioral field, that is, with respect to the asymmetry of the body, we would observe that the two maps are virtually identical. As a general principle, the mapping from eyes to tectum in the coordinates of the behavioral field is relatively invariant; this mapping of visual loci also maps a topography of points of entry into the action system.

The confluence between seeing and doing was highlighted earlier in Lee's chapter and that between hearing and speaking was critically examined in MacNeilage's. A further, though brief, comment on the perception-action relation is warranted. The problem of coordination is the problem of controlling the enormous number of degrees of freedom that the biokinematic links—the skeletomuscular hardware—can attain (Bernstein, 1967). In view of the indeterminancy of the peripheral motor apparatus it is most unlikely that executive processes coordinate movement through the individual control of each degree of freedom. In short, action plans are probably not written in terms of individual muscle contractions. The alternative view (Gelfand, Gurfinkel, Tsetlin, & Shik, 1971) is that action plans are written in terms of muscle linkages, that is, muscle–joint complexes whose activities covary and whose kinematic characteristics are similar. Such linkages may be referred to as coordinative structures (Turvey, 1977). The role of these structures is to reduce the degrees of freedom requiring control, for a coordinative structure behaves quasi-autonomously and, therefore, from the perspective of an executive procedure it represents but a single degree of freedom. But coordinative structures provide only a partial solution to the degrees-of-freedom problem. In the performance of acts the degrees of freedom are regulated with precision but, as noted, an action plan, necessarily, is specified crudely in the language of coordinative structures. Therefore, we ask: how are movements performed that are precise in their timing, velocity, and displacement? Obviously perception must modulate unfolding action plans but in order to do so perceptual information must be parsed in ways compatible with the nested components of the evolving act and must be injected into the action system at the right place and at the right time. How this is done is not at all apparent but we may regard Trevarthen's comments on somatotopic organization and on the contrasting capabilities of focal and ambient vision as preliminary steps in the direction of an answer.

Let us conclude our summary of this volume with the shared insights of Trevarthen and Halliday on the nature of infant behavior. An appropriate backdrop is provided by a brief consideration of Gibson's (1966) shift away from perceptual psychophysics. In common with his predecessors, in his early writings, Gibson (1950), adopted the causal chain theory of perception: perceptual experience was caused by stimuli. However, as he developed the concept of the optic array, it became evident to him that the formulation "stimuli trigger perception" was incorrect and that a more judicious formulation was that "the ambient optic array *supports* the regulation and coordination of activity." The significance of the reformulation is that it emphasizes exploration and selection with the animal as agent rather than the animal as reactant.

Suppose that we do adopt an agent or algoristic-oriented view of the relation between what there is to be perceived and how it is perceived. Do we mean to hold to this view for all stages of ontogeny? Popular scientific and not-so-scientific opinion would most likely respond "no." For the agentlike qualities of the adult perceiver–actor are said to result from a lengthy apprenticeship: the infant human *reacts* to stimuli, in the ageless story, and only comes to plan and regulate behavior with respect to information after the slow process of enculturation. The contrary and, perhaps, radical claim of Trevarthen and Halliday is that the infant is inherently purposive. What we witness in Trevarthen's and Halliday's behavioral and protolinguistic analyses, respectively, of infant life, is the infant as algorist possessing and deploying a stock of fundamental strategies or modes for selectively operating upon the world. The disposition of these strategies rests on the capacity to distinguish between animate and inanimate objects as affording different possibilities of interaction. Thus, the infant communicates, vocally and gesturally, with animate objects but reaches for and manipulates inanimate objects. What we learn from Halliday is that the inchoate vocalizations of early childhood are actually basic acts of meaning intended, in part, to procure material ends and to maintain contact with and regulate the behavior of those who enter into the communication scenario. To the claim that the infant is inherently agentlike we add the claim that the infant is inherently social.

NOTES

"Mode" has many synonyms, of which "style" and "fashion" are perhaps the most common. We speak about this and that style of dress and we will often pass comment on how fashionable or unfashionable a given style happens to be. Such comment is intended to relate the style in question to the context of contemporary living. It is a matter of whether the style is compatible with some broader context of constraints, although the criteria for adjudicating on this subject are rarely unequivocal.

Patently, fashionableness is a passing quality although there are no fixed time limits on a style's period of grace. Nevertheless, it is fair to claim that the longevity of a style of dress is considerably shorter than that of other "styles," such as the style of eating. Other "styles" are even more perpetual; the style of human locomotion, for example, has undergone relatively little change.

Styles, therefore, may be said to lie on a continuum from persistent to transient and, we may propose, in addition, from immutable to docile. But consider a further aspect: given several styles of dress, a person cannot be dressed in more than one style at a time. In short, different styles of dress are mutually exclusive. But styles are also said to be stereotypic, invariant, ways of doing things. A not uncommon reproach of haute couture by those excluded is that they, the in crowd, all dress or act alike. But the epithet "stereotypic" must be handled cautiously for its use is likely to blind one to the important fact that to be in style does not mean that one is a carbon copy of one's comrades in fashion. Rather, one's dress differs perceptibly from that of the others in ways, however, which do not violate the prescribed, although often ineffable, conventions. We may say, therefore, that to be in a style is to be in a certain "ballpark" of states, and we will proceed to define a style as *a set of constraints which ensures the realization of an invariant condition over variable instances.* Unfortunately, equating style and constraint does not carry the bonus of a simple way in which to classify styles. Constraints—and thus, by definition, styles—vary on a scale from light to severe with the severity of a constraint measured by the reduction it causes in the number of possible configurations, that is, the extent to which it freezes degrees of freedom.

Consider the relation between style of dress and style of dance. We have remarked already that one cannot be in two styles of dress simultaneously: one excludes the other. Similarly one cannot be dancing in two styles simultaneously. Nevertheless, one can be in a style of dress and dance in a certain style at one and the same time if one of two conditions exists. First, when the style of dance and that of dress do not affect one another, as is the case when one's style of dress does not restrict movements, then one is perfectly able to do a certain dance while in a certain style of dress. Second, when the style of dress does restrict movement in some particular way, one can still perform a certain dance if the dance constrains one's movements *in the same way* as does the style of dress. For example, one can do the currently popular hustle while wearing platform shoes, since the constraint on bending one's foot is the same for the hustle as for platform shoes. However, an Irish jig and platform shoes are not compatible, since the constraint on bending one's feet imposed by platform shoes is not compatible with dancing the jig.

Speaking more generally, *two or more styles are compatible (that is, they can coexist) if: (1) they govern different degrees of freedom; or (2) they selectively freeze the degrees of freedom which they have in common in the same way.*

Returning to our dress—dance metaphor, we intuit that when neither of the conditions are satisfied, styles behave in a coalitional (free-dominance) fashion. That is, styles are not organized in a strictly hierarchical manner: any one style may take precedence over any other style, it depends on the event in which the two styles take part. Thus, one may be intent upon wearing platform shoes in which case the jig is modified to avoid bending the feet; or, if intent upon doing the jig correctly, one may remove the platform shoes and dance in bare feet.

Substituting the term "mode" for that of "style," we may summarize as follows: a mode is a set of constraints which guarantees the realization of an invariant condition over variable instances; such sets of constraints may range from temporary to permanent and from flexible to unchangeable; two or more such sets of constraints may operate simultaneously if certain conditions prevail; generally, the organization of modes is coalitional.

In terms of the preceding we may approach the question of how "mode" is to be understood in psychology by asking: What constraints are operating when an occasion of perception—a perceptual condition—is labeled as an instance of this or that mode? Ideally, we seek to identify those constraints that are both necessary and sufficient for applying a mode label. As a rough strategy, we can ask initially what constraints are necessary and then inquire whether they are also sufficient.

Reference has been made in this volume to a speech mode and a nonspeech mode, and, in the case of vision, to a focal mode and an ambient mode. It is roughly apparent that the constraints governing the information available to a perceiver (that is, what there is available for the animal to perceive) are necessary for defining a given mode. However, it is also roughly apparent that those constraints are not sufficient (in and of themselves) for the application of a unique mode label in each particular situation where those constraints occur. Indeed, we argue that while the set of constraints corresponding to the set of answers to the question "*what* is the animal perceiving?" is necessary for the application of the label for a given mode, it is not sufficient. As a case in point, a musical sequence is easily recognized as such even when the notes of a melody are presented as a speech signal. It has been shown that when the fundamental frequency of a melodic line is inflected on a high-quality synthesized syllable ("tea"), indices for a "nonspeech mode" are obtained even in the presence of overall conditions of stimulation normally associated with a "speech mode" (Darwin, 1969).

Perhaps we should look at the set of constraints governing *how* information is processed as well as at the constraints on *what* is processed. In this way, we circumvent the problems caused by attempting to define mode strictly in terms of informational constraints. For example, it has been shown that indices for a "nonspeech mode" can be obtained with a natural-speech stimulus if the perceptual task is a nonlinguistic one (Haggard & Parkinson, 1971). Apparently, a given input is processed in a different way when the nature of the perceiver's task changes. A less equivocal example is provided by the following experiment. When "O" is embedded in a list of digits, it can be found more rapidly if the observer is told that he or she is looking for a letter than if he or she is told that the target is a digit. Conversely, when "O" is a member of a list of letters, latency of search is considerably shorter if one is looking for a digit zero than if one is looking for the letter "O" (Jonides & Gleitman, 1972).

We see, from the above examples, that the set of constraints governing *how* information is processed is by necessity linked with the intent of the perceiver (the epistemic *who,* as defined by Shaw & McIntyre, 1974), as well as with *what* information exists in the surrounding medium. An illustration of the coimplicative relations among the what, the how, and the who of perception is provided by the hermit crab's "attitudes" toward a sea anemone. The description of these attitudes is due to von Uexküll (1957). To preface, let us identify the what of perception as the affordances (see Gibson, 1966) specified in the ambient optic array structured by the sea anemone; the how of perception as the exploratory and performatory measures taken by the crab in detecting and exploiting the different uses of the sea anemone; and the who of perception as the intents of the crab. In the first case, the hermit crab has been robbed of the actinians which it normally carries on its shell. These actinians serve to protect the crab from its enemy, the cuttlefish. In this case, the crab is described as assuming a "defense tone," and it plants the sea anemone on its shell. In the second case, the shell has been taken from the hermit crab, and the crab attempts often unsuccessfully to crawl into the sea anemone, the crab having assumed a "dwelling tone." Finally, the crab, who has been left to starve for some time, assumes a "feeding tone" and proceeds to devour the sea anemone. Thus, if "defense," "dwelling," and "feeding," are mode labels it would seem that answers to each of the what, how, and who questions are necessary for the application of one of the mode labels and, further, that answers to all three questions are sufficient for the application of a unique "mode label" in each particular situation.

In these notes we have attempted, in a most elementary and approximate manner, to sketch the metatheory of modes. To this end we pursued the general concept of style, teasing from it several principles that we hoped might prove useful to the understanding of the more specific concept of mode in perceptual theory. Of these principles, the most fundamental equates "mode" with "set of constraints." We were motivated, therefore, to ask whether, in defining a mode, the information for perception exhausted all the constraints or whether the information for perception together with the algorithms for its analysis exhausted all the constraints. Our tentative answer to both of these questions is "no." Unfortunately, that which appears to provide the full complement of constraints defining a mode is not something that we understand very well at all, namely, the relation among the what, the how, and the who of perception. Nevertheless, it is our hunch that an appreciation of the aforementioned relation is the proper departure point for a rigorous analysis of "modes of perceiving."

REFERENCES

Anderson, J., & Bower, G. H. *Human associative memory.* New York: Academic Press, 1973.

Bernstein, N. *The coordination and regulation of movements.* London: Pergamon Press, 1967.

Chistovich, L. A. Classification of rapidly repeated speech sounds. *Soviet Physics and Acoustics,* 1961, *6,* 393–398.

Darwin, C. J. Auditory perception and cerebral dominance. Unpublished doctoral dissertation, Cambridge University, 1969.

Gelfand, I. N., Gurfinkel, M. S., Tsetlin, M. L., & Shik, M. L. Some problems in the analysis of movements. In I. M. Gelfand, V. S. Gurfinkel, S. V. Fomin, & M. L. Tsetlin (Eds.), *Models of the structural–functional organization of certain biological systems.* Cambridge, Mass.: M.I.T. Press, 1971.

Gibson, J. J. *The perception of the visual world.* Boston: Houghton Miffling, 1950.

Gibson, J. J. *The senses considered as perceptual systems.* Boston: Houghton Mifflin, 1966.

Gibson, J. J. The information available in pictures. *Leonardo,* 1971, *4,* 27–35.

Gibson, J. J., & Radner, M. Adaptation, after-effect and contrast in the perception of tilted lines I. Quantitative studies. *Journal of Experimental Psychology,* 1937, *20,* 453–467.

Gross, Y., Webb, R., & Melzack, R. Central and peripheral contributions to localization of body parts: Evidence for the central body schema. *Experimental Neurology,* 1974, *44,* 346–362.

Haber, R. N. Where are the visions in visual perception. In S. Segal (Ed.), *Imagery*. New York: Academic Press, 1971.

Haggard, M. P., & Parkinson, A. M. Stimulus and task factors as determinants of ear advantages. *Quarterly Journal of Experimental Psychology*, 1971, *23*, 168–177.

Halwes, T., & Wire, B. A possible solution to the pattern recognition problem in the speech modality. In W. Weimar & D. Palermo (Eds.), *Cognition and the symbolic processes*. Hillsdale, N. J.: Lawrence Erlbaum Associates, 1974.

Hoy, R. R., & Paul, R. C. Genetic control of song specificity in crickets. *Science*, 1973, *180*, 82–83.

Johansson, G. Projective transformations as determining visual space perception. In R. B. MacLeod & H. L. Pick (Eds.), *Perception: Essays in honor of J. J. Gibson*. Ithaca, N. Y.: Cornell University Press, 1974.

Jonides, J., & Gleitman, H. A conceptual category effect in visual search: O as a letter or a digit. *Perception and Psychophysics*, 1972, *12*, 457–460.

Kelso, J. A. S., Cook, E., Olson, M. E., & Epstein, W. Allocation of attention and the locus of adaptation to displaced vision. *Journal of Experimental Psychology: Human Perception and Performance*, 1976, *1*, 237–245.

Lappin, J. S., Bell, H. H., Harm, O. J., & Kottas, B. On the relation between time and space in visual discrimination of velocity. *Journal of Experimental Psychology: Human Perception and Performance*, 1975, *1*, 383–394.

Liberman, A. M. How abstract must a motor theory of speech perception be? *Status Report on Speech Research SR-44*. New Haven, Conn.: Haskins Laboratories, 1975. Pp. 1–16.

Luce, D. A., & Clark, M. Duration of attack transients on nonpercussive orchestral instruments. *Journal of the Audio Engineering Society*, 1965, *13*, 194–199.

Luce, D., & Clark, M. Physical correlates of brass instrument tones. *Journal of Acoustical Society of America*, 1967, *42*, 1232–1243.

Neisser, U. *Cognitive psychology*. New York: Appleton-Century-Crofts, 1967.

Pfafflin, S. M., & Matthews, M. W. Detection of auditory signals in reproducible noise. *Journal of the Acoustical Society of America* 1966, *39*, 340–345.

Pittenger, J. B., & Shaw, R. E. Aging faces as viscal-elastic events: Implications for a theory of nonrigid shape perception. *Journal of Experimental Psychology: Human Perception and Performance* 1975, *1*, 374–382.

Posner, M. I., Nissen, M. J., & Klein, R. M. Visual dominance: An information-processing account of its origins and significance. *Psychological Review* 1976, *83*, 157–170.

Rosenbaum, D. A. Perception and extrapolation of velocity and acceleration. *Journal of Experimental Psychology: Human Perception and Performance* 1975, *1*, 395–403.

Saldanha, E. L., & Corso, J. F. Timbre cues and the identification of musical instruments. *Journal of Acoustical Society of America* 1964, *36*, 2021–2026.

Schubert, E. D. The role of auditory perception in language processing. In D. D. Duane & M. B. Rawson (Eds.), *Reading, perception and language*. Baltimore, Md.: York Press, 1975.

Shaw, R. E., & McIntyre, M. Algoristic foundations to cognitive psychology. In W. Weimar & D. Palermo (Eds.), *Cognition and the symbolic processes*. Hillsdale, N. J.: Lawrence Erlbaum Associates, 1974.

Turvey, M. T. Constructive theory, perceptual systems and tacit knowledge. In W. Weimar & D. Palermo (Eds.) *Cognition and the symbolic processes*. Hillsdale, N. J.: Lawrence Erlbaum Associates, 1974.

Turvey, M. T. Perspectives in vision: Conception or perception? In D. D. Duane & M. B. Rawson (Eds.), *Reading, perception and language*. Baltimore, Md.: York Press, 1975.

Turvey, M. T. Preliminaries to a theory of action with reference to vision. In R. Shaw & J. Bransford (Eds.), *Perceiving, acting and knowing: Toward an ecological psychology*. Hillsdale, N. J.: Lawrence Erlbaum Associates, 1977.

von Uexküll, J. A stroll through the worlds of animals and men. In C. H. Schiller (Ed.), *Instinctive behavior.* New York: International Universities Press, 1957.

Verbrugge, R. R. Perceiving invariants at the invitation of metaphor. Paper presented at the meeting of the American Psychological Association, Chicago, 1975.

Webster, J. C., Woodhead, M. M., & Carpenter, A. A perceptual constancy in complex sound identification. *British Journal of Psychology,* 1970, *61,* 481–489.

White, B. W., Saunders, F. S., Scadden, L., Bach-Y-Rita, P., & Collins, C. C. Seeing with the skin. *Perception and Psychophysics,* 1970, *7,* 23–27.

Author Index

Numbers in *italics* refer to pages on which the complete references are listed.

225

Subject Index